Blaming Japhy Rider

Memoir of a Dharma Bum Who Survived

Philip A. Bralich, Ph.D.

BALBOA.
PRESS
A DIVISION OF HAY HOUSE

Balboa Press books may be ordered through booksellers or by contacting:

Balboa Press
A Division of Hay House
1663 Liberty Drive
Bloomington, IN 47403
www.balboapress.com
1-(877) 407-4847

ISBN: 978-1-4525-4051-1 (sc)
ISBN: 978-1-4525-4052-8 (hc)
ISBN: 978-1-4525-4053-5 (e)
Library of Congress Control Number: 2012900061

Excerpt from HOWL by Allen Ginsberg. Copyright © 1956, 2010 by Allen Ginsberg LLC, used by permission of The Wylie Agency LLC. "Copyright © 1955 by Allen Ginsberg. Reprinted by permission of HarperCollins Publishers."

Printed in the United States of America

Balboa Press rev. date: 01/21/2012

This book is dedicated to the elucidation of "the best minds of my generation destroyed by madness," to those who have sought to stop the madness rather than exacerbate it, to the best minds of the Eastern and Western traditions who never succumbed to the madness, and to the victims of those who did.

He*rd Said.

He said she said that they said I said … but
What I really said
Is I think it's you instead.

I saw the best minds of my generation
destroyed by madness . . .
—ALLEN GINSBERG "HOWL"

CONTENTS

1

Our Second Anniversary: Peace Corps—Togo, 1978

It was 1978, and nearing Deb's and my second anniversary. October 30 was the exact date; we were planning a big reunion/anniversary celebration for the event, and we just wanted to aim for near that date. I cannot remember the exact day of the party. Our close friends new it was our anniversary, but for us the best way to celebrate our anniversary was to throw a reunion. This reunion was to be celebrated in the Peace Corps in West Africa—Lama Kara, Togo, to be exact. We weren't sure it was going to work out, but, little by little, we organized a party as an excuse to bring together all the other Peace Corps volunteers we could find in the area, or even from around the country, if they could make it. It would be a reunion of the volunteers from our two-month training, and also an opportunity to meet and get to know other volunteers in the area. In those days a good party included a theme, food, and lots of alcohol, and what we were planning was no different: Western-style beer, local millet beer, and a barbecue of an entire cow. The cow was the highlight *and* the theme. The 1970s also included lots of drug-taking, but neither Deb nor I was into that—and, besides, drugs were virtually nonexistent among the other volunteers, given the harsh penalties in the country and the unavailability of drugs in West Africa. This to me was a relief, because I didn't want to have to deal with the embarrassment or risks as a result of someone else's drug use at our party.

Stewart, an English teacher like I was, had a houseboy who was the son of a butcher. His father agreed to butcher the cow for us in exchange for the skin, brains, guts, bones, hooves, and so forth—all the things we didn't know what to do with. My understanding was that this was a very good deal for the butcher. The animal-traction volunteers were able to donate the cow, our houseboy and the boy across the street were able to dig a barbecue pit, and the construction volunteers came up with the rebar so that we could properly build a barbecue pit in our yard—and then cook up that cow.

The boys laughed at me when I offered to help dig the pit, which I actually thought would be fun. Trying those half-size poles and digging the pit for the barbecue appealed to me. They laughed because it was inappropriate for me to do that sort of work when kids were around to do it for me, and they also thought I could not handle the handheld, half-size hand plows they used for the job for more than a couple of minutes. A couple of the construction volunteers agreed to search out the best local millet beer, and I set up a deal with the SGGG to keep a huge refrigerator he had full of beer, and any of us with motorcycles would run the beer back and forth throughout the day so that we could keep it cold. We only had a half-size refrigerator, and that wouldn't be sufficient to provide cold beer for the thirty or forty volunteers we were expecting. We were lucky, though, in that we actually had electricity and an electric refrigerator—ours was much better than the kerosene *frigos* that many volunteers had to make do with, but it was still too small for the party.

The monks and nuns of Chaminade and Adele, our bosses, took care of us rather well. We had a large, one-story, two-bedroom cement-block house with a light in every room, and even wall switches. The house, which belonged to the monks of College Chaminade, was for housing "civilian" teachers. Changing a lightbulb one time tossed me about six feet across the room; after that, I remembered to be sure the electricity was off whenever I changed one. In any case, as I said, our refrigerator was too small to hold the beer and drinks necessary for the thirty-plus volunteers we were expecting, so the deal for the refrigerator with the SGGG was quite useful.

The volunteers who went to search out the best millet beer disappeared for three days. They turned up at Maureen's hut stone—drunk, stumbling, disheveled, and bearded—announcing triumphantly that three days of drinking millet beer had been successful: they had found the best in the area.

From the start, being in Africa was an adventure. "The best job you'll ever love" is more than just a sales pitch for the Peace Corps. It is every bit as challenging, adventurous, and enjoyable as any bunch of idealistic twenty-somethings could dream up. Deb and I both were twenty-five when we joined, perhaps just slightly older than the average age. We were the only married couple.

. . .

Getting to Africa was an adventure in itself. We were in Lake Geneva, Wisconsin, when we decided to join. We both had finished college about a year before: Deb with a degree in French, and I with one in linguistics. I was working for the Playboy Club as a food-and-beverage management trainee; she as a cashier . . . I forget where. I remember talking to her at the counter, but I don't remember where it was. We were both getting sick of the corporate mentality.

Although I liked the Playboy Club philosophy in general, like all the other hotels, it was pervaded by a growing problem of reward for politics, rather than reward for a good job. Long story short, I was beginning to see that the food-and-beverage trainee thing was falling apart. The jealousy generated by three guys being fast-tracked to management caused no end of problems from room managers and chefs who had been there for years, and who were interested in management themselves. It was an interesting job, though. I was picked mostly for my experience with fine wines, my knowledge of liquor, and my experience in restaurants and hotels, which I got while I working my way through college. I am not sure why the other two were picked, but there were three of us in all, and we were meant to spend a year doing all the different jobs in food-and-beverage service—from dishwasher to head steward, from line cook to chef, and so on—and then, at the end of that year, we could expect a management position in one of the clubs around the country.

In any case, the job seemed to be falling apart under the weight of the jealousy and politics, and Deb and I were looking for a real life, something with substance and meaning, and at least some longevity. We looked into the navy briefly, but there was not much they could do with married couples at the time. The Peace Corps was a well-known option in those days, so we gave them a call, which started the rather long application process: references, doctors and dentists appointments, interviews, and so forth. We finally got to the point when they sent us job descriptions from around the world. We had chosen West Africa and perhaps South America as our areas of interest, and English teachers— ESL teachers, that is—as our job of choice, but we were really motivated to go to French-speaking West Africa, as we both wanted to improve our French while serving in a Third World country.

As an interesting highlight to our relationship, even though we both were from Wisconsin—she from La Crosse, and I from Oshkosh—we first met in Paris. France, that is. It was about five years earlier. The University of Wisconsin Oshkosh offered several study-abroad programs. After failing to find the money for a year in Vienna (where my friend, John, was attending school at the time), I grabbed a summer-school, first-semester French class and then a first-term, second-semester French class Finally, I was able to get student loans to cover a one-semester trip to Reims, France, the champagne capital of the world and home of the cathedral in front of which Joan of Arc was burned at the stake.

Deb, still unknown to me, was in La Crosse, Wisconsin, simultaneously going through a similar process; but she was a French major already taking lit classes when she signed up. She told me one time after we met that she noticed me at the orientation meeting in Oshkosh. She had remarked on the then-unpopular fashion of white socks and sandals I was wearing. I think she had sort of an "e-w-w-w" feeling about me because of my fashion, or lack thereof, and we didn't meet at that point. And, actually, come to think of it, I am not sure we even met before Reims. We were in Paris at the Sorbonne's École des Mines for the first month of the trip, but I do not recall meeting her there except perhaps briefly. The whole group was housed in a foyer called FIAP, and there was every reason to believe I had met her there, but we didn't really have the same group of friends.

It was not until we had our modest studios in Reims that we met on the stairway one day when the elevator was out. She was coming up the stairway, and I was in my room. She was a good-looking neighbor, and I wanted to ask her out. I was sitting at my desk, working on a giant crossword puzzle, and I left my door open. As she passed, I greeted her to see if I could engage her in a conversation. She took the bait, and we started talking about my crossword puzzle. Little by little, we began to talk about other things. She used the long stairway trip as an excuse to stop by so she could talk to me. Within a few days, we were dating. I still like to say we met in Paris. We were both quite romantic and, later, very much in love. Two years later at twenty-one, we got married.

Deb was a good-looking Midwestern girl, brunette, cheerful, bright, wholesome, and homey. She had a tendency to gain weight, which she constantly fought and which occasionally gave her wide-eyed, smiling face a pink roundishness. She wanted to have a busload of kids. She was very friendly and outgoing, always looking for fun people—people who would sing songs from musicals they had memorized, other French majors, literary types—but not the arrogant ones; she gravitated more toward readers than writers. She was fond of many authors and was not at all into the avant-garde type of foolishness that was so popular in the seventies, though she was on board with feminism and with antiwar, Peace Corps–type movements. She and I both were very on board with the movements toward hobbies like macramé, homemade beer and wine, and so forth. As I said, she was very wholesome and homey, even sewed a lot of her own clothes. Her future plans at that time were to get a master's in French, but later they would change to becoming an RN and then a midwife. Her interest in childbearing and so on was greater than most young women our age, but it never hit a weird or overdone point. It was something that interested her both personally and generally, and it was the Peace Corps experience that got her more interested in nursing and midwifery. In those days, too, a lot more women openly expressed an interest in motherhood, even feminists and hippies.

Deb and I were quite similar in many ways, except for the maternal part. In college in the seventies, I did my bit with long hair and a bit of drug experimentation—Deb had done virtually none—but I soon became disenchanted with the need to conform to nonconformity. I gave up the drugs, cut my hair, dressed as what I thought a beatnik would dress like, and continued to hang out with the nonconformists. I never bothered to ask about or research beatnik fashion; I just figured a jean jacket or polo-type coat with jeans and sneakers would suit the bill. The white socks and sandals had to do with the beatnik fashion statement as well, though I really had no idea what they thought of white socks and sandals.

I, too, liked the antiwar movement, the Peace Corps, feminism, and things of that nature; but I did not go into it too radically, either. I remember when the Vietnam protests were at their height before I met Deb, and the discussions often turned toward the consideration of the value of violence to shock the culture into a realization of the seriousness of the problem. They would talk of "trashing" stores, tearing up streets, burning cars, protesting, and more. The SDS was prevalent, and the realities of violence were in the news almost daily. However, there were also the hyper-peaceniks, the Gandhi wannabes, and I remember making a conscious and heartfelt decision to stay with that group no matter what transpired. That stance appealed to the idealist in me, and I really bought the Gandhi-type arguments that things could be accomplished both without war and without violence. Certainly, the Vietnam War had to go. As I mentioned, I was also into the hobbies of the time: fine wine, fine food, gourmet cooking, making beer and wine, and so forth. A friend bought one of those K-Tel bottle cutters, which I thought was a little déclassé, but in the long run it turned out to work for him and actually was entertaining.

Both Deb and I were from middle-class families. My father always worked in factories—first as a skilled laborer, then as a buyer, and then in sales. We were, in fact, lower middle class, but I always tended to associate myself more with the working class. At the time, I had thick, wavy, dark hair that the girls always liked, and my looks reflected my Croatian background—like all the people on TV during the war in Bosnia. I was a little ripped and flat-stomached, but not too much. I stopped working out in high school. I was only about 5'7". Deb was just a little shorter, or maybe just a little taller; we would often argue about that. I would off and on have a beard or a mustache. There were always girls who liked my look, but because of my problem with self-esteem, I didn't avail myself too much of the opportunities of the sexual revolution. Not that I missed it totally: In the course of my life, I guess I have had a total of twenty or thirty girlfriends, but only one wife. As it was popular to say in those days, I was a serial monogamist. I was always looking for a girlfriend for dates and hobbies, not one-night stands. Some of my joking at that time—a very sexualized time in American history—would seem otherwise, but I just preferred a relationship to a one-night stand.

I had a number of gay friends in college, but, after a swish or two (no sex), I decided that I knew from a very early age that I was straight. Gays were quite out at the time, a new thing for them, and it was a mark of a liberal to be tolerant and to have black friends, gay friends, and so on. I even had one grotesquely obese female friend who was a source of introductions to the poetry and arts world. She was a poet herself and knew a lot of the teachers and students in creative writing. I met one guy I didn't know was gay. Later, I found out he was, but that was after we had already become friends. I then noticed I was a welcome straight guy in a gay crowd—not my only crowd, but one that I was welcome in, and they were fun, and there were always plenty of good-looking straight women around them, their "fag hags." It was refreshing to have male (not necessarily masculine) friends with whom you felt no competition for the girls, and therefore no jealousy of. They seemed more like a source of, rather than an obstacle to, women. I worried a bit about whether people would think I was gay, but in those days there was not that much concern about that, and there were plenty of straights with gay friends.

A few years later, after returning from France and moving to Milwaukee, I decided to get my degree in linguistics: I liked learning foreign languages but was not that interested in literature, so I moved to Milwaukee and changed my major to theoretical linguistics. My friend, John (who happened to be gay), had returned from his trip to Vienna about a year before, and he'd moved to Milwaukee. So he was about the only person I knew when I arrived, and he helped me get set up, which also meant more gay friends and parties, but at college campuses at the time this was not at all rare. At a gay guy's party, I was caught kissing two women at the same time in a closet. It was the sort of thing that kept me at the parties and on board with the gay crowd. They just wanted to see if I was good at kissing or not, so we ducked into the walk-in closet for a demonstration. Both were quite good looking, one American Indian and one Jewish, a good argument for liberal attitudes as well. They did actually conclude that I was good at kissing.

That was actually a year or two after Deb and I returned from France, but it does describe the era. Early on in France, Deb and I became an item, but it only lasted until it was time to leave. I had run completely out of money, but she loaned me seventy dollars so that I could join her and another member of our group, who had a Volkswagen, on a trip to the south of France. We ended up in Toulon, just west of Nice, in a little bungalow on the Riviera. We stayed few of days and then headed home; she went to La Crosse, and I went to Oshkosh.

Deb and I kept in touch after we returned to the States, trying to maintain a long-distance relationship. I eventually convinced her to move to Milwaukee. We later moved in together. While on a camping trip, just for fun, somehow the conversation changed to marriage; before we got back, we were engaged. Much of the talk at the time was antimarriage, free love, and that sort of thing, so it was a surprise to both of us. Neither of us, as far as I know, had any thoughts in that direction beforehand—marriage being somewhat on the outs in those days, as I said—but we came back engaged. I didn't ask her, and she didn't ask me. It just sort of came about. It still seemed romantic to both of us.

I thought about our time in France. The classes there had been good. I spent a good many evenings drinking, mostly with members of the group, and got less out of the classwork than I could have, but it was a good experience, and it left me with a taste for travel that would ultimately lead to about four years outside of the country, most of it as an ESL teacher. Deb was a more serious student than I was, and a better French speaker. I found that my interest in languages, both German and French, waned when I got into the literature. I enjoyed the grammar and the pronunciation but little else at the time. It would be years before a serious interest in literature of any sort would develop, though I did have my mandatory classes. I had very little money the whole time, and spent a lot of the time bemoaning my lack of access to a fuller experience of France. I was quite jealous of the richer kids who had charge cards from their parents, Eurail passes, and all that sort of thing. I was especially interested in having a moped, and, even though a used one would cost as little as sixty dollars, I simply never had that much money at one time.

I also remember eating mostly in the student cafeteria, which was quite cheap. I hung out a bit with some Chinese guys and had my first of a long series of exotic eating experiences. One time, I didn't quite know what was on the menu but ordered it, anyway. I sat with the Hong Kong guys, and as I ate this gray, fleshy, roundish chicken-fried substance, they started laughing. I asked them what was so funny, and, continuing to laugh, they said, "Americans don't eat that!" I asked what it was, and, after learning that it was a pig's brain, I opted for a candy bar or some such substitute for lunch, much to their continued amusement. Much later in my travels, I would develop a taste for odd eating experiences, but I couldn't take it quite yet. This was a decade before anyone had even heard of sushi. The taste of the time was still for European foods and more complex American ones. This was when the mood was shifting from the commune and the brown-rice mentality to that of the tastes of the world: gourmet cooking and European restaurants.

I still recall the trip to the South of France. The drive from Paris to Toulon was excellent: vast, countryside fields exploding with red poppies and yellow mustard; winding roads through quiet villages; French people not used to tourists; and a beautiful cut through the mountains, the Vosges or the Pyrenees—I am not sure which any more. We arrived in Toulon, immediately heading for the beach. I had no shorts, and we wanted to enjoy the beach; Deb cut the pant legs off my jeans, and we were off. The French found it amusing and a little odd, in their friendly, accepting way. We had, by that time, become accustomed enough to the ways of the French that we no longer got the scowls the average tourist gets; instead, we got to see the friendlier side of the culture. The trip took us about seventeen hours.

Later, in Milwaukee, while attending the university and working on my degree in linguistics, I worked at a liquor store as the stocker in the afternoons and fit my classes around that. I had talked Deb into moving to Milwaukee so that we could continue our relationship. I was the principal stocker for a very large liquor store that specialized in fine wines of the world. The manager was quite well versed and experienced in wine, and it was easy to keep the conversation turned to that subject, as he constantly wanted to hone his talking skills on the topic. The manager and several of us at the store and our girlfriends and wives formed a wine-tasting club. I was reading heavily on the subject at that time, as were several others. The manager would give us wines at cost, and we would then all go to one of our houses, break out bland cheeses and French bread as palate cleansers, and the manager would give a lecture on the region or grape variety we were sampling. We tried some of the best wines in the world, including Europe and California, within a budget of from between ten and forty dollars per bottle—1970s dollars, that is. In the beginning, these parties were quite staid, informative, and formal; but, as the evening and the wine tasting progressed—and as we became looser—they became more like drunken parties, with laughter and conversation on the state of the world, friends, and so on.

We were not so poetry bound as the beats, hippies, and so on. Kerouac and pals were quite popular, as were poetry readings and poets. We were much more the ordinary Americans, bound for less-exotic lives. Deb and I had some interests in that direction, but no one else really did. I got my degree in linguistics, worked in wholesale wine for a while, and then took a job as the weekend wine steward at the Pfister Hotel, one of Milwaukee's oldest and best-known four-star hotels. I wore a tux and sold wine in the gourmet room on the weekends, and, during the week, I ran the wine cellar. It was this experience more than anything else that got me the job at the Playboy Club in Lake Geneva as the food-and-beverage management trainee. Deb had finished her French degree but was still working in restaurants.

By this time we were already married, just six months after the engagement, I think. It was a homemade wedding: Deb and her best friend made the dresses, the decorations, and so forth. It was a classic seventies wedding. I wore my tux from work. We got married on October 30 to a harvest theme. The ceremony was in a Lutheran Church, her family church in La Crosse. We had it approved by the Catholics, both to assuage my lingering Catholic guilt and to ensure that my parents would attend. They did not attend my brother's wedding because he had become a Quaker and got married in that church without the Catholic sanction, which would only have taken four meetings with a priest and a promise to raise the kids Catholic. The stance my parents took may seem extreme these days, but all through my brother's and my growing-up years, we were taught at home and in school that anyone who was not Roman Catholic was going to hell. I believe that stance by the church softened considerably in the seventies, but my parents were slow to change, quite dogmatic, and inclined to think they were doing the right thing for all concerned—and in the eyes of the church and God.

After college and a bit before, I had an interest in reading Eastern Philosophy: the Tao Te Ching, Yoga books, D.T Suzuki, Alan Watts, things like that. Pretty typical for the time, but I avoided things like the Egyptian and Tibetan Books of the Dead, or anything that would later be called New Age-y. Those things were a little too spooked out for my tastes, and they always attracted people I didn't like—people who would talk their heads off about gurus, astrology, and so forth. They would never let you get a word in, and they always had plenty of unwelcome, unhelpful advice about your life situation. Their lack of social and conversational skills was generally only rivaled by their lack of character judgment.

There was still quite an active drug culture at that time, with lots of LSD and marijuana. Cocaine was just beginning to become popular. The more problems people had with those drugs, the more they would turn to the weirder side of the spiritual arena, so I stuck with things that struck me as more established and less prone to wrap you up in the overly talkative, bad-advice mentality of unmitigated arrogance. Deb read a little of it, liked to hear a bit about it, but mostly stuck to novels and sewing and hobbies. We both liked classical music but knew little about it. We were exploring that a bit during our time at the Playboy Club. We were also part of the crowd that liked to experiment with gourmet cooking for ourselves and friends, and we had a growing collection of cookbooks.

The gurus were beginning to turn up in larger numbers as well; Rajnish, Ram Dass, and a few others were becoming commonplace. Jim Jones was operating. The Hare Krishnas, rather miraculously in my eyes, were still managing to get Americans to put on orange robes, shave their long, hippie hair into a top knot, and prance around like lunatics singing just one song. The Maharishi Mahesh Yogi seemed to attract a more responsible crowd, and I even thought about trying it but never really got around to it. Flirty Fishy was happening around the country, and there were dozens of born-again cults cropping up all over the place, with that intense, painful, pushy argument style that wouldn't allow anyone to respond except the way they wanted. Zen was well known and more widely respected as a serious discipline and a serious spiritual endeavor; at that time I never really tried it, though I read in the area a bit. There were scandals, cults, televangelists, and a growing movement that would later be called New Age before it died out around the first decade of the new millennium, probably from exhaustion and failure to deliver anything but narcissistic, knowing nods and stupid grins.

My reading also included a fair amount of philosophy, though at that time I didn't have much direction to my reading. I would just go to the bookstores, look around at the religion and philosophy sections, and see what struck my eye. Though I went to Catholic grade school and high school, I had been pretty much a nonpracticing Catholic, sometimes experimenting with atheist arguments but never quite being sold on that either.

In the seventies, besides a rather wide tolerance of drugs and the leftover mentality that there was a government conspiracy preventing marvelous new drugs from hitting a legitimate market, there was a tremendous tolerance for drinking. AA was around, but generally considered more low-life than life as a homeless wino, and homeless winos were considered the only ones who would join. The eighties brought a decade of twelve-step programs of all sorts: AA, NA, SA, etc. This was due in part to the psychological and financial meltdowns that came from the abuses of the sixties and seventies.

The drinking in the seventies was everywhere: rich and poor, old and young. Six-martini lunches, tolerance for those who would turn up drunk at work, and tolerance for those with massively debilitating hangovers—all were the norm. Working at the liquor store for those four years, I saw a lot of it. People around Christmas would buy as much as a hand truck full of hard liquor, mixes, and snacks, and the beer would come on a second. Everyone knew the hard liquors, the beers foreign and domestic, the liqueurs, the wines, both foreign and domestic—and everyone was expected to drink. Parties at work and at school would all have bars. Wine tastings were popular. There was even a time when the taste for the European included cheese stores, and the new and growing trend toward coffee shops with a European flavor. This was easily ten years before Starbucks-type chains. Deb drank far less than I did, and she trusted me to be the one that had all the knowledge of liquor and wine; socially, this was a door opener for both of us. We had a large circle of friends drawn from our own circles at our jobs, in our classes, and from our hobbies. It was a great time, filled with parties and hangovers and jokes and socializing. The conversation was basically about socializing, a little bit about politics, a lot about the hobbies, and a little about the arts. Decorating was in.

As a good example, at the Playboy Club, it seemed everyone was corrupt in a cute sort of way. Anyone who had access to liquor was a source, and everyone else traded what they had. While I was working as a line cook, I would skim some prime rib off the big one, feed a bartender and a busboy, and the busboy I fed would bring me glasses of wine hidden in coffee cups from the bartender I fed. I never saw anything more serious than that, and that sort of thing was very common. Not to say that we were all drunk and fat. There was some restraint, and there was the built-in restraint that a little prime rib really didn't merit more than a couple of glasses of wine—and more than a little prime rib would be missed. What was most interesting was the degree to which it was tolerated. Everyone either turned a blind eye to it or participated. There were rumors that there were some bunnies who would pick up keys left on tables by visiting stars for secret rendezvous, but these were likely just rumors.

Working with the bunnies was fun as well—lots of beautiful women in their sexy outfits. I never socialized with them, as Deb and I had a different circle of friends, and they had their own. All in all, it was an interesting job and quite fun, and, until it began to look like it was going to fall apart, it seemed that Deb and I were starting a life as food-and-beverage people. The corporate mentality was there; it was unpleasant but tolerable, but it also did not fit in well with the idealism that had not yet been quashed by cocaine, corporations, and the madness of Reagan and the new right wing, which no one saw coming. But as it began to look bad, the Peace Corps and the return to idealism looked better. Deb and I were both antiwar, but we were not antimilitary or antiservice to the country. For us, the Peace Corps also represented a chance to build our resumes with service to the country without military service.

While working at the Playboy Club, we were receiving job descriptions for French-speaking West Africa. One from Senegal said you would have to survive on peanuts and millet, and that was a bit too much for us. Another one came from Togo, specifically asking for a married couple. I didn't really notice it much at first, but I showed it to Deb, who became immediately excited. "We should act on this one," she said. I took another look, and agreed. A few more phone calls, another interview, and we were on our way to the US Army draft center to get the required military physical for entry. I remember the doctor at the last step of the process asking me what service I was joining. "The Peace Corps," I told him. He was disappointed, telling me I would have been a good candidate for the military. That surprised me but somewhat built my ego; be that as it may, we were off for the Peace Corps, more French, and training in teaching English as a second language.

Togo . . . We didn't even know where it was. We checked it out on the map, went to the library, and generally were quite high on the whole idea. Our lives were on track again, and we didn't have to worry about anything for two years—just teaching, learning and speaking French, and connecting with a Third World culture. Not only were we on track, we were also way cool once again. Everyone received our idea with enthusiasm, seeing it not so much as a dangerous risk, but as an idealistic chance to serve our country and another country.

We had about six months to prepare before going to Africa. Leaving the Playboy Club, we moved back to Milwaukee, got table waiting jobs (because that was the best and fastest money we could get), paid off all our bills, sold pretty much everything we owned, bought knapsacks and duffel bags for the trip, and even went to the local army surplus store to buy khaki jackets and pants so we could look the part. We were worried that might seem a little colonialist or silly, but that never really materialized; most people just thought it was fun. We were enjoying the process and getting ready to go. We had a party with invitations that read "Going to Go to Togo to Teach." My mother had a cake made: a white cake with white icing, it had a map of Africa, with Togo drawn in blue. A few days later we were off to Philadelphia for a three-day orientation preceding the two-month in-country training, the stage (pronounced like the French). Her parents and my parents saw us off from my parents' house. The last thing her father, or anyone else, said to me before we left was, "Take care of my daughter." He said it in a warm, paternal way.

In Philadelphia, we began to meet the group that was going over, and we quickly became friends. The seventies were much friendlier than today. The passive-aggressive, constant jealousy and competitiveness that so characterizes American socializing today was correctly seen as foolish and unsocial; it was not tolerated and not much indulged. We all became fast friends, taking the orientation seriously. On one of the first days, Deb had one of her many pregnancy scares. I was all shook up thinking the whole thing would fall apart at the last minute before we even boarded the plane. Deb was crazy to have babies and was always missing her pill. I didn't know if this scare was just cold feet, a real pregnancy, or just a fluke. She disappeared for a couple of hours and came back mysterious and relieved. The trip was back on. She wouldn't talk about where she'd gone; I was much into denial in those days and just wanted the trip back on. My head reeled a bit trying to think if she could have had an abortion in that short time, if it was even legal in that state, or whatnot. I suspect she found a nurse or a doctor to relieve her fears. I also don't think she would have considered having an abortion, given her desire for kids, but her silence kept me scared. She was mysterious, so perhaps she just decided to wait it out on her own. Sex was still not much spoken about in those days. We had a healthy sex life. Nothing exotic, but we could rattle the walls on the odd occasion. In the new age of the sexual revolution, we were more talk than action.

2

Going to Go to Togo to Teach—1978

". . . starving hysterical naked, dragging themselves through the negro streets at dawn looking for an angry fix . . ."

—ALLEN GINSBERG, "HOWL"

I still remember the sweltering, windless, humid, thick air when we stepped off the plane in Lomé, Togo. The air actually seemed to have an added weight, and everything was thick with sweat and humidity. The airport was stark and poorly lit. I went to the bar to have a beer and look at the crowds a bit, while everyone else milled around waiting for luggage and the bus that would take us to our quarters. There was a crashed military plane a little off in the background, and everyone was kind of nonverbally indicating that we shouldn't look at it. Togo was a military dictatorship run by a mostly popular leader named General Gnasingbe Eyadama. We would later learn that it was best not to refer to him directly, because the walls had ears. Everyone was a potential informer, and the American penchant for exercising free speech would have to be curtailed. We would use the code name, Stevie Wonder, anytime we wanted to talk in a freer manner about the man.

We were told the story of a volunteer who had said something derogatory about the general in a letter home, only to find armed members of the military waiting for greet her in her classroom to escort her back to the capital. She was given the choice of either going home or facing trial in Togo. On the trip to the capital, however, the military personnel who had arrested her stopped at their homes to introduce the interesting American they had met; they even had nice meals prepared for her. Togo was full of those sorts of contradictions.

It took us a week or so to realize that these events were not actually spontaneous; the Togolese had one planned for every evening of the stage. We were hoping to have an occasional evening off, but they seemed to want to keep us as busy as possible, like a kind of Peace Corps boot camp. We did have weekends off; but, with the heat, the study assignments, the culture shock, and so forth, it was a grueling yet rewarding challenge.

The two-month stage actually took place in three cities—Lomé, Atakpame, and Sokode—with a few weeks spent in each. We had gotten most of our shots in the States and kept our WHO cards updated, but our typhoid shots preceded the transfer from Lomé to Atakpame. What resulted was a several-hour ride in a hot bus with everyone having a minor case of typhoid. We were all draped over the seats and languishing, looking more like a busload of injured military than Peace Corps volunteers. *What timing,* we all thought. In retrospect, I think there may have been some method to their madness, in that they wanted us to have some experience traveling sick so we would have the wherewithal to travel back to the capital from our posts to see the Peace Corps doctor if we were sick. But then again, maybe they were just hard-pressed to fit the typhoid shot into the schedule, or maybe they didn't get it on time. My penchant for finding a benevolent plot behind every mishap might have led to that first conclusion; the latter deductions were far more likely.

During the stage in Lomé, we quickly learned of the only ice cream and pizza parlors, and a few other sources of food that could lessen the withdrawal from Western food. We ate cafeteria-style mostly, but on the weekends we would explore the town.

The pay was modest, but it went a long way in Africa—about two hundred dollars a month at that time. That was even enough for most volunteers to hire a houseboy. This may sound a little decadent or colonialist, but they were only paid in school uniforms, school supplies, and occasional gifts. It was a great work reference and connection for the houseboys, and it took some of the burden off needy families. It was also necessary because of the amount of work caused by the rapidly growing bush, the blowing dust, and a thousand other miscellaneous problems that the new volunteers wouldn't recognize or know how to deal with. The houseboys were also important ambassadors to the local village. They knew the village leaders and chiefs, as well as the neighborhood good guys and bad guys.

I remember our houseboy, Jean Paul, warning me about the local *maraboo,* a Muslim shaman whom we sawing walking down the road one day. Jules told me I should be nice to him or he would throw demons at me, and, almost as if he had overheard from one hundred yards away, the man twisted his fingers in his hair and made a tossing gesture toward us. Another woman in the neighborhood was introduced as a witch, which was laughingly accepted by those around at the time. In the markets, there were vendors who would spread out small blankets with dead birds and animal skulls, and we were notified, quickly and nonverbally, not to stop or look at them, as they were intended for local magic rituals and shamanistic medicine—things that Westerners weren't expected to understand.

Deb and I each had a salary, so we were in the catbird seat financially. Only those who had cash reserves or rich parents were in a better position. We had neither of those benefits, but neither did a lot of other volunteers who only had one salary.

I learned my first word in an African language on one of our first few days in Lomé. The word was *mapalo,* an Ewe word that means, "I am going to beat you." This rankled my liberal sentiments a bit, as I thought we should be examples of nonviolence and all, but I was informed that there were homeless beggar children who would follow you around all day, regardless of whether you gave them money, until you said, "*mapolo,*" and shooed them away. I never really needed to use it, finding that a couple of centimes would take care of the situation, as most of these kids were savvy enough about Americans to see that I was not the sort who beat them.

The vendors at the markets, I learned, could recognize the volunteers from the tourists and the European engineers, and they could also recognize those who were new to the country, which meant that they would exact higher prices. It was necessary to get your attitude right—that is, the attitude of a country-savvy volunteer rather than a new one—in order to get good prices. I was a good bit naive and a little childish, so it was a bit difficult for me to affect that attitude at first, but it became easier after a while. Things like cleaning your fingernails with the mandatory Swiss Army knife helped.

The markets themselves were a mix of fascination: beauty and ugliness, filth and charm. Baskets filled with fish or peppers, tables laden with goods of all sort. Lomé had a particularly large market that looked like a large three-story parking garage. Most markets were all outdoors, but the one in Lomé was in that garage-like structure, and it had a lot of the supplies we needed. Some of the evening meetings helped us understand what we would need for sure, so that we could buy them even before we learned where our posts would be. The posts were to be assigned once we finished the stage. They wanted to see our French-speaking levels, our general abilities, and our willingness to take different posts. Hardship posts—that is, posts that were particularly stark and barren, and/or off in the bush—were the hardest to fill, what with large dropout rates, tremendous poverty, and little support for the volunteers. Naturally, we all felt a mix of hope and fear regarding our potential posts, but we had little advance knowledge or opportunity to affect the process in advance. All we could do was show our best abilities, and wait. There was to be some degree of choice, but not a lot.

The personalities of our fellow volunteers quickly came to light. Some minor affairs started. Deb and I were put up in a hotel, as we were the only married couple, and so we were spared the dorm experience. Deb was worried about feeling like an outsider, but I didn't like dorm-style living. In the long run, we were quite accepted, and no one resented the special treatment. Deb might have preferred to be closer to the action in the dorm. She loved the markets, checking out all the goodies like a teenager in a mall, but her pleasant, amiable style kept her chatting with the vendors, looking for friends among the volunteers, and basically just cheering up everybody around her. She was always like that. I always was and still am rather quiet, but I enjoyed her ability to make friends, because it always gave me a larger circle without putting pressure on my introverted nature.

. . .

Life in Togo was quite severe for the locals. Thievery was dealt with particularly harshly, whether it resulted from hunger or anything else. If someone stole or someone shouted "thief," the entire crowd would descend on the culprit and beat him to within an inch of his life. I only saw this happen once. I was quite shocked, as it occurred at our dorm/ eating facility in Atakpame. One night at dinner, one of the former Peace Corps volunteers involved in the training came into the room, announcing that someone was upstairs robbing the dorm rooms. The entire crowd of Togolese men—there were a lot of them because they were training native ESL teachers along with us—ran up the stairs, pulled the thief out of the room, and beat him in front of the dorm porch. Everybody tried to get in a punch or a kick. When it was over, the thief was all bloody, swollen, and bruised. At first I didn't want to even go out, but I stood on the porch and watched. A big part of me wanted to shout for them to stop; however, the combination of culture shock, the awareness of the dynamic in the culture, and the silence of all the other Americans who just stood watching, prevented me. Our understanding was that the police would give him another beating. What shocked me more than anything was the fact that it was an experienced Peace Corps volunteer who announced to the crowd that the thief was there. Why on earth did she not just run him off herself, or get a couple of male volunteers to do it, and thereby prevent such a display? I was utterly shocked. Afterward, most everyone in the room was silent. Some attempts to excuse and justify the behavior came up, but I kept silent. I wanted to say that, as Peace Corps volunteers, we should have said or done something to prevent or stop it, to give people an idea of what Americans were all about, but I never did voice that opinion. At all. I wanted to have, and win, an argument on the subject, one that would change minds and sway opinions, but nothing came out of my mouth—or anyone else's.

. . .

Lomé, Atakpame, and Sokode passed pretty much like that. We were in class most of the day and at meetings in the evening. Every day at dinner a message in French on the blackboard would announce the evening meeting: *"Il y aura une réunion ce soir a partir de 7:30."* We were all getting tired and would've liked an evening off, but that never materialized; no one told us that a meeting was planned for every evening of the stage. I organized a small rebellion among the volunteers in Sokode near the end of the stage. We wrote on the blackboard: *"Il y aura une rébellion ce soir a partir de 7:30."* And when the time came, about ten of us skipped the meeting, walking out and singing a song—I think it was some patriotic American thing, but I can't remember for sure. I also don't remember if we were coaxed back in or not, but we probably were.

The massacre at Jonestown occurred while we were in Atakpame. The news made the rounds, but even that was not enough to cut through the sweltering heat and the demands of the stage. We were not news deprived, but there were no TVs. Some had radios. We were not allowed to have shortwaves—it would look too much like we were spies. Guns and shortwaves were the only forbidden items, also a past history with military intelligence. I suspect military bearing was weeded out as well during the interview process. We all looked like liberal idealists. No one looked ex-military, and I don't recall anyone speaking of previous military experience. When we got to our posts, we would be pretty much alone. A few volunteers were in the area, but it was certainly not like being in the military where hundreds of compatriots surrounded everyone at all times. We had to avoid the appearance of appearing to be a threat or a spy. We also had to avoid those who actually *were* spies, as they might seek out a volunteer, looking for information on that volunteer's local area or populace. That was simple enough. We were to avoid anyone who showed excessive curiosity about our areas, whether such curious types were American, European, or African.

The evening meetings also included a fair amount of first-aid training: how to fix a splint, manage a tourniquet, and avoid malaria, as well as what to do if we got sick, and so forth. We were given pretty good first-aid kits and, of course, a large supply of Aralen, the antimalaria pill. We took this pill weekly while in-country, and then we would take the cure when we left. In that part of Africa, everyone gets malaria; the best we could do was to suppress the symptoms until it was time to leave. I remember hearing a story that the mosquitoes that stood parallel to the skin were not carriers, but those that stood at a slant were. I don't know if that was true or not. One evening at the first-aid training, a rather timid volunteer at the back of the room tentatively raised his hand, and asked in a quivering voice, "What about the green mamba?" This was a dangerous snake indigenous to the area. Togo had all the major snakes of African fame: cobras, pythons, boas, and mambas. We were told that carrying a flashlight, avoiding high grass, and walking with loud steps would be sufficient to give the snakes warning, and they would slither off without causing any trouble long before we would even know they were around. In response to the specific question about the green mamba, we were told, "If you are bitten by a green mamba, you have twenty minutes to get to an iron lung, or you will die." The nearest iron lung was at the air force hospital in Wiesbaden, West Germany. I heard that one volunteer who didn't keep the grass in his yard short enough was held partially responsible for the death of a neighbor boy, because the kid had been bitten by a green mamba hiding in the grass—hence the need for houseboys, as they knew all about this sort of thing.

We were also informed that, as Peace Corps volunteers, we had access to the military medevac system. In case of a real emergency, the Peace Corps doctor could call for a medevac to fly us to Wiesbaden. This was a relief, but the first-aid classes did bring home to us the dangers we faced. Largely alone, disease and danger were everywhere, but that was part of the adventure; most of us twenty-somethings just ignored it. We were cautious and followed the guidelines, of course, but we all just pretty much assumed that nothing would happen to us that we couldn't handle.

I met a few locals during stage, mostly young guys looking for a Peace Corps guy to hang around with, hoping for a few free beers or to practice their English. I found them culturally quite different, always smiling, never saying no, and not wanting to argue about anything. Everything was to be superficial and pleasant.

One of the French teachers told a story about her grandfather, a great sorcerer who had a fight with a bad sorcerer. It was a long and interesting story that involved the two sorcerers turning themselves into various animate and inanimate objects in order to battle one another. Her grandfather finally won by turning himself into a twig and falling on the back of the other sorcerer, who had taken the form of a bull. I didn't get much of a point out of the story, but I was fascinated by her matter-of-fact belief in the story, which led her to expect us to believe it just as automatically as she did—as readily as one would accept that a car will run when the key turns in the ignition, or that a lightbulb will light up a room with the flip of a switch. She was probably aware that Americans didn't easily believe such stories, but she told it the way they told such stories there, as if she expected us to believe.

. . .

In Atakpame and Sokode, there were no ice-cream or pizza places, but by the time we got there, we were getting used to the local food. I was actually becoming quite enamored of street food—beans, beignets, rice, sauces, and so on. There was some danger of disease, but, as long as you were sure that the food had been thoroughly cooked, the danger of parasites would be significantly diminished. The beignets were my favorite, and they were quite cheap. Seeing your lunch on the hoof was new to me, and it was also a little shocking. I didn't go vegetarian, but I saw a very cute goat tied up outside the kitchen at the Atakpame dorm, soon realizing the little fellow was going to be lunch and dinner. Until then, I'd found goat to be quite good, but I couldn't really eat it without guilt after that.

As I said, Deb liked hanging out with a crowd who knew all the words to musicals, and she would often get a singing match together. I would join occasionally, but I rarely knew the words. She was a bit more diligent than I was but quite considerate of my lesser discipline. Oddly enough, she never much criticized me. We did bicker a lot, but this was never all that critical of me; it was more about what we were doing or going to do, and, of course, our finances. All in all, it was a welcome relief from the relationships I'd had in the past. Deb was always pleasant and supportive; she always looked for more to do—more cooking, more decorating, more people. I liked going places with her, but I also liked beer and bars. She rarely came with me but was amazingly tolerant of my indulgences. We were lucky in that Togo was once a German colony, and so it had its own brewery, Byre de Benin. It was quite good and inexpensive, so it made its way to all the Peace Corps parties and socializing.

There were those who had to go home because they couldn't hack it. I was worried that Deb and I might come across something that we couldn't handle, but, as the stage progressed and we met more of the already in-country volunteers, those worries melted away, giving rise to a heady feeling that all was not only going to be all right, but challenging, rewarding, and successful as well. Deb and I talked about our future—grad school for me, and nursing school for her; or maybe jobs with the State Department when we finished, if we couldn't afford school, as we'd heard that Peace Corps service was a foot in the door to some jobs in that department.

. . .

One guy dropped out as soon as we'd landed. After a few hours in Lomé, he knew he had made a mistake. Another bailed a few weeks later; unable to understand why the Togolese parents wouldn't buy their kids shoes, he couldn't resist calling them to task for it.

One of my favorite friends there was a really intelligent, interesting, humorous guy who liked to argue politics and philosophy. His name was Liam. At one point, he confided in me that he was gay. A bit of a pass might have been mixed into in his confession, but I had no trouble fielding it, and we remained good friends. A few weeks into the stage, the staff published a list of the schools that we all had graduated from.

"Hey, Liam, look at this!" I said. "Someone here went to Yale."

He said, "*Shh!* Don't tell anyone."

"It's you? C'mon?!"

25

Not that I thought he couldn't have gone to Yale; I just never thought anyone from Yale would hang out with the likes of me, a guy from a state college in the Midwest. But Liam confirmed that he was the Yale graduate; in fact, he'd already been accepted at Harvard Law School, but he had taken two years off to join the Peace Corps, wanting to serve the country and also build his resume for a future in politics. He said he had presidential aspirations, thus wanting to keep the fact that he was gay a secret. This was even more important in Togo, as the prejudices were quite severe about that sort of thing.

In a nutshell, Liam was more interesting than anyone I had ever known up to that point. He had a great sense of humor too. He didn't like snakes, and he had an odd fear of stepping barefoot on a fish.

As the time in stage progressed, we all got our sea legs, so to speak; we could walk through markets without attracting beggars and or paying high prices, and we could recognize Peace Corps volunteers from others, even on the fly. It wasn't necessarily a hardened look; it was more of a comfortable, liberal, at-ease-in-the-atmosphere look. No more eyes darting back and forth trying to drink in everything, our eyes now were wary of trouble, yet comfortable knowing that we "knew our way around."

. . .

At the end of the stage, the list of assignments was printed out. Everyone had a bit of a choice. Of course, we all would not get exactly what we wanted, but we each could put in for what we wanted, and then it would be decided if we could have it—or not.

Deb and I, however, were not given a choice. We were told that the reason they'd requested a married couple in the first place was for two Catholic high schools up north in Lama Kara: Deb was to have College Adele for the girls, and I was to have College Chaminade for the boys. The previous volunteers had been a little wild for the Catholic atmosphere, and they thought a married couple would solve the problem. We were a bit miffed at first, but we quickly warmed up to it. Feeling special for having been requested, we learned that the schools were considered the best in the country and, even better, Lama Kara was relatively well supported. We'd escaped assignment to a hardship post, much to our relief.

Togo liked the Peace Corps and was generally quite supportive of it. A Peace Corps ID opened doors, getting volunteers through inspections and roadblocks that other whites couldn't get through. Basically, the corps had four kinds of volunteers: ESL teachers; construction volunteers, who built bridges, schools, and dispensaries; nurses; and animal-traction volunteers. The Togolese, at the time, did most of their farming with handheld, half-length plows, and the animal-traction volunteers would provide cows and training on how to use them. Many of the Togolese would have preferred to jump straight to motorized tractors, but animal traction was the best we could do. The nursing volunteers dealt with pregnancies, infant care, and basic first aid. This also meant countering superstitions. For example, many pregnant women would not eat snake or eggs, because they were afraid their kids would be born with feathers, or never be able to walk.

When the post assignments had been completed, most of us were satisfied and ready. We had time to go up to Lama Kara, merely an hour or so from Sokode, and spend the night at the house of one the ESL teachers already up there. His spare room had a bed with a straw mattress. It was quite hard and uncomfortable to sleep on, but it was an interesting experience. Deb and I looked around the city, liking it quite a bit. We visited our schools and met some of our respective bosses and co-workers, all monks and nuns. The nuns wore white habits, but the monks dressed more casually—what today would be khakis and polo shirts. They were all Marionists, a Swiss order famous for missionary work and education. A few days to a week later, we moved up there.

The discussions of culture shock in the evening meetings of stage (French for "training," [pronounced *stahj*]) proved particularly useful. We'd learned that the main symptom was hating everything about the culture: the food, the people, the weather, the lifestyle, and so forth. We were further informed that the greatest amount of culture shock usually occurred at the three-month and six-month points. Thus, if we made it through the six-month point, we were statistically much more likely to make it through the full two years. Knowing the warning signs and the time periods made it seem much easier to get through.

We had left a lot of friends and family behind, and everyone made time to write letters back home. This was long before the Internet and e-mail, obviously. We all quickly noticed that we were more likely to have things to write about than those we left at home, where life was much more routine, leaving far less adventure to report. Nevertheless, there was enough return mail to keep it interesting, and we all kept up with our correspondence. We mostly used aerograms, but we sent longer reports of our adventures as well. Even though e-mail wasn't an option at the time, this was a more rewarding way to keep in touch. We had a lot to write about—the food, the people, the stage, the weather—plus, it was also quite pleasant to tune in to our own experience by trying to describe it to friends.

Overall it was overwhelming: everything was so new. It was a Third World country. There was poverty, cruelty, and harsh government, and everything was interesting. Once in Sokode, I saw one of our schoolrooms abuzz with large bugs. As I watched these bugs flying out of the room, I then noticed a young boy standing in the doorway, completely oblivious to the hundreds of bugs bouncing off him. I walked up to him, not sure if I should say something, and then I noticed his father inside. He and the boy were collecting the easy-to-catch bugs, tearing off their wings, and throwing them in a pot. He informed me that a termite nest had broken open, and that they made a very delicious soup. I then had to muster the wherewithal to stand in the room, with hundreds of the giant termites bouncing off me as well—not a typical experience for a guy from Wisconsin. He invited me over to have some soup, but I just begged off. My developing taste for street food notwithstanding, I was not quite ready for such exotic local delicacies.

. . .

The bugs in Togo were countless, mosquitoes and flies the most notable among them. If you sat in a local open-air bar, you'd spend all your time swatting the dozens of flies that circled your beer. We got used to it pretty fast. The locals were amazingly oblivious to it. The flies carried parasites, so there was good reason to keep them from landing. One bout with fifteen-times-a-day diarrhea that required a trip to the Peace

Corps doctor in the capital was sufficient to keep you swatting. There were bot flies, which carried some form of sleeping sickness; malarial and regular mosquitoes; giant termites; giant flying cockroaches; and the list went on. But, strangely, we didn't see it as a big deterrent to our enjoyment of the challenge. It was just one small, annoying part of it. The flies were the most distracting; the cockroaches were numerous but tolerable, not like the swarms in Wisconsin. Deb one time stepped into a line of ants, which quickly swarmed all over her, but she jumped out of the stream and wiped them off. Fortunately, they did not bite or sting at all, just swarmed. Giant termite hills were commonplace sights, but mostly on the plains.

. . .

Atakpame, the second city in our stage, had a bar that was famous for actually having a men's room. It had a trough with a pipe for drainage. What was funny about it was that the pipe merely went through the wall and onto the road out front, but it was at least a hint toward modernity. One of the projects of the construction volunteers was to build public toilets, but no one would use them because they seemed unhygienic compared to a trip to the bush. At one point, we wanted to walk along the beach in Lomé, but we were quickly warned against that, because the beach very often used as a public toilet.

Liam had brought a Frisbee, a very new toy for African kids, and one day he and several other volunteers got a game of Frisbee football together. Some African kids joined us, and it was quite amusing to teach them to play and to watch them catch on to the new toy.

There was a kind of reverse racism everywhere; but, rather than being hated and discriminated against, we were loved. The locals considered us quite wealthy, as well as good sources of information and handouts. Little children, mostly from three to five, would spontaneously, and almost invariably, jump into a little song and dance whenever they saw a white person.

"*Yovo, yovo, bon soir.*"

"*Ça va bien, merci.*"

It was quite adorable really, but some volunteers felt it was racist, and they resented it. *Yovo,* in slang, meant "white person." It was not usually derogatory, but some of the volunteers and the Europeans resented it. The Red Cross would give out free clothes in some markets, and this was called the "dead *yovo* market," because it was unimaginable to the locals that anyone would give away his clothes unless he was dead.

Every market had a section with bolts of beautifully patterned cloth sold to be made into dresses. The Lomé market's section was particularly good. The dresses and the cloth were called *pagne,* and he patterns and colors of these fabrics were striking; occasionally, you still see them here in the States. Naturally, Deb bought some and had her own wraparound *pagne.* It was a jungle-green shade with a pattern in it. I remember that *pagne* in particular because she'd jokingly wished that she would get dysentery so that she could lose some weight. She did lose about thirty pounds, and was in the best shape of her adult life. She looked so great that we took a photo in which she's wearing that jungle-green *pagne.* The *pagne* outfits were usually made of three of the cloths, and there was a fair amount of variability to the possible styles.

Many of the local women went around bare breasted, which was commonplace and widely accepted. It was casual enough for the twenty-something volunteers not to stare or make a scene. Our interest in cultural sensitivity also helped on that score. During stage, we were warned not to have affairs with any of the locals, because that could ruin a girl for life. Dating a white person was tantamount to killing any chance for her of marriage, and the chances of her enculturating in America were quite slim, both because of the need for extended families and the complexities that would result from going from a relatively primitive setting to a modern civilization. This was especially true in the hardship posts. Some of the construction and animal-traction volunteers talked about prostitutes a bit, but this was quite limited, and, given the liberal, culturally sensitive nature of the Peace Corps, more than a little uncool. There were enough women in the Peace Corps to make dating a reality without interfering with the culture—or ruining some local girl's life. Some of the women volunteers did date local men, which was considered to be a good bit more workable.

Deb and I were able to move to Lama Kara about a week or two after the assignments were given. Stage was over, and we were ready for our jobs. We found that we were actually getting a nice housing assignment: the two-bedroom, one-story place I mentioned earlier. It even had running water of sorts. There was a cement holding tank dug into the ground at the side of the house for water; it had a hand pump that allowed us to pump the water to the roof, from which point, gravity would take over to run the shower and the faucets. It was a simple cement-block building with slatted-glass windows, but we were very pleased. The fears in the backs of our minds about living in a mud hut were immediately alleviated. Not only did we have modern accommodations, but our digs were what could only be described as "Peace Corps Deluxe." There was even a quaint screened cabinet in the kitchen made out of *fufu* pounders. *Fufu,* one of the staple foods of most of West Africa, was pounded yams. They have these large yams—about eighteen inches long by about six to eight-inches in diameter—that are as common as potatoes in the Midwest. Women stood over a giant pestle, pounding the yams with giant mortars. The *fufu* came out a sticky ball, not unlike Japanese *mochi*. You then dipped this in a sauce which may or may not have a few pieces of meat in it, but which is usually red and made with tomatoes and peppers.

In Togo, people primarily ate with their fingers, quite cautious about using their right hands for everything, because the local custom was to eat with the right and clean with the left. Toilet paper was a luxury most couldn't afford, and water was often in quite short supply; as a result, offering your left hand, giving money with the left hand, and so forth, could be taken as a grievous insult. From very early ages, children received sharp slaps on their left hands if they ever used them for the wrong purpose.

· · ·

We inherited a houseboy from the previous PCV (as volunteers are called), a very nice sixteen-year-old boy named Jean Paul. He was bright and hardworking, and spoke French and several languages of the area too. I don't think he spoke that much English, but I don't really recall anymore. I think I remember him preferring to speak English with me, and French with Deb. He was Kabye, the main tribe in that area. There were dozens of other tribes. Ewe, Mina, and Kotokoli were the most common. They would distinguish themselves with various facial scars. The Yoruba, a Muslim tribe, had very intricate and copious facial scarring, and they were the main merchants throughout the country.

We stayed in our new quarters the first night. When we woke up the next morning, we started taking inventory of what needed to be done: a few broken slats, some sweeping, a huge ant nest in the spare room between two doors that lay on the floor, and a lot of other things. We weren't overwhelmed; we looked forward to the project, but we just weren't quite sure about how to do a lot of it. There was virtually no furniture. Before that morning was over, we saw Frere Cattin, the Frere Adjuant (Assistant Director), marching over, brisk and businesslike, with a bevy of uniformed students marching behind him. They greeted us in rapid French that I couldn't follow, but Deb seemed to understand. They walked around the house, taking inventory of everything that was there and making a list of what we needed. Within a couple of hours, he was back, accompanied by more students who carried chairs and tables and tools to fix all that needed fixing. The Frere Adjutant supervised; the kids did all the work. All in all, a very impressive display of taking care of what needs to be taken care of in a crisp, efficient manner. Almost military in its precision. We were relieved and pleased, and felt quite welcome in the atmosphere.

We were to start working in a few days. We had dinner with the monks that night at College Chaminade, my school. It was quite enlightening. The monks were serious but not humorless. They had wine with the meal, and a very good European-style meal it was, with cheese, French bread and so forth. I saw one of their rooms, dorm-like quarters with a bed, a desk, a bookshelf, and a closet. I rather admired the mix of civility and monkish lifestyle they displayed. I was a bit intimidated by them, and I worried about how well I would do with a real classroom full of real kids.

My ESL training went well, but my first lesson was a huge bomb. I was to prepare a fifteen-minute lesson but finished all I had in just five, and then I stood gaping and looking stupid when it ran out that fast. It was my first teaching experience, other than a few wine tastings; however, I knew myself well enough, even at that young age, to know that whenever I did something the first time I would bomb, but then I quickly found my way to a more natural level after that. I got a couple of desperate, pitying looks from some of the volunteers, but the Togolese and the trainers were not that worried about it: they just explained what I needed to do and how to conceptualize a lesson plan. Deb's major was French, but she also had a minor in teaching, so things went much more smoothly for her, and she had much more confidence in her upcoming job. I did not mention to her that I was a bit frightened, but she might have known, anyway.

The dinner was good, the house was set up, and we were ready to go.

. . .

Our first classes in Lama Kara went well, and I began to feel more and more comfortable in the environment. I had two classes of twelve-year-olds and one of fourteen-year-olds, which meant that I only two preparations a day. And the students actually had books. In many other schools, the students had nothing but blank notebooks, and they had to copy everything on the board. This meant that the teacher had to write out the entire lesson plan, in order to turn the notebooks into textbooks. We had it easy! Our students were considered brighter, more motivated, and more hardworking than the students in most of the other schools. The schools Deb and I were assigned to were a bit more expensive, and they offered a doorway to a secondary education. Secondary education was the main reason that English was studied in West Africa. Togo only had one university and few trade schools, which offered a very limited number of possible majors or careers, so many of the students needed to go to English-speaking countries like Ghana or Nigeria for further education.

Some days it was just too hot to teach or study, but we plodded through the lessons, anyway. I didn't know to what degree I could let the students languish, slouch, and lay their heads down in the heat, but I certainly did sympathize. I was not a tough disciplinarian, but

I also wanted to make a proper impression on the monks. They had emphasized that it was prohibited to have sex with the students or to beat them, hastily explaining that they realized Americans wouldn't do such things, but they wanted be clear—they also explained that the Togolese teachers sometimes had problems with that.

The twelve-year-olds were sweet and eager to learn, slapping their hands on their desks and avidly waving their hands to get called on to practice or recite. The fourteen-year-olds provided more of a challenge with discipline, but nothing like in the States—a little too much joking, some smart remarks, and inappropriate giggles—all in all, nothing that couldn't be handled. Talking in class and minor cheating were some other small problems. Le Frère Le Directeur informed me that the students were very grades oriented; all I had to do was take out my grade book and subtract a point for misbehavior, and that would end the problem. It did. I caught two kids cheating on a test, took their tests away, and gave them each a zero. They complained to the Directeur, which scared me, but he supported me, and that ended any further problems.

A particularly disturbing introduction to the culture took place when one student was kicked out for being a discipline problem. The Frere Adjuant called me aside one morning to tell me not to let this boy into class that day because he had been thrown out. I went to class, and, sure enough, there he was. He was lying on the desk with his face buried in his arm. I guess he had hoped that I would not notice him. I began walking toward his desk to say something, and all the kids waved at me to stop. Their faces bore looks of very serious concern. I got to his desk, and he looked up. In all my life I had never seen anyone beaten so badly, and certainly not a child. His face was swollen and purple, both eyes were blackened, and he was tearful and terrified. It seemed his father had tried to intimidate both the boy and the school with the beating. I decided to let him lie on the desk while I began class, feverishly thinking about what to do. But just a few minutes later, the Frere Adjuant arrived, and he asked me if the student was there. I told him the boy was there but so badly beaten that I didn't have the heart to toss him out. The Frere Adjuant told me to fetch him out; they would send some monks to escort him home, which, hopefully, would prevent any further abuse.

I was not too religious in those days, as was the fashion with liberal PCV types, but I was quite fascinated by the monks, who reminded me of more religious times when I was younger and had gone to Catholic schools. I was actually quite moved and inspired by my experiences in the school and with the monks.

. . .

The Togolese system of communicating different from ours, and they are much more articulate than we are with their gestures, some formal and some not. Whenever a teacher walks into a room, the student closest to the door slams his hand on his desk, and they all leap to attention, where they remain until the teacher arranges his books and is about to begin the lesson, at which point the teacher bids them sit down. This was not optional, even for PCV teachers; it was a bit of discipline that was expected of all classes throughout West Africa. Secretly, I rather enjoyed it but didn't tell anyone, because it was not a sufficiently PCV attitude. Whenever they walked with a teacher, the students were expected to carry his books for him. If they did not, neighbors and other classmates would call them on it, but they obviously enjoyed both carrying the books and being seen with the teacher.

One time a student who thought a test was too hard stood before me, imploring, "*Ça chauf! Ça chauf!*" ("That's too hard!"), all the while slapping the back of his right hand on the palm of his left in a gesture of begging. It was quite cute, but it did not make the test any easier. All the boys watching enjoyed the attempt. My fears of teaching and pleasing the monks were alleviated when the Directeur sat in two observe two of my classes. He was older than the rest of the monks, white haired and thin, with a stern but accepting countenance. After observing both classes, he left without a word; but I had the feeling he found my work acceptable. It seemed that things were going fine.

Deb, however, was really sweating. The previous teacher had gotten sick and gone home early, and so all her classes were about six weeks behind in their work. Deb had to struggle to get them caught up. She was a real advocate for the girls, offering after-school tutoring for those who wanted it, and generally being a supportive feminine force. She was very well liked by the students and the nuns.

By October, we were all settled in, as was everyone else.

We had arrived in Togo in early June, been in stage for another two months, and, by the end of October, we had three months of teaching under our belts. We were about to celebrate our second wedding anniversary, and that was when we got the idea for the party. Word went around to all the volunteers throughout the country. We had the cow coming from the animal-traction guys, the butcher arranged, and the beer all set up. We even had the heroic exploration into local millet beers to guarantee that we would have the best millet beer that could be found. It arrived in two clay jugs that held approximately twenty gallons each. Naturally, we would be drinking the beer out of the traditional calabash cups.

The beef and the *ignames* were the next to arrive. This in itself was quite exciting. We were used to seeing people carry anything on their heads, from sewing machines to tubs full of water, but, in this case, four women from the area were walking down the dirt road in front of our house, each one with a quarter of beef in a large tub on her head. I was lucky enough to get a photo of the women carrying the beef, and, as usual, they found this amusing. Also as usual, there were some kids gathered on the road, just sitting and standing there, watching the *yovos*. This was commonplace. Without televisions and with a scarcity of toys, one entertainment for the children was to stand around watching *yovos*. Occasionally, we would give them ice cubes, but we didn't want to become the local boys club or girls club, so we saved that for immediate neighbors and friends' kids. The *ignames* were cut up and deep-fried like giant French fries. For some reason, I had a sauce made of the cow's blood, some sort of macho thing, I guess.

Volunteers began arriving. Some arrived the night before and were staying in the area with other PCVs. A bunch stayed in sleeping bags in our place. When the party was off and running, everything went smoothly. Lots of friends from stage, volunteers we hadn't met before, and so on. The beer supply was fine, and anyone with a motorcycle—nicknamed the "Peace Corps Cadillac"—would make runs for cold beer. The barbecue pretty much took care of itself, as animal-traction volunteers and others took turns supervising—or, rather, took turns dominating, ruminating, and commenting on it. I pretty much started the fire, and that was it; I spent the rest of the day eating, drinking, and talking. This was a great day for Deb too. She was really in her element, with lots of friends around. She variously played hostess and enjoyed the company of her friends. One girl from stage arrived, breaking into to tears as soon as she saw everyone. She had accepted a hardship post way in the north of the country, had been living in a hut, and had no contact with any Westerners, let alone American PCVs, for three months.

One of the animal-traction volunteers spoke Fulani, the language of the nomadic herders of West Africa. Another, who had been bitten by scorpions three times and was relatively fearless in his approach to the environment, had suddenly turned paranoid because he was just two weeks from leaving. He was afraid even to sit under a coconut tree, for fear one would drop on his head. The guys who sought out the millet beer were there. The whole thing was great. No one complained, and it went on until the next morning, with just a few volunteers left.

We discussed survival and "PCV gourmet." We learned there was a shop in Lomé that sold block cheese, and we arranged to get in on a deal for someone who was going to bring some back for us. We shared information about a lady with a small flour mill who, for a small fee, would grind peanuts into peanut butter for us.

With our knowledge of the area growing, we continued to work on the house. We had screens made at our own expense, and Deb planted flowers on the front lawn. The neighbor ladies liked this quite a bit, but one of the husbands warned Deb that it would make everyone jealous. She was miffed, but she went on undeterred, remaining as pleasant as she could. I was very interested in the screens, because, in spite of the embroidered, mosquito netting over our bed, three or four mosquitoes always managed to get in, and they delighted in disturbing our sleep.

. . .

One time when Deb and I were walking home, we saw about six of the neighbor women on our porch, which was only about ten feet by four feet. They were stepping on millet to get the grains out. At first, I felt a little imposed on, but Deb thought it was great, so I figured I'd just ignore it and let her have her fun. It was neighborly, and it was difficult to know when you were, or were not, being imposed upon. There was tremendous poverty in the area; by all comparisons, we were quite rich. The needs were real, and it was always difficult to turn down a request. We had requests for money, for blankets, and for medicine. No one seemed to understand that we had a limited supply of these things, but we got used to it—and, eventually, we learned how to tell when to help and when to refuse.

We paid to have lunch prepared for us three times a week by a family close to my school. They lived in a compound of huts, with lots of kids and a large extended family It was a great opportunity for us to get to know the culture and ease the time demands of taking care of the house, doing our class preps, and socializing. Plus, there was no shortage of cultural experiences. One time one of the women of the compound was showing off her watch. The others kept saying, "Ask her the time! Ask her the time!" When we did, she made a large, exaggerated gesture toward the sky, looked at her watch, and then told us the time. Everyone laughed. Deb and I didn't see why it was funny, but then we were informed that she was a prostitute, and a customer had given her the watch. The funny part was that she didn't know how to tell time, and so she had to look at the sun in order to give a response; hence the expansive gesture.

Another time we had come for lunch, and one of the girls had her head shaved. We asked her why, and she explained that she'd had a malaria attack, and that the shaved head helped with the headaches. The tribes in the area all distinguished themselves with facial scars, as I said. They would make the appropriate slits, and then put a ground-up leaf in it so that the wound wouldn't heal too quickly. A scorpion bite had a similar remedy.

One particularly baffling experience occurred one day while we were at lunch at the compound. The eighteen-year-old girl took me aside. I thought she was going to ask for some tutoring, but she took me into one of the rooms in the compound. The room had no furniture, and she stood facing me from the back wall, while I stood with my back toward the door. She proceeded to tell me that her father wanted me to know that I could have her as sort of a sideline girlfriend. I knew this could ruin her life I agreed to it, but her matter-of-fact delivery was quite baffling to me, as was the fact that it was her father's idea. I declined as politely as I knew how. I can't remember for sure if I told Deb, but I probably did. I went back to lunch, and everything went on as usual.

Another time, everyone was passing around a picture that was making the rounds all over Togo. It was a picture of a guy sitting on the ground, holding a severed head in his lap. I was quite shocked. They explained that the man had caught his wife with another man, and decapitated him. He was sentenced to death, but, before the execution, he was to sit in all the major markets holding the head in his lap. Of course, he was beaten by the police at each stop as well. Again, I had to restrain my liberal intention to criticize and try to uplift the situation. There really was no room for anything other than quiet acceptance. I hoped that the Peace Corps work, in general, would help with everything.

I discussed it a bit with one of the other male volunteers. He told me a story that in Ghana, just a year or two before, a major chief had died. Shortly thereafter, four farmers out in the bush turned up decapitated, supposedly for some sort of ritual for the deceased chief. The monks assured us that the Peace Corps was in no danger; yet, in spite of decades of missionary work, the locals would go to church and claim believe in God, but they still performed many of the same rituals of times past—and there were those who still practiced sorcery.

I remember the first day we had our motorcycle. I had this weird, deep-seated sense of foreboding, which I told Deb about. Rather than being her supportive, soothing self, as I'd expected, she rather surprisingly became very frightened. She told me not to talk like that, and then she dashed back into the house. I just thought that maybe she was catching some of the local superstitiousness.

Our neighbor across the street was an ambulance driver and a Muslim. That was a good job, so he could afford four wives. He had a dozen or so kids, whom we rarely saw. His compound was across the street, basically, but it was a little hard to see into. One of his boys would come around and do odd jobs for us. He killed a rooster for us one time when we wanted to have coq au vin. The boy had an odd reputation. He seemed a little delinquent, but he was a neighbor, and so we wanted to be helpful. He was known to be able to pick up scorpions by waving his fingers in front of them to distract them, and then picking them up by the tail. We had a tiff one time about him shortchanging me on an errand. Deb straightened it out.

One time the family who served us lunch asked us for some blankets and some malaria pills. It was as though they thought all we had to do was ask, and the Peace Corps would resupply us. I can't remember what we did. We didn't give up the malaria pills, because it was difficult to go all the way back to Lomé to get more—an eight-hour grueling drive in a bachet or a station wagon crammed with as many people as they could fit. I had to make the trip one time with a case of giardia. I didn't know what I had. All I knew was that I had the fifteen-times-a-day diarrhea that signaled a parasite, and I had to go to the Peace Corps doctor. I loaded up on Imodium for the trip and headed south. We were told not to trust the local bush clinics. The trip down was miserable, but I felt better after I took the medicine, and so I had a couple of days on my own in Lomé. Given my introverted nature, this was a bit difficult for me. I went to some restaurants, read a bit, and, overall, breathed a huge sigh of relief when it was time to go back.

One night a building in the neighborhood burned down, and I stood and watched a little bit, until a neighbor boy came by and told me to leave or people would think I had set it. This kid's father had a pet monkey, tied up in the back. He warned me the monkey was dangerous, so I decided not to fool with it at the time. It was pretty cool, though. I wondered what the father was thinking, keeping a dangerous monkey with little kids around, but I felt I was too new to say anything. There were lots of things you wanted to comment on, but it made little sense to do so, as nothing would make a lasting point. It was best to stay with the Peace Corps agenda, where you would occasionally have a chance to present a different view of things. The boy attended the local public school, but he liked me and would hang around a little. He was a very cute kid with a good sense of humor.

I think he hung around the party a bit, as did a bunch of other kids, but the animal-traction volunteers and the construction volunteers were more likely to shoo them away than let them stand around staring. The English teachers were a little more tolerant and a little more used to the locals' behavior.

Carol was one of Deb's friends, and she and Deb spent a lot of time catching up and creating chatting circles throughout the party. Naturally, they all spoke of their future plans, their current experiences, and so forth. Deb's cats were around, but, with the party going on, they were probably scared and hiding a corner somewhere. Deb was always having pregnancy scares, but I figured cats were better than kids until we were more settled and had more money. She even wanted to have a kid in Africa, an idea which I shot down because of the dangers. She still tried to talk me into it on occasion, but there were other occasions when I would see her popping three birth-control pills at once. I said, "I thought you were told it didn't work that way," but she just ignored me. I wondered if it wasn't some kind of a test of my tolerance of an in-country pregnancy.

She had a bad malaria attack one day. I went to her school to tell them she wouldn't be able to work, and they sent the sister nurse with a shot of some sort. She was miserably sick. It was the kind of attack with alternating fevers and chills, and the inability to decide which was the more pressing symptom: vomiting or diarrhea. In spite of the challenges, the sickness, and the culture shock, we still felt that we were making a contribution and that our future was on track. Even better, we had particularly good situations: a good house, jobs at the best schools in Togo, off in a city that was far enough from Lomé to be exotic but not so far that we didn't have Peace Corps friends in the area. There were three others in the vicinity and a half dozen more nearby; they all were in small villages, some of which were only an hour way, some quite a bit farther. Sokode was only an hour away, and a lot more volunteers lived there. Liam was about an hour away.

We had only recently gotten our motorcycle. The Peace Corps supplied them to animal-traction and construction volunteers, but they weren't considered a necessity for the teachers, so we had to buy our own. We got a black 90cc Kawasaki. It was way cool. Deb liked it and liked the freedom it offered, but she was afraid to drive it. I got her to try one time, and it ended in a mini-disaster. I took her to a large, flat, dirt-covered vacant lot, and I told her what to do. She took off across the field, completely out of control, and ended up having to fall off it in order to stop. I figured she'd want to pick it up again another time, but I was content to be the sole driver for a while.

There were a couple of very odd experiences with some of the construction volunteers shortly after the party. I never did figure them out. I was trying to get to know them in order to enlarge our circle of friends, so I wasn't too critical of them. They seemed to have a bit of a hazing mentality, and so I thought I'd just be tolerant and wait that out. I also had some notion of spending my second year as a construction volunteer for a more hands-on kind of Peace Corps experience and also to get something a little different on my resume. I don't remember the circumstance, but one of them was giving me a ride back from Sokode, and on the way he stopped at some friend's house, a Togolese local. He was very sharp and convincing, saying that I should wait in the truck. He went inside and didn't come back for hours. I felt like an idiot for sitting there and not going in, but I was somehow frozen in my style of socializing, where I wouldn't be my usual critical self until I got to know people better. He came back—finally, after three or four hours—and he didn't offer an apology or a word of explanation. When we got back to my house, he again told me to wait in the truck. He needed to talk to my wife; it was a matter of grave importance. I again complied, feeling even dumber and more timid, especially since I thought some of the construction volunteers had been overly solicitous with her in the past, crowding around her in an excited social exchange while subtly excluding me. This time I only waited about fifteen or twenty minutes before I went inside. I gave the guy a glare, but Deb wouldn't tell me a thing. I sulked over a beer and then went to bed. It was the seventies after all, and there was need to be more tolerant of those overly solicitous behaviors, because the one who complained was the one who was most likely to be taken to task. The others were "just being boys," or something of that nature.

In any case, the party was over; we were back in the routine of things, and our second wedding anniversary was a memorable one with lots of photos. Almost as good as the wedding itself. Deb and her friend, Joyce, had designed the wedding themselves. Because it was in October, they'd decided on a harvest theme. Deb's and the bridesmaids' dresses were harvest gold; rather than cut flowers, they carried sheaves of wheat, and so forth. Deb made her own dress, as did the others. It was a real homemade seventies wedding.

3

The Accident—December 7, 1978

". . . angel headed hipsters burning for the ancient heavenly connection to the starry dynamo in the machinery of night . . ."

—ALLEN GINSBERG, "HOWL"

I woke up in the hospital in Wiesbaden barely remembering the flight from Togo; a nurse was having trouble placing an IV. I guessed I had been there for a couple of days. I was informed that Deb was still on her way, but as I attempted to ask about her, the nurse gave me yet another shot of morphine, and I passed out. Just before I went out, I heard her say that I was in intensive care.

The next time I woke up I was in a regular room. The bed next to me was empty. At first I wondered if Deb would be sharing it, but then I thought that would be a bit odd; it was a hospital, after all, not a hotel. The air force doctor came in shortly afterward to inform me that I was in Wiesbaden. He told me not to worry about my leg: they were still trying to save my life. I was shocked and baffled because, over the five days or so, I'd had no idea that either my leg or my life was in danger. Before I even had time to think this through, Dr. Kilgade, the Peace Corps doctor, walked in. At that moment, the gravity of the situation hit me: why on earth would he be there in Germany with us? *This is just a couple of broken legs,* I thought, *not enough to take him away from all the other volunteers.* He sat down on a chair next to me, informing me that Deb was dead and that I was still dying. She'd died of a combination of shock and gas gangrene. They had tried to save her by amputating her leg, but this was to no avail. After that short, matter-of-fact explanation, he was gone—or maybe I passed out.

Next came my first awareness that I actually might be dying. I didn't realize how serious the situation was until Dr. Kilgade came to talk to me. Shock and denial—and constant shots of morphine every time I'd woken up during the past five days—had kept me blissfully unaware and more motivated to heal than if I had known the truth. Now I felt quite ill, and I turned to the side. I felt like I was really drifting off to death, and I had the first of several near-death experiences. When I looked to the side, I could see through the walls. I saw nurses in the hallway and other people scurrying about, and I saw through the hall to the other rooms. Everything still had the same colors, but it all was see-through. I wondered if I wanted to die, if I should die to try to follow Deb, and so on. I really had no idea what to do or how to do it, though, so I resolved that if I could do anything, I would try to live. At that moment, I saw Deb—by that I mean an image of her, which appeared to be about forty feet high. She had on the green *pagne* she always liked so much—the one she wore for that photo after she lost those twenty-five or thirty pounds from dysentery—and she looked great. I looked at her image, and then I drifted off into that weird see-through world.

When I woke up, my arm was swollen, red, and quite itchy. The antibiotics they were pouring into my arm were causing a reaction. I called the nurse, who put the IV into my other arm. She gave me a soaked towel to put on the swelling, explaining that the antibiotics could not be stopped. My ribs hurt; two were broken, I guess. The pain in my leg was awful, and I asked for pain meds. They seemed to have changed from morphine to Demerol. The nurse informed me that I had an operation coming up. They were going to put an external fixation device on my leg so that the large wounds on my lower left leg could be treated daily. That is, they were going to drive four spikes through my leg, two of which would stick out from the top in order to make a double tripod device that would serve as an external cast. This contraption would hold the bone together, and then the wounds, which I had not seen since the accident, could be dressed and cleaned every day.

I wanted to think about Deb, about my leg, about this whole thing. Was I going back to Africa? Would I be going back alone? Could I go back alone? What would that be like? What would people think? Would they blame me? What would Deb's family think? There was far too much to process, not to mention the loss. What would I do without her?

What in God's name had happened? I actually remembered everything in the minutest details. It was not a matter of not knowing what happened, literally; but, rather, the unanswerable question of what had happened to our nice life, our future, my wife, my job, our cute little house. What had caused such a wonderful situation to turn so horribly bad? I wondered about black magic—if I had inadvertently or naively angered someone—but I didn't really believe in that sort of thing. I pushed all this back as, once again, my arm began to swell and itch from the antibiotics. I checked my body for other wounds: just a few cuts and bruises. My leg was in a long cast stained with blood and yellow pus from what I'd been told was still an open wound. The leg and the ribs were the only serious injuries. I was also informed that I had picked up many very serious infections from the accident, and perhaps from the bush clinic in Lama Kara and the hospital in Lomé. This accounted for the copious yellow drainage and orange tinge to the bloodstained cast. Deb's wound had closed, but mine stayed open. A closed wound provides a better environment for gas gangrene, which is why I never got it—but she did.

The accident was quite clear in my mind. It still is, even now, and repeats itself in its entirety all the time—quite involuntarily, I might add. Pausing at the entrance to a small bridge, noticing a car coming a long way off, wondering whether or I should wait or go, suddenly feeling a wave of macho come over me because I was thinking that Deb thought I was a wimp—all because some of the construction volunteers seemed to be hitting on her. I elected to go, only to discover a deep rut on the right side of the road that I could not cross without tossing us, and then noticing that the car had turned onto the road coming toward us and going far faster than I had thought. I bore down on that rut, keeping as close to it as I could without toppling us in front of the oncoming car or into the dry riverbed below. (Much later, I would learn that Deb had been distractedly looking to the right, enjoying the scenery, and had no idea whatsoever of the impending accident.) The car sideswiped us, and we were thrown into the riverbed. I landed with about six inches of bone sticking out of my lower left leg. A huge, ever-growing pool of blood formed, and the flesh on my calf was torn open and bowed back in an impossible way. Deb was crying, asking me to come and help her, but I told her I could not because my leg was broken.

I don't really recall going into surgery, but when I woke up afterward, my leg was covered in bandages. Instead of a cast, the external fixation device was there. My leg was covered in a large bandage, but I could see the four pins going straight through the sides of my leg, the two protruding out from the top, and the bars that turned the whole thing into a wire-cage cast. I was somewhat shocked and confused; I had no idea what to think or feel about this or anything else that was going on. My arms kept swelling and itching terribly, and they would alternate the arms for the IV, but they could not stop the antibiotics. All the distractions and the drugs made it nearly impossible for me to think about the reality of the situation: Deb's death and my condition.

At the time, I was not very involved in religion, and I had virtually no knowledge of psychology. I didn't really believe much of anything, spiritually; I was rather science-minded. The only strategy I had for dealing with it all was to push everything back. The idea was to keep out any painful feelings until I was better. This made me strangely flat but cheerful. I wondered what the nurses and doctors thought of me. Did they think I was heartless or cold? Did they think it was all my fault? They were all quite nice and sympathetic, which I thought was genuine. They seemed to think well of me, but this fear gnawed at me—that I had done something wrong, or that they thought I had done something wrong, and that this had led to the accident. But this, too, I eventually pushed back, in favor of flat and cheerful. I never cried. I thought of suicide occasionally, not too often, and I pushed this back also, as I had enough of a religious background to worry that things could actually be worse if I tried.

I tried to ask about my prognosis, but didn't receive much of an answer except that, as long as I was an emergency, I would be kept in Wiesbaden. I remained there for twenty-one days before I was taken by medevac to Wisconsin and given a medical discharge from the Peace Corps.

The most painful part of the stay was every morning, when the doctors would come in to do a debridement of my leg. This had to be done every day for about a week; I think it was eight days, but it might have been six. The two doctors would come in with four nurses. The nurses stood two each on either side of the bed. Their job was to hold me down if I couldn't take the pain, or if I squirmed too much. The doctors had to cut away dead flesh and black bone, which were being rotted away by the infections. They were also still finding and removing dirt and stones in the wound from the original accident.

The nurses actually never had to hold me down, even when the doctor would hit that nerve below the knee that caused my whole body to spasm in pain. He always apologized, assuring me that he was getting better at avoiding it; he promised that, as soon as the nerve was exposed, he would be able to avoid it completely. I didn't want my bone or my flesh being hacked at. I didn't want the pain. I didn't want the infections or the device. And yet, my mind did not reel at all this. Rather, along with the emotional pain that I was able to stuff, I also was able to stuff my reactions to the physical pain. I could lie quite still through all the debridements, never moving, crying, or screaming in pain. Throughout the day during the week or so that I had to endure this process, I did have some fear of the procedure that would occur the next morning, but this fear was crammed inside me along with everything else. The air force doctor, who had served during the Korean War, said he'd never seen anyone who could take pain the way I could.

It seemed that I was somehow consciously able to access the shock that had swept over me at the site of the original accident. I recalled the scene again. I remembered lying in the dirt below the bridge. Deb was crying; she kept shouting at the crowd that had gathered. She was behind me, I think. I looked down at my leg, seeing about six inches of bone hanging out; my calf was torn open and bowed back in the weirdest way, and the puddle of blood that had formed kept getting

48

bigger. I tried to look at Deb, but I couldn't turn in any way that would allow me to see her. I heard her ask me to come to her, and I told her that I couldn't: my leg was broken.

I was in extreme pain and on the verge of panic. I was afraid I was going to cry and scream like a little girl. But then, just at that moment, my whole body seemed overwhelmed by this feeling that I realized must be shock. I completely froze: the pain was there, but somehow it didn't seem to matter, and I was able to remain calm and focused. I tried to address the crowd that had gathered on the bridge above us. Thoughts of being off in the bush in Africa, bleeding quite copiously with no ambulance and nothing but bush clinics in the area, all failed to get through to me. The shock took over my mind as well as my body.

Deb kept yelling at the crowd, because, rather than trying to help or even do anything, they just stood on the bridge and stared at us. I tried, in my most formal French: "*S'il vous plaît, monsieur, nous avons besoin d'un camion.*" We had to get someone to flag down a truck. We were a bit out in the bush, and there were no ambulances. Fortunately, a short time later, two fellow PCVs from Lama Kara turned up, and they were able to flag down a truck. I guess they must have applied a tourniquet—I would have bled out otherwise—but I don't actually recall their doing this.

My hospital strategy of cramming every emotional and physical reaction into that memory of shock seemed to be working. In addition, I was quite lucky in that John, an American friend who was working in Berlin, was able to take time off and come and sit with me. He got in a few days after I arrived and was able to stay until my medevac back to Wisconsin. John was a good friend and a very good-humored person. He was a good friend of Deb's too, and, thankfully, he was as good at denying the facts and the emotions of the issue as I was. We stayed with superficial, cheerful conversation. He stayed in town at his own expense. He was gay and a bit of a drunk, and the staff allowed him to drink scotch in the room, as he entertained everyone with his bon vivant gay style and drinking. People were quite soft on drinking in those days, as I said, even in the hospital.

Several times a day, one or the other of my arms would swell up and become itchy from the antibiotics. It was hugely uncomfortable, but they informed me the infections were still raging; the antibiotics were still necessary, and so were the debridements. As I said, all these distractions, along with the drugs, made it nearly impossible to think about what had happened.

When I finally saw my leg, it was quite a mess below the knee: About three inches of exposed bone, two inches of which were black on the edges, and a trough in the center where the bone was missing. The leg was swollen to about four times its normal size, and there was a huge amount of exposed muscle where the skin had been torn off in the accident and as a result of the various operations I'd had—two in Africa, and one in Wiesbaden (at least one that I knew of, I should say). The daily debridements were done with just a local, as no one can undergo general anesthesia every day. These debridements were necessary, but they probably made my leg look worse. The section of exposed muscle was about fourteen inches long and four inches wide at its widest point. It ran along the side of my leg, and I could see it quite clearly when the bandages were changed. The blackened parts of the bone, and the even blacker parts of the muscle, were what the doctor had to clean off during the debridements.

The accident had happened on December 7. Deb had died on December 9. On Christmas Eve, I was still in Wiesbaden. John was visiting me, and he got up to look out the window. On the way, he noticed a large pool of blood under the bed. It's a good thing he got up, as it wasn't visible from where he was sitting. I could have bled out if he hadn't seen it. John called the nurse. I felt bad that the eighty-something-year-old doctor had to be called in on Christmas Eve just for me, but nothing could be done about that. Just one stitch fixed the problem, and, once I was sewn up, the nurses gave me a couple of bags of blood to fill me up again.

That whole night was just one more thing to stuff—Christmas Eve in Wiesbaden with John, rather than in Togo with Deb. I was pretty much in a mode that would last for thirty years: emotionally flat, cheerful, a little childish, and tremendously cramped. For years, people would describe my countenance as looking like a bomb about to go off, and yet I appeared cheerful and a little childish; perhaps I vacillated between explosive and cheerful more than they were simultaneous.

In spite of John's presence and the friendliness of the nurses and doctors, I was quite lost, everything seemed quite bleak, and I could not bring myself to think about or feel anything—not the accident, not the past, not the future, not the debridements, not who was paying for all my care, not what I would do, not when I would actually be able to walk again, not what would happen when I did decide to process all this, and on and on. I simply remained frozen in shock, a cramped misery in the deepest denial. Anytime I felt threatened by a thought or a feeling, I would push it back again. The painkillers helped a great deal in this regard. I might have had a few drinks with John, but not many—if I had any at all. They allowed us both to smoke in the room. Perhaps they didn't want the complication of nicotine withdrawal added to everything else I was dealing with. Maybe they were just being nice; or, maybe, it was still okay to smoke in hospital rooms in the seventies.

When I was no longer an emergency, they asked me where I wanted the medevac to take me. I thought about DC, as it would offer some semblance of connection to the Peace Corps and all our plans for the future. But, ultimately, I chose my hometown of Milwaukee—I dreaded this, because I didn't want to be the one to tell people that Deb had died, and I also felt that the accident was my fault—or that others might see it as having been my fault or a sign of my failure.

But, in any case, the medevac would take me to Milwaukee. The first hospitalization there lasted a total four and a half months, largely because they wanted to keep me on high dose antibiotic treatments for the osteomyelitis that had developed, and also because they had to keep doing operations to continually replace the bone that the infections rotted away. One of these surgeries involved cutting off a portion of my fibula and placing it inside the tibia, where the huge trough had been chiseled during the debridements in Wiesbaden.

They put me in a hyperbaric chamber, which actually caused me to kind of freak out at one point; I refused to go in. My hesitation had something to do with death and graves, I think, but I wouldn't think it through or even look at any associated images. I just stayed with the situation and refused to go in. They later brought me Valium, and I was able to complete the treatments when I took it.

At one point, the plastic surgeons who were reconstructing the leg, along with the orthopedists, suggested that I have a portion of my calf from my right leg attached to the gap in my left, and then leave the two plastered together in some kind of weird double cast. This I refused. It was just too much: too much of a reminder of my helplessness and too much of a threat to my good leg. I also didn't see any reason to believe that this operation would take any better than the others.

They used to take me down to the physical-therapy room for baths, where I would be loaded bodily on a winch into a bathtub full of Betadine to cleanse the wound and fight the infections. I remember this being particularly painful after the first bone graft, when they had chiseled bone from my hip to try to heal the bone in my leg. My hip was particularly painful, and it was difficult to be constantly transferred from the bed, to the carts, and then to the baths.

I also had twice-daily bandage changes. I was lucky that I was at St. Mary's in Milwaukee, the hospital that housed the burn center. Because of this, they had a doctor who was an expert in difficult-to-treat infections, and he had me on many, many antibiotics, both oral and intravenous. Blood, antibiotics, blood work, catheters after the operations, but not for too long after. He wanted me to eat five thousand calories a day, but I was hardly eating at all, so he hooked me up to a subclavian feeding tube so that they could pour the five thousand calories a day straight into me, just below the neck.

I maintained the same cramped, cheerful, somewhat childish countenance through it all, but the experience was one of constant assault, with no let-up. Something was always rotting, or they were poking or prodding me, or I was on my way to another operation. One night, I woke up in a pool of diarrhea. I called the nurse, and then I passed out, I thought from embarrassment. The next night, the same night nurse informed me that I had almost died again. "From what?" I asked. He wasn't sure, but the doctors were on it. I think I had about eight operations in Milwaukee—that's in addition to the ones in Africa and Wiesbaden, as well as all the debridements. Drugs were constantly pouring through my system. The operations seemed like assaults, as did everything else. During the day when I was alone in my room, there was just a pervasive feeling of bleakness and hopelessness, along with some suicidal thinking, but, again, my religious background was still strong enough to make me worry that things could actually be worse if I took that route. It felt like my body was writhing without moving. Still stuffing everything except that general sense of hopelessness and bleakness, I'd tell myself, *I'll just make it to lunch. I can handle that much. I'll just make it to dinner. I can handle that much. I'll just make it to the sleeping pill. I can make it that far.*

It would be a total of three and a half years before I was finally off crutches, out of the cast, and walking on my own—that is, with a mutilated, crooked leg that wound up two and a half inches shorter than the other as a result of all the surgeries. My total time spent in the hospital was about eight months. The whole time, I kept stuffing everything, not seeking any support, just trusting the doctors, even when they kept saying "six more weeks" every time another six weeks had passed. Throughout this time, my only therapy was drinking beer and hanging out in coffee shops and restaurants. I could hardly stay at home anymore, and even with the full leg cast and crutches and the Wisconsin weather, I would make it out every day to bars, coffee shops, and restaurants.

In the hospital in Milwaukee, I was lucky in that I had a lot of friends in the area, and many came to visit frequently. This was very helpful. I was allowed to smoke in the room, and I had a doctor's order for two beers a day. I often had a couple more, and this helped as well. My friends, too, stayed superficial and cheerful—maybe this was just the Midwestern style of socializing, or maybe it was out of consideration for my condition. They were quite nice, not exactly psychologists, but sensitive enough. Coffees, beers, and friends would help. Ordering a coffee during the day from the nurses would help as well, as I could usually squeeze in a little superficial conversation. The infection specialist called me a survivor, and this bucked me up. I wanted to be in the good graces of the doctors, whom I saw and treated as demigods of sorts. The nurses complained of the doctors treating themselves in the same way, but I kind of liked it.

In any case, after four and a half months of all this, I was able to leave. Four and half months of having no other end in sight than "six more weeks" or "one more operation." After having been on my back or in a wheelchair for that long, I had to go to physical therapy to get used to standing and walking with crutches. I would still have the external fixation device for a few more months, and I found this tremendously embarrassing. On top of everything else, I thought I looked like a freak with that contraption on my leg; besides, it would always lead to curiosity and the need for me to mention the death of my wife.

During the stay, I found out that I was getting workers' compensation and the federal government was paying all the bills. I don't think I ever had to pay a cent. There were no co-pays in those days, not even for the countless prescriptions I had to take throughout the whole ordeal. I had a small insurance policy of ten thousand dollars from the Peace Corps, plus another few thousand from the money from compensation that was not spent while in the hospital. I felt I couldn't work because of the constant impending hospitalizations, as well as the need for time to put my leg up, change bandages, and on and on. I also felt funny about the money, as it involved Deb's death; I wanted to do something productive that she and I both would've enjoyed, rather than just blow it on a car, stereos, and things of that nature. After a while, I started a small business, because, with myself as boss, I could work around the hospitalizations and medical appointments.

I began a small arts-and-entertainment magazine for the city of Milwaukee. In six months, the money was all gone. This happened just as advertising contracts began to come through, but they were not enough to keep the business going. I had started a city-activities magazine modeled on the *Parisscope* of Paris. An exhaustive and well-organized weekly presentation of everything there was to do in the greater Milwaukee area: arts, dance, bands, local events, and so on. It was a good run, and I was able to keep it going, even with a short stay in the hospital in the middle of it all. It was staffed by friends with relevant talents, and we successfully completed and distributed four weekly magazines, but the money just wasn't enough. If I had hired a proper, experienced ad salesman in the first place, we might actually have made it, but we closed and the money was gone. I felt bad, of course, but at least the money had gone for something that was productive. I also felt somewhat relieved of a burden, because the money, having resulted from a tragedy and the loss of my wife, mostly just made me feel bad. I wondered if the lack of success was also part of bad luck or a curse, just as the accident had been, but I still didn't really believe in curses. In the end, I figured I was just naive and underfunded.

Before the first four-and-a-half-month stay in the hospital was over, a volunteer from Chicago who had finished her tour in Togo came to visit me. Others had felt that I needed to know the whole story, and she had been with us during that time. She had been a good friend of Deb's. I came to learn that the reason it took three and a half days to get a medevac was because the Peace Corps doctor had trouble getting through to actual doctors in Wiesbaden. He kept getting dismissed by operators who didn't think two broken legs were serious enough for the service. One could argue that Deb might have survived if it hadn't been for that delay. They might even have been able to save her leg. Wiesbaden had a hyperbaric chamber, and that would have helped with the gas gangrene. Deb's friend gave me a long detailed account of how they'd kept Deb and me in the Peace Corps offices, rather than in the hospital, because it was considered more hygienic and less traumatizing. I recalled that, at one point, I woke up in a large ward in the Lomé hospital with about twenty other patients, men and women both, of all sizes and all in various degrees of disrepair. I also recalled wondering if I was going to have to stay there, but then the Peace Corps doctor showed up, and he ushered me—us?—out of there.

Hospitals in Togo don't provide food, so families bring it in. The hospital in Lomé was divided into a number of one-story buildings, rather than one building of several floors, to inhibit the spread of infection. I also remembered being on an operating table, with what looked like an old-fashioned cylindrical dentist's light over me. I don't know if I woke up just before or during the operation, but they put the gas mask over my face, and I was out. I was aware of being in a hospital in Africa and of all the dangers that entailed, but I did not have time to think that through or fret over it.

I remembered being in the Peace Corps offices as well, but every time I woke up and tried to get information about Deb's condition or my own, I quickly received another shot of morphine, and then I would pass out or drift off to sleep again. Due to the more obvious nature of my wounds, everyone thought I was the more seriously injured, but the fact that I had an open wound made me less susceptible to gas gangrene, as I said.

Deb's friend had been a nursing volunteer of some sort, and she also told me how, in spite of the African dislike of needles and superstitions about puncture wounds, many of Deb's students turned up to donate blood because they liked her so much, She told me of Deb's concern for me and of all that had happened to her; when the gangrene spread to her lymph system, they'd had to amputate her leg at the hip. I found this particularly disturbing, as Deb had always felt her legs were her best feature, and she liked showing them off. She was quite attractive, and her legs were very shapely. This bit of information was very hard to take, and I felt morbidly awful. I didn't know any terms like "survivor guilt" at that time; but, after the visit, although I was thankful for having been filled in on things, I felt awful overall. I thought back to being in Wiesbaden, before the doctor there had told me about the gravity of the situation. I had fantasized that Deb and I would stay in Wiesbaden until we were off crutches—after all, it was just a couple of broken legs. Soon, we'd be back in Africa, once again the married couple with the cool house, cool jobs, cool friends, and a great future. Our dual broken leg stories would just be something we'd tell to entertain other volunteers, and, later, our friends back home.

After the business closed, due to a lack of funding and my inability to understand sales and a sales team, I was back to the routine of "six more weeks, six more weeks, six more weeks." I was drinking heavily to self-medicate; I took mountains of pills but avoided painkillers, as I wanted to drink instead. Drinking helped, and always being in public helped me maintain my cramped, cheerful, childish countenance.

People would ask me about the external fixation device and the accident, but it was all too much to bear. It invariably got to the point where the death of my wife came up, and that was too difficult to talk about. I would dismiss questions by answering that I had been captured by UFOs and was slowly being transformed into a navigational device. Around that time, I had an image sufficiently graphic and explanatory to describe how I felt during the whole situation. It was like having had open-heart surgery and being forced to walk around with my chest open while it slowly closed over "six more weeks, six more weeks, six more weeks," and I was the only person on the planet who had to walk around with that open wound. This was the first time I experienced such an image; I never told anyone about it, but I have carried it with me ever since. In those days, however, the image plagued me, and I was afraid other people could see it—that they would see my image and think me mad. I was worried that people would think everything was my fault, that I had done something wrong—or, even worse, that I had done something wrong *deliberately*. These thoughts were hard to push back, but with beer and memories of the initial shock, I was able to.

I remembered the actual moment of the accident quite well. We had been out to Pagoda to see Liam and some other volunteers. There was a six-day market out there that was famous for a white-embroidered cloth that Deb wanted and also for *wagosh*, a native kind of cheese that I wanted to try. Cheese was a rarity natively in Africa, but, for some reason, there was a leaf in the area that naturally fell into jugs of milk, producing cheese. It was later developed a bit, and they sold it in that one market. All in all, it had been a very good trip. Pagoda was about an hour from Lama Kara, and we made the trip on the Kawasaki. It was hard to figure exactly when the market was open, because it was operated on the six-day African week, rather than the seven-day European week.

Somehow, we never quite got to the market. I remember being on the lanai of some outdoor café, and we tried to order beers. The kerosene *frigo* was broken, so the beer was hot, and we could only manage a couple of sips. While we were there, there was some sort of small local festival with a costumed dance, which we enjoyed. We then went to another volunteer's house for an afternoon party. We didn't stay long, because it was getting near dark, and there were only dirt roads all the way back to Lama Kara. I was still too new with the motorcycle to chance the roads. Deb wanted to stay a bit longer, and I wanted to leave a bit earlier. We bickered over this a bit. I was especially motivated to leave, because those construction volunteers were playing that game again, where Deb was engaged in a lively conversation, and I was subtly excluded. I had a feeling they were trying to break us up, that one of the construction guys had his eye on Deb, and he was behind it all. I didn't know who, specifically, but I just had that sort of feeling, and so I resented the whole thing.

Again, this was the seventies so a lot of that had to be tolerated. If you said anything, everyone would say the complainer was paranoid or imagining things or whatnot. There would not be much support for the complaint. Deb would only see it as socializing and enlarging our circle of friends, and even helping with my interest in doing my second year as a construction volunteer.

We left both a little miffed and a little disappointed with the time of departure. A few miles out, there was a small bridge. I saw a car off in the distance around a corner, and I was going to wait for it to pass. But then, at the last minute, I decided to cross, because there seemed to be plenty of room. My wounded macho from the party made me feel I was being too timid in hesitating, and so I crossed. We were already on the bridge when I noticed the car had turned onto the road; it was coming toward us at a tremendous speed. I saw it was going to be close, so I pulled way to the side, even though there was a rut in the road that could have toppled us. I was riding the edge of that rut, trying to get as close to it as possible and also trying to get off the bridge. The car didn't slow in the least; actually, it came tearing straight at us. At the last moment, we were flying in the air. I shouted Deb's name several times as we flew, and then we landed in the dirt of a dry riverbed, a particularly good breeding ground for infection. I didn't know if shouting her name was asking for help, offering help, or just calling out.

Later, when Deb's friend visited me, she informed me that Deb had been looking at the scenery in the opposite direction, and she'd never even seen the accident coming. That was how I learned about that; I was glad to know that part, at least. The two other volunteers I mentioned came along, and they took over, as the crowd gathered on the bridge did nothing to help us. These volunteers had been at the gathering in Pagoda as well, and I figured one of them must have tied a tourniquet for me so I wouldn't bleed out. They loaded us onto the flatbed truck. I held Deb's hand, trying to reassure her. I made a sign of the cross, but I stuffed any real feelings of the possibility of serious harm, let alone death. One man who helped lift me onto the truck wore a Togolese military outfit. I later realized that he was the driver of the car that sideswiped us. It turned out that he was a chauffeur for a major in the Togolese army; he was driving the major's kids home from school, at about 110 kilometers per hour—or 85 miles per hour—on roads that simply couldn't handle that speed. No one knew what happened to the driver after the accident. The position of his family would determine the degree to which he would be subject to penalties, and the Peace Corps would not be included in those discussions. The military would have their own actions in such matter. Later, the US would conduct its own investigation and conclude I was not at fault.

I remember there was a military parade that forced the flatbed to stop, and, even though there were injured people in the truck, they could not interrupt the parade. We finally got to the bush clinic in Lama Kara, where I remember getting blood, having my pants cut off, and getting morphine. I had not thought much about the pain in my leg, but I kept complaining about my foot, which actually was not injured. I woke up a while later in a hospital-type room in the bush clinic. The Peace Corps doctor was there, and he informed us that the president of the country, the one we called Stevie Wonder, was sending his personal plane to fly us to the hospital in Lomé. I looked down at my blood—and pus-stained cast, and pushed back some thoughts of roaches, bugs, and infection. The last time I saw Deb was on the president's plane. I looked over to the side, and she was on a litter across from me. Her blanket had dropped off, and her breast was exposed; I tried to tell her, but the nurse covered her up before I could. The nurse gave me another shot of morphine, and I was out. Except for waking up in the group ward and on the operating table, my next memories were of being in the Peace Corps offices, but Deb was not in the same room. No one spoke of the gravity of the situation. They said they were going to call our parents, and I asked them to wait. I didn't want to worry our folks, and I wanted to know more of the story before we called, but they insisted. Every time I woke up and inquired about our situation, I was met with more morphine.

On a somewhat spookier note, Deb's friend also informed me that the director of the Peace Corps had made sure that the amputated limb was transported with the body. She seemed to be allaying any fears I might have had of someone using the body parts for magic or sorcery or something of the sort.

About a year after the business folded, and about two and a half years after the accident, I was still in a cast and on crutches, and I asked the doctor to just cut the leg off so that I could have a life. I didn't want to hear, "six more weeks, six more weeks, six more weeks," anymore. He talked me into one more operation, promising that, if it didn't take, he would amputate. I was informed that, in Africa, they would usually amputate in the case of an injury as serious as mine, but because I was going to Wiesbaden, they'd just patched me up, hoping that the air force doctor would be able to do something for me. In Wiesbaden, they ordinarily would have amputated as well, but I was going to America; so, once again, they just patched me up. In America, they said they ordinarily would have just amputated, but, as I'd had it so long, they were going to try. I honestly preferred to have the leg, and the desire to have it amputated just to have a life seemed a little macabre to me, but I really wanted to do something—anything—other than sit in restaurants and bars while waiting for my leg to heal.

That last operation finally took, and, with the additional therapy provided by an electronic stimulation device twelve to fourteen hours a day, I was finally free of cast and crutches, and was able to walk with a cane. There was some promise of not needing that, either— eventually.

I had been dating a woman at the time. She was a neighbor who stopped by to borrow something, and within a few hours we were having sex. She was a massage therapist or something like that. I soon found out that she was quite nuts, emotionally unavailable, and very manipulative, but the sex was good, so I didn't fight her too much. It was actually quite difficult for me to think seriously about an emotional attachment, but, at age twenty-eight, I was able to manage a sexual one.

I decided it was time to start working again, figuring the compensation would stop soon, now that I was out of the cast, and the operations were done. I was getting a Peace Corps jobs newsletter, and I found a job teaching English in Japan that offered an English teacher's visa. I was driven by the idea that I had to pick up my life;

I wanted to get back to where we had been. I wanted a wife and a future and a cool house. I liked to travel, and except for the accident the experiences in France and Africa had been quite stimulating. I also wanted to prove myself again, get through something the way we'd originally planned. It wasn't as good as the Peace Corps, but I had my Peace Corps training and experience. I was also driven to fill my days with something productive: a real job with a future. I still harbored plans of getting a master's and a PhD.

While at the University of Wisconsin Milwaukee as an undergraduate studying theoretical linguistics, I had come up with an idea about a theory of word boundaries, which I never talked too much about, and which I hoped would not be discovered and worked out before I actually got into grad school. Because of that one idea, I didn't consider any alternatives besides those that would build toward a PhD in linguistics, and ESL fit the bill. I also felt that the work would be less trying than school, and it would ease my return to normal life. In any case, shortly after starting the affair with the massage therapist, I was off to Japan. I don't know if she harbored any hidden animosity, or if she had any hidden thoughts of more of a relationship, but I was off to Japan for at least a one-year renewable contract.

A few weeks before I was to go, giddy with my newfound freedom, I leapt to catch the top of a swing set in a playground we were cutting through, and I fell and broke my leg. At first, I had fears of the whole thing happening all over again, but I was pleased to learn that it was just a twisted fracture of the femur as a result of the atrophy from all the time that I had not been able to move around. It hadn't affected my lower leg at all. I felt stupid and a bit horrified, but I soon managed to cram all that with everything else I kept stuffed, and, once again, I was joking and cheerful and cramped. I also wondered if there was a jinx or curse that was behind it all. I think that was about the time when people started telling me I was angry, or when I began hearing that I looked like a bomb about to explode. I thought I looked cheerful and friendly. Some people were jealous of my disability compensation, and they treated me like I was faking, but this didn't bother me much then, as the reality of my situation was known to my friends, family, acquaintances, and anyone whose opinion really mattered.

4

Japan—1982

"... who poverty and tatters and hollow-eyed and high sat up smoking in the supernatural darkness of cold-water flats floating across the tops of cities contemplating jazz..."

—ALLEN GINSBERG, "HOWL"

Japan was as fascinating as Africa, not at all Third World, but as different from America as Africa was. I only knew a couple of phrases of Japanese when I arrived, but I was determined to set the land speed record for learning a foreign language. I was all about systems, and I wanted to invent my own system for rapid learning of the language. The boss, who was the owner of the school, seemed affable enough, as did his wife. The school was quite nice, located about 70 miles northwest of Tokyo in Utsunomiya, a town of about 350,000. Even at that size, it was still considered a small town and a bit rural. Heavy drinking was commonplace and widely accepted among the ESL teachers and students, and the boss and his wife were on board with it. They even encouraged it, as the students were quite interested in socializing with the teachers.

The culture intrigued me as well. I was interested in Zen and martial arts, even though my leg would prevent me from actually doing any martial arts. I was also interested in Noh and Kabuki. There was plenty to look forward to. I learned there was a group of American English teachers in the area—lots of drinking, and lots of fun. It was close enough to Tokyo to make semiregular weekend trips. I felt that I was back on track. There was plenty of culture shock, and it wasn't until I started working that I noticed how stressed I was. I was constantly on edge, and the smallest things were the source of tremendous stress: cooking, buying basic supplies, and so on would fill me with stress and dread, but I managed to keep it all hidden beneath that cheerful and cramped countenance. I also had some thoughts that I might soon be able to start thinking about the accident, Deb's death, and so forth. I had no idea how I'd go about it or what that would do, but I decided to put it off again, at least until I got used to my new environment. I really had no idea of religion or psychology except what I remembered from grade school and high school, and this I didn't access very much. There were still a lot of unresolved issues in my mind about all of it.

By that time, I'd had many dreams of the accident, the hospitalizations, and Deb in various forms. Sometimes she was angry at me, sometimes not. Over the years, one of the most disturbing forms of my recurring dreams was that Deb was still alive but had been kidnapped and kept in Africa and needed my help—or that she had been kidnapped and was now in Russia, where she'd been sold as a white slave and needed my help. Regardless of which variation, I had no idea what to do about these dreams. I also had dreams where she had been alive and living happily in Wisconsin all these years, but she was just too mad at me to bother to tell me. These dreams followed me as fantasies in daily life as well, being almost too real to ignore and pressuring me to actually do something. There was yet another where I saw her with her leg sewn back on in a cartoonish kind of way, and she was on crutches and quite angry with me. This image would follow me for years in something I would come to call "the frozen part of my imagination." Whenever I wanted to look at this part of my imagination—and sometimes even when I didn't—it would have images stuck in it. A giant cockroach to my left, a cluster of spiders up in front, the image of Deb on crutches with her leg sewed back on, and so on. I also had a pretty regular sense, or maybe it was my imagination too, that Deb was with me in one way or another—but most of this, too, I would ignore, giving myself the excuse that I was not ready to look at it. I kept looking forward to the future or at the present, but I never let myself look back.

And, in Japan, there was plenty of drinking to help me keep it all at bay. There were even outdoor beer machines that you could access anytime you wanted. Because I was working, my drinking actually decreased. The job turned out to be pretty good. I would study Japanese in the mornings, teach in the afternoons, and socialize at night. And there was plenty of socializing at night. This was 1982: ESL teachers were still pretty new in Japan, and the Japanese were avid to get to know the English teachers. Constant invites, many paid for by the students, and even some relatively high-priced invites to very posh circumstances with well-placed members of the community.

. . .

I heard about a Shingon priest who was studying English at the school. After asking around a bit, I was able to meet him. He was very fun, very cool, and a well-known calligrapher. His family owned and ran a Shingon temple for the neighborhood behind the train station. A nice, quiet, very traditional neighborhood, with this beautiful temple that he was in line to run when his father retired. I didn't really get to meet or know this priest much until a few months after I was there. I first met him when I had a party at my house for students and ESL teachers. The party was reminiscent of the party Deb and I had in Togo, but without the cow. There were about twenty or thirty of us seated on *zafus* around the main room of my house. It was bring your own booze and food, a concept pretty much unheard of in Japan, except for those who knew English teachers. I had a cool house—the job came with a modest salary and a housing assignment—I had to pay the rent, but it was a great house, small yet full. The floors were all tatami mats, and I slept on traditional Japanese futons that I would lay out on the floor at night. There was also a *kotatsu,* a small table you sat at cross-legged, but it had a blanket for the edges and a heating element underneath. The winters were cold; it down to around 30 degrees at night, and any dishes left out would have ice in them the following morning, so the *kotatsu* was necessary. That, plus a kerosene heater in the bedroom/front room, was all that most people used to keep warm.

That gives a pretty good idea of the setting for the party, which went well. The students were unused to that sort of thing. Just lots of people sitting around drinking and eating and chatting, but they liked it. They particularly liked the mix of people that ESL teachers could bring together. In the strict atmosphere of Japanese society, it was often difficult to meet people except within a rather narrowly defined social system, but the ESL classes gave them an opportunity to meet a wider range of people. We even had a guy who everyone said was *yakuza*, the Japanese version of the mafia. He was learning English as a hobby. I taught one of his classes. When we started the introductions during the first class, I'd asked him, "What do you do for a living?" He'd replied, "I make loans." Everyone was good natured about it, but you could tell he was talking about something other than being a banker. He wasn't scary or threatening; more than anything else, he was fun, but he did look pretty tough.

. . .

Most people in Japan had hobbies, so one of the standard questions in the introduction classes is, "What is your hobby?" In the US, we pretty much make do with work and socializing, or work and play, but the Japanese have work, play, and hobbies. It is important to them to have hobbies, to pursue them, and to make them a part of socializing. The hobbies include flower arranging, martial arts, calligraphy, sports, all the traditional arts, and all the modern ones. Everyone pursues one or two hobbies. Learning English was quite popular at the time, to the point of being a kind of hobby. In any case, the hobby thing seemed very good to me, and I enjoyed the Japanese pursuit of hobbies, seeing the American way of just work and play as a little shortsighted. Although many of us in the US had hobbies, we didn't pursue them as seriously as the Japanese did. Thinking this was a little narrowing, I decided the Japanese way was a bit more fun. The hobbies in Japan often reflected the culture's interest in discipline: not just a rigorous, frozen nod at discipline, but a considered effort to be disciplined, to understand discipline, and to work with it. The whole culture was built around it—the jobs, the hobbies, the approach to socializing, all were conducted with an attitude toward discipline. Even the drinking and partying were disciplined. The only time people were off the hook was when they were really drunk. The Japanese were amazingly forgiving toward outbursts, slovenly behavior, and pretty much anything that occurred if a person was very drunk. You could even yell at your boss, which was pretty much unheard of otherwise.

The Japanese were very pleasant toward Americans—toward all foreigners, really. The *gaijin,* as we were called, were excused from almost all societal rigors, so we were allowed to be ourselves. In some ways, it seemed like a great, national, social experiment to enjoy the company of the *gaijin* while they acted and lived as their cultures of origin dictated. Getting to know foreigners was also a hobby. A lot of Japan was just like the movie *The Last Samurai,* but without the swords and guns. Everything was a test or a challenge or an experiment, and people were always being called on to be intelligent and disciplined.

The pleasantness was quite genuine. It never seemed forced—not with the hobbyists, at least. Some classes were conducted at corporations and civil offices for those who needed English for their jobs. These were more demanding, and you could meet the Japanese who didn't necessarily see the *gaijin* as cute. The Japanese were good to each other and to us, but with each other they had a much stricter social code. I had some interest in dating Japanese women, but I was still quite cramped emotionally, and the women didn't often come forward as they might in America, so I was pretty much stuck to myself. It was not as bad as it was Africa, but even in Japan, dating an American could ruin a woman's chance of making a good marriage. Dating was still pretty casual in America at that time, but it was best not to be casual about dating in Japan. There was prejudice too, but you didn't see it much when you were traveling among ESL students and teachers. The Japanese courtesy wouldn't let it show too much, anyway.

This was the early eighties, and cocaine and corporations were beginning to be the next big thing in America. Disco was out, and singles clubs were in. Carlos Castaneda was popular, and I read several of his books, but they scared me, somehow making me feel that I could, at any minute, fall into the same weird experiences as Castaneda did, but without the drugs. I read several samurai books as well. *The Book of Five Rings* by Musahsi, Japan's most-famous dualist, was one of my favorites. The Japanese took well to people who were reading up on their culture, and the samurai books were treated as particularly important.

I had gotten into the habit of having dinner at a small restaurant near the school and close to the railroad station. It was run by a widow and her son, and they both were very interesting and very fun. The restaurant was a *robata yaki* place: they had little charcoal barbecues in each table, and they would bring out a variety of vegetables, fish, and meats that you cooked at your table. I got to know the owner and her son a bit, and we even went on a couple of tourist trips together.

I also hung out at a jazz bar called Jazz Groovy, and got to know the regulars there. It was good for my Japanese and good for their English. I had a friend who had learned English by listening to rock and roll, and she had a charming and wonderful way of making do with very broken English. We spoke half English and half Japanese, filling out our conversations by drawing pictures and pointing when we didn't have the necessary vocabulary.

At Jazz Groovy, one of the American ESL teachers and I started talking about learning the Japanese writing system, *kanji*. We were both a little unmotivated, so we challenged each other to a *kanji* contest, but when we met about a week later, I was soundly defeated. I challenged him to a rematch two months later, and he agreed. During the ensuing two months, I invented a system to memorize the characters as quickly as possible. I spent as much time working out the system as memorizing the characters. I had to be able to both read and write them. My competitive juices were flowing, and I spent two or three hours every morning memorizing characters; on the weekends, I often spent the whole day. I also saw it as part of my bid toward getting on board with the Japanese sense of discipline and hobbies. My Japanese was getting better as well, and many people were impressed with the speed with which I was learning it. There were occasional classes that went too slowly for my taste, so I just kept working on my own. I paid the school secretary to come over and help me do exercises, but I soon found that was also slow. Eventually, I realized that working on my own was better, because I could rely on the evening socializing to provide sufficient practice. When the date of the rematch came, I won quite handily, and the Japanese at Jazz Groovy were impressed. They quite enjoyed the spectacle of the "*Gaijin no tame ni kanji contesto.*"

So the time began to pass quite nicely. I was extremely tense and cramped, but I had a life, and it reminded me sufficiently of what I wanted to get back to in order to satisfy myself that my life was once more proceeding—cool house, cool job related to linguistics, and cool friends. I had everything but Deb, or even a new wife or girlfriend. Dreams of Deb and the accident and the hospitalizations were commonplace, but I could still stuff everything and keep going. People thought I was eccentric and angry, but it was easy to pass it off in the accepting, amiable atmosphere of Japan at that time. I really kind of objected to being called "angry," because I thought that was inaccurate. I was tense—or perhaps intense—but not angry.

. . .

Around Christmas, things began to change. I don't know why, but pretty much out of nowhere, I began to write a Christmas card to Deb's family. I became overwhelmed with a strange kind of mania that felt like my entire body was on fire. I poured my soul out on that card, which I never sent. It seemed everything I had stuffed for the last four years was pouring out of me physically and verbally—and without any choice on my part.

From that point on, the world seemed to change. Everything had a deep significance, everything was spiritual and symbolic, and everything seemed like a potential threat. I wondered if hadn't I had some kind of break with reality. The arrogance that came with it was amazing. I thought I was everything and everyone, from a samurai to a cowboy and whatnot. I knew that these thoughts were not normal. I did everything I could to hide them, but I could not stop them. It all changed so suddenly—from everything being a struggle to hold back thoughts and feelings of the accident to everything being a struggle to keep from mentioning or showing the madness that was raging in my head. It seemed that I was in a new, spiritualized, frightening world, while everyone else remained in the previous, "more real" world. I couldn't let on at all what I was thinking or feeling. I read more Buddhism, thinking I might find some clue as to what was going on, and also how to resolve it.

It was around this time that I got to know the Shingon priest a little better. Because of my involvement in memorizing *kanji,* he said he would teach me some calligraphy, which I took up quite excitedly. He had me over to his temple a couple of times; we usually met in his study. In some strange way, he seemed to know that I was going through some sort of veiled crisis, but he only talked about it in helpful hints. I lived in constant fear of going stark-raving mad from it or acting out on it, but I kept all this pretty much to myself.

The first time he had me over, he gave me a tour of the temple. It was quite beautiful and lavishly decorated with gold, as is the tradition with Shingon temples. He did a small ceremony for me, having me place some ashes on my forehead and do a couple of bows. I was fascinated and very pleased. I was having a genuine Japanese cultural experience, and this guy was very interesting and fun. His father still ran the temple, and he taught calligraphy at a local junior high school to earn a living. I considered that little ritual my introduction to Buddhism, and it has moved and inspired me ever since. Everything around the Shingon priest and most of the Japanese was like the movie *The Last Samurai,* but without swords and fists, as I've described. Everything was discipline, all of it a trial or a challenge of sorts.

Shortly after arriving, I realized that, even though the Japanese were very forgiving of Americanisms, the culture opened up and became much more interesting, and much more challenging, the more you used Japanese and the more you tried to do things within their social boundaries. I did this with the Shingon priest, and I was rewarded with the lessons and the visits to his temple. On one occasion when I was visiting there, he got a call. It was some calligrapher buddies of his, and they wanted to go for drinks. He brought me along. On the way to the bar, he was suddenly accosted by two seeming muggers or attackers; I was shocked, and had no idea what to do, but, knowing he had a black belt in judo and was judo teacher, I wondered what would happen. I quickly found out that these were his two calligrapher pals, and they were just joking around.

My Japanese was still pretty rudimentary, so we made do with the priest's English, my broken Japanese, and the graciousness of Japanese culture. At one point, the older of the two calligraphers—he was probably about seventy at the time—took out a very expensive gold pen and a piece of paper, handed them to me, and solemnly and ceremoniously told me to write my name. I took it very seriously and, with the raging arrogance that I was trying to suppress and my interest in impressing the Japanese and participating in their culture, in a dramatic and exaggeratedly ceremonious way, I wrote my signature. The older guy looked at it and, in a very convincing way, indicated that there was something very impressive about my signature and something unique about me. He handed it to the other guy, as though there were something of great importance about it. When the other took it, he looked at it and then dismissed it as though it were garbage. I was a bit dumfounded, but it was obvious they wanted me to treat the whole thing seriously, which I did. It was a moment that would follow me for years as a means of working with the arrogance that was raging in the background. The Shingon priest also took it seriously; by that I mean as more than just a couple of guys fooling around in a bar, and, rather, as a kind of introduction to the world of calligraphy and one of their many tests. On another occasion, several of us were visiting the same priest, and he had us all write our names. He was quickly and easily able to imitate everyone's signature, a fun little parlor trick on the surface; but, again, there was something a little deeper about it, just as there had been that night in the bar with his two friends.

It wasn't just the raging arrogance that bothered me; it was the growing fantasy world and my drifting into it, combined with the arrogance and a fear that it all could take over. I believed that, rather than my external fixation device turning me into a UFO navigational system, I was slowly being turned into some kind of guru, and I would have to fend off the weirdoes and devotees that turned up around people like Ram Dass, Rajnish, and Jim Jones—people I did not think much of, and a lifestyle I did not want. And I certainly did not want to attract that sort of crowd, with their spooky eyes, goofy guru ways, and what seemed to be the same arrogance that I was battling—and yet, strangely, they didn't battle it, but, instead, seemed to indulge it as some kind of "God's truth" or "deep wisdom." I was worried that I would give into it, fall into it, or in one way or another be overwhelmed by it. It was entertaining and seductive, but nothing close to what I wanted in my life. I saw Japan as a chance to reconnect and rebuild from the point of the accident. I didn't want to go off on some kind of idiotic guru trip, though I did want to connect nicely and properly with the arts and religion of Japan.

. . .

The widow and her son who ran the restaurant I often went to took me on an outing one time, and we stopped at a Shinto shrine dedicated to Kami, the god of foot health. I clapped my hands a couple of times, made a bow and an offering, and left a shoe. Quite interesting. There were festivals dedicated to Buddhism, different Shinto gods, and so forth. Shinto is as big as Buddhism in Japan. More accurately, the Japanese participate in both. They may identify themselves as members of one, more or less, but they use both variously for marriage, funerals, and other rites of passage.

At a party at the Shingon priest's house one time, he had hung one of my calligraphies over the door of the party room. It was one of my novel uses of *kanji* which people found amusing. I took the character for "nuance" and the character for "echo" (which is pronounced *shinkyoo* and is a homonym for the word that means "religion"), thus making a new combination and a personal meaning. He was quite nice to people that way. Always paying for everything, always gregarious and fun, he also very naturally and unaffectedly expressed genuine concern and compassion for people while still remaining totally devoid of the arrogance that I had so associated with gurus and whatnot. He gave me my major first impression of Buddhism, and also was—and still is—my major inspiration for studying it more deeply.

The Shingon religion is not Zen. It is more like Tibetan Buddhism than Zen, with deities and visualization practices, embracing ritual much more than Zen does. Actually, Zen can be quite stark and even opposed to ritual in many ways, seeing it as a distraction from attaining the Zen mind—the mind of ordinary reality, the "beginner's mind" versus the "expert's mind," as they call it. The expert's mind can't learn anything, but the beginner's mind can. The simplicity and beauty of Japanese arts and religions really attracted me.

The last time I saw the Shingon priest, he pulled out a large stack of *shikishi,* the twelve-by-twelve-inch cards on which much calligraphy is done. He had me go through the stack to choose one that I could keep. I chose one on which the calligraphy extended the boundaries of the internal circular border of the card. This situation also had a tone of ceremony and significance to it, and I chose quite carefully. When I had chosen, he was quite pleased. I don't know why, but he treated it as a choice of great importance, as well as a good omen.

He had given me instructions on how to mix ink, and he'd also shown me how to do calligraphy a bit, giving me some copies of the heart sutra that he had done for me to practice copying. He also gave me a fan with the characters *wa kei sei jitsu* on it, which he said was a kind of name. His generosity, his pleasantness, and his genuineness are still quite unmatched in my experience; more than anything else, it all seemed so natural and uncontrived. I was definitely inspired enough to take up a serious study of Buddhism, and yet I never had the slightest sense that he wanted to impress me or convert me. Very pleasant fellow and wonderful experiences. And always there were those hints that he somehow was aware of the turmoil I was experiencing, that he was trying to be helpful, but that we also were just having some fun.

On one occasion, I told him about the accident and the death of my wife. It would later become a habit of mine to tell people like him about the tragedy. I had no clear ideas about what life after death was, or how to get a fixed belief in it, but I thought that at least mentioning it to people like him could only be of value.

. . .

I continued in this way for the full year; but, at the end of the year, I decided not to renew my contract, as I had begun fighting with my boss, and the new teacher was not exactly my cup of tea. She, too, was a former PCV and had completed her full tour. She was manipulative, domineering, and overly competitive, and the boss was able to get along with women better than with men, so I went back home. This time, I'd fully completed my contract, had a wonderful series of cultural experiences under my belt, and gained significant experience with Japanese language and writing. I was quite pleased.

The madness and arrogance still raged in the background—this was a sense of being outside the real world, of needing to constantly fight to hold onto that part of me that was committed to reality—it continued, and even worsened. It probably had to do with the added culture shock from Japan, and, later, with the reverse culture shock when I returned to the US. Everything had a spiritual significance to it, and the air, the environment, and my own mind were charged with ghosts and spirits, with Kami and other gods, and I had no way to sort through any of it.

There were also seemingly weird occurrences in the natural world. One time at my house near the school in Japan, I was plagued by wasps. They seemed to be hunting me down. I wondered if it wasn't revenge for the two wasps I had killed rather cruelly in Africa with a spray can of DDT, as if somehow the wasp world new I was a wasp killer. I mentioned the wasp problem to the landlady, and she called an elderly carpenter to take a look. He found the nest and removed it, pointing out that it was odd that they should be there at all, as it was several months before wasps should hatch. In my bloated state of mind, I wondered if I wasn't somehow psychically at fault for this.

5

Home from Japan—September 1982

"... who bared their brains to Heaven under the El and saw Mohammedan angels staggering on tenement roofs illuminated ..."

—Allen Ginsberg, "Howl"

I returned to Milwaukee, found a place to stay, and began looking into getting into graduate school. I also wanted to find a Zendoo somewhere so that I could start the actual practice of Buddhism. The massage therapist was still around, and we dated a bit. She was caught up in the New Age mentality, though, which actually I could not stand, and so it did not last long between us. She introduced me to a couple of Transcendental Meditation (TM) practitioners, and her roommate was quite odd and quite New Age. Everyone around her seemed to give the "spooky eyes" treatment, and they all were experts on whichever one New Age book they had read on a particular subject, all giving unwanted, useless advice on spiritual matters they clearly did not understand.

At this time, I was becoming quite paranoid and saw annoying New Agers everywhere. They all seemed to want to talk to me, to follow me around, or to convert me to believing one dumb idea or another. In spite of this, I was undeterred in my efforts to find a Zendoo. I heard about a group that would meet in one another's houses, and I had a Zen teacher stop by once in a while. Before I could find an actual Zendoo, I noticed a Tibetan Buddhist center next door to a New Age bookstore where I often shopped for Zen books.

The center happened to be open, so I went in to look around. An eight-week Introduction to Buddhism class would start the following week, and I accepted the invitation to join the center and take the class. It all seemed perfect, as the center offered instruction in meditation, where a regular meditation instructor would sit for a full hour before each weekly class. I quickly fell in love with the place, and there was a pretty nice group of people there. "New Age light" at their worst, they were basically what I imagined American Buddhists would be like. It was called a Dharmadhatu, and it was sponsored by a group led by a kind of wild, young Tibetan named Chogyam Trungpa Rinpoche. I quickly learned that there were close connections to Zen and Japan, via a teacher named Shunryu Suzuki Sensei and Shibata Sensei, the twentieth-century bow maker to the emperor of Japan. The leader was quite fond of Japan and things Japanese. I was quite pleased with this, and soon I was ready to settle in and learn to practice Buddhist meditation.

I took the eight-week course, and several others subsequently, and began to read books by the leader of the group and by other Tibetans. I was interested mostly in the quiet, calm elegance of Japanese-style Buddhism, but quickly became enamored of the Tibetan style as well. Tibetan Buddhism is ornate and colorful, quite a contrast to the quiet, somber Zen. I would go down for the hourly sitting sessions, and I also attended the ones on Sundays, which were three hours long. I found it quite difficult to sit at home on my own. It is actually quite different. For beginners, sitting is never an experience of calm, but, rather, one of an agitated mind—given my state of mind, added agitation was the last thing I needed, but I was inspired and wanted to continue. I also saw it as a way of finally sorting through the rampage that was going on in my mind, continually, behind the cheerful, cramped, somewhat childish outer countenance. I saw it as making a serious attempt to finally work through the reality of the accident and Deb's death. This was four years after the accident.

The Buddhists talked about "impermanence"—the fact that all things pass away—and this is an important part of their philosophy. I had, by then, evolved my own theory of "fragility," which was rather similar; so much so, in fact, that I gave it up in favor of impermanence. Fragility was basically a pessimistic view of the world that I couldn't shake: no matter what you had or how good you had it, one moment could take it all away. I was unable to trust the world or put myself fully into anything, thinking that all would be lost. The fact that one day you can have a cool wife, a cool house, a cool job, and cool friends—but that then, in a moment, it can all be gone, and you can be constantly assaulted by tubes and pain and infections and operations, all was quite real to me. The note of reality that the Buddhists struck on the subject was quite appealing to me. Impermanence seemed to imply that bad things can pass away as well, which made it a little more reassuring than fragility.

If I was able to practice at home at all, it never really lasted more than five minutes. The practice is simple enough, and, at the time, it was quite attractive to me: you just sit as close to the posture as you can, rest your palms on your thighs, and then every time you breathe out, you label everything that occurs in your mind as nothing but "thinking," getting used to noticing the entire thought process as nothing other than just "the entire thought process." If you can do this more than a couple of times, you are doing well, and then you're off and running. At the center, the other people in the room and the embarrassment of ducking out because I couldn't handle it, enabled me to actually do it. I would have some weird experiences—one time I saw the entire room glow, and another time my crutches seemed to magically slam themselves on the ground behind me—but I chalked all this up to the bizarre qualities of my experience, and to my mania, and I just labeled it all "thinking." The Buddhist discipline is not at all about indulging such things, but, rather, about getting back to an ordinary, five-senses reality.

They also had these remarkably cool chants with protector deities, which I loved. Giant spirits with sparks flying out of their beards, skull cups, swords to kill evildoers, and commitment to support the religious. Quite fun and really quite convincing, a drum beating a primitive beat in the background, and so forth. I imagined the protector spirits taking care of the wilder part of my mind, while I did the necessary reading to sort through things on my own.

The world was abuzz with New Age lunatics, ex-hippies, and burnouts, but it was the eighties now, and, as I'd learned in Japan, cocaine and singles clubs were beginning to take over. Disco was dying out, and the eighties music was coming up. The polyester leisure suits were out, as were disco haircuts, and the eighties love of money and coke began to take hold. I hated the New Agers and the burnouts. I also didn't think much of the coke mentality. I always pretty much figured, if you can't entertain yourself with what's legal—nicotine, caffeine, and alcohol—you just weren't trying. This was about ten years before sports bars took over the whole of the bar scene across America.

For me, the New Agers were the worst; they were such a drag on ordinary conversation and socializing, and to spend any time with them meant hurting your social circle. There were posters everywhere for New Age gurus, Christian evangelists, Kabbalah, anything with a mysterious ring to it. New Age bookstores and psychic fairs and shops for palm readers all were commonplace.

I had rented a room from an old acquaintance of mine. Over the years, she had grown obese and also become more and more bizarre, but at first I had not recognized it. She was caught up in the New Age foolishness, and, even worse, immersed in gossip and innuendos. She quite enjoyed threatening people with them. She began to threaten me with them, and I am not even sure why. Possibly it was because she wanted to coerce me into participating in that foolishness. I had never even tried, because it was obvious to me that the whole thing was based on a bastardization of the guru principle; it was a pyramid based on manipulation and control, rather than a hierarchy based on respect. I just ignored her, determined to get my money together so that I could find a different situation as quickly as possible. I had only planned to be there a couple of weeks while I got things sorted out, but I wound up staying for about six weeks.

At that time, the news and TV shows were filled with fears of satanic cults, sex cults, and the like, and there were a number of sensationalized trials for child molestation that captured the country. It seemed that all the innuendo and gossip surrounding these took on either a supportive tone or an accusatory one. Those who were accusatory were as deluded and irresponsible as those who supported the cultishness. No one seemed interested in letting the system work, or in letting experts handle it. As I had suspected, most people were wrong on both sides of the issue, as later evidenced when some of the same stories that were in the news at the time would be shown to have been based on coercive techniques of investigation. Many of the children came forward in later years to recant their stories, and easily a half dozen people who had spent fifteen years or more wrongfully imprisoned were freed. Not that there weren't those who deserved it. I am merely trying to highlight the madness and confusion, and the fact that crowds who were so cocksure of their innuendos were creating problems, and I am unsure if they solved any. Such problems as the question of guilt or innocence seemed far too important to trust to the innuendo mongers, who were more than happy to admit that they were more than happy to slander or spread slander. Some even seemed to want to excuse molestation as culturally determined. I was disgusted with this, and I would argue against it if anyone brought it up—but no one ever actually did bring it up to me directly, except through insinuation.

One time before I was able to move out, I was home watching television while my roommate babysat the Down syndrome adolescent from across the street. I didn't mind, as it was only for a short time, but then my roommate ducked down to the corner store, leaving me alone with the girl. I really didn't like the impression that would make, and I told my roommate so, but off she went, anyway. When she returned, she again began threatening me with slander and innuendo, almost implying that somehow she was going to use that five minutes alone with the Down syndrome girl as her ammunition. I was incensed, but I also found it extremely difficult to address, as she did it all by means of implication and innuendo. I was not sure if it might not be better not to address it all, in order to take any strength out of the threat. I do think that was the best strategy, but she was known to all the gossips in the neighborhood and at the university where she worked, and none of them cared the least bit about the truth of the rumors they spread, only about maintaining their jobs and their lifestyles by means of their gossip at the expense of anyone who got in their way or could entertain them. She also seemed to imply that she would try to affect my relationships with her maliciousness.

That event was a catalyst. Very soon after that, I moved to a different apartment where I lived through the rest of winter and spring, and then I went to Boulder, Colorado. I ended the relationship with a massage therapist I was seeing, and the friendship with the obese woman—my former roommate—drifted off into oblivion. I stopped calling both of them, and if either of them called me, I would be too busy to talk. Eventually, I never saw or heard from either of them again. Actually, in an odd twist, the massage therapist started hanging around the meditation center and doing a lot of the practices; I felt as if she were almost following me around, but, then again, I felt that about everyone. I even felt that about the obese woman, imagining that she would try to have her gossip circles try to find any gossip circles that were around me, and then they would try to share stories. Remember, I said I was paranoid.

In any case, at the time, it also seemed that a large part of the dynamic involved deliberately targeting other people, as though somehow that would make the whole thing work. If the innocent were targeted and the guilty were exonerated, the slander would fly better than the other way around. People would say you had to engage in the perversions and the slander in order to avoid the gossip. Some would say doing something just once was a kind of vaccination, referring to any of a number of possible perversions of which strangers could be accused. Somehow they either believed, or tried to convince people to believe, that doing something perverse just once would act like a vaccine, and then the person would be able to join in the gossip wars with impunity, which sounded to me like a heroin dealer saying, "First time it's free." I had no interest in the perversions and no interest in the gossip, except to do what I could to end it around me, without becoming grotesque or gossiping or perverting myself. All through the years that I had to endure this foolishness, I always preferred dating women to trying to participate in the bizarre behaviors: get a number, make the call, go out for lunch or coffee, and, if anything happened, have more and better dates. This was quite typical for anyone before the New Age madness took hold.

As the gossip and perverted storylines grew, it became more and more difficult to find ordinary dates, and everyone was suspicious of everyone else. After a while, it seemed like the laziest and least datable were finally finding a world where they could dominate the most datable and the most willing to work at a relationship, rather than the other way around.

There were still posters of gurus and New Age lectures in all the bookstores. This was back when there still *were* a lot of bookstores. This was before e-tail bookstores, which, in their pretense of creating jobs, actually destroyed thousands of bookstores across the country, ruining entrepreneurs, and putting neighborhood workers out of jobs. Even Shambhala Bookstore, a great little place in Berkeley established by some members of the Trungpa group, couldn't make it in the face of Amazon. Jobs for geeks and corporate schmucks and the entrepreneurs and neighborhood workers were out. I am sure they destroyed far more jobs and integrity than they created, but they wouldn't want that sort of news to get out.

In the workplace, the key dynamic was dominance versus skills, and this eventually dominated the scene of what used to be dating behaviors. It was not about charm and poise and being interesting and winning hearts, but about finding and capturing a woman. These were behaviors that quickly degenerated to rather typical pimp behaviors, and to a rape mentality that always blamed the object of the attentions for the attentions. There was talk of sadomasochism, vampire clubs, sex clubs, key clubs, and any sort of thing a deluded imagination could dredge up, along with all the rest of that. People said it was necessary for business; that Wall Street, Madison Avenue, and the Beltway all were full of it, and that there was no way to avoid it. Economic success was impossible without perversion and slanderous aspersions. It called to mind Sodom and Gomorrah, as well as the book of Revelation, where no commerce would take place except for those who had the mark of 666 on their foreheads, and the perverts and innuendo mongers were the mark of the coming of the end of the world. I also remembered the whore of Babylon; at the end of the world, people would be drinking from the cup of the filth of her fornication. I am not much of a Bible reader, but bits of drama like that stick in my head.

Jerry Farwell had a Christian explanation for the 9/11 fall of the twin towers that was different from mine. He blamed libertarians; I blamed the innuendo mongers and their perverted storylines, seeing the fall of the towers as a warning to stop those behaviors. I saw the spin of the right and left wings, but particularly the right wing, to be the deception of the Great Deceiver himself. It was not just deception; it was great deception, and it derailed America, setting up the economic depression of the early twenty-first century. The angels of Revelation had poured out the vial of plague upon the masses, and none but those who could resist the spin and the deception and the perversion would survive.

I saw those Christians, Jews, and Buddhists who could stay out of all this as those who would survive. I preferred to think the end of the world would be an end of the deception, and so forth, rather than a nuclear disaster or something like that. There were Christian themes running throughout the crowds. The crowds really didn't care what they accused people of, merely that their accusations prevented them from being accused themselves; they were tremendously entertained by a sadistic schadenfreude that was frequently mistaken for an achievement of spiritual bliss and membership in an elite mainstream.

I was still drinking a lot, as a kind of self-medication for the ongoing leg pain and the raging nonsense in my head. I was getting better and better at maintaining my social front and, given the Buddhist practice, had shifted my style to revealing nothing to anyone, except what came from a matter-of-fact awareness of the five senses and good manners. I would sometimes act out or speak out of the nonsense. It was seductive, and it would constantly want to take over, to turn me into a New Age loony or a guru of some sort; but, whenever I noticed it either creeping up or taking over, I would push it back and reassert my commitment to the five senses and good manners.

The Buddhist practice was quite good for this. Rather than trying to see lights in your head, other worlds, or anything magical, the basic purpose of Buddhist practice is boredom and the five senses. This appealed to me tremendously, given my latest strategies of holding on to reality. You were not looking for just *any* sort of boredom; you were looking for a particular kind: "cool boredom" versus a hot, agitated boredom. This, along with the good protectors of the Tibetan pantheon, motivated me and kept me going as much as I could. The Tibetans are not without the lights in your head and other practices, it was just that with this group at the center, you had to go through a long series of sitting practices and study before you could approach such advanced practices. I assumed this was to mitigate against the less-attractive side of New Ageism, and I approved of it; I thought I might even be interested in exploring these advanced realms if things remained staid, calm, and ordinary.

I was also trying to get into graduate school but was a good bit disorganized. In spite of the Buddhist practice and the cool boredom, the paranoia was getting worse, as was the wildness of my mind. The Buddhism, however, gave me more and more strength to maintain a good front; my loyalty lay more and more with that good front, but the seduction and power of the madness were still raging. I was still often afraid that I would get lost in it and become a permanently ranting New Age lunatic living on the streets, hollering at boogeymen and friends who would duck across the street to avoid me.

As time went on, I did a semester of grad school in linguistics in the English department at UWM, but I found it difficult to study anything but Buddhism, and sitting in a classroom and relating with the crowds was too much. They were all out to undermine me in some way or another. They were all trying to prove that my façade was just a façade, and I was a crazy in hiding. Some of this actually happened, but a lot of it did not.

This was in the winter of 1982-83. The Dharmadhatu in Milwaukee was connected with the larger group centered in Boulder, Colorado. They had established Naropa Institute, which was offering a bunch of summer-school classes. I made it through the semester at UWM, and then I decided to go to Boulder for the summer to take an intensive in Tibetan and Sanskrit and to meet more Buddhists, including the guy in charge. I was on workers' comp again—I forget why; probably another operation—so I was able to afford the trip and the courses.

I had my plane set up, a place to live set up, and some classes to take. I got to Boulder, found my room, and went down to Naropa to check it out. When I got there, the Tibetan and Sanskrit class had been canceled, but no one had bothered to tell me. I was suddenly reeling, anticipating another accident-type scenario where everything would be lost, but the administrator I was talking to said a *dathun* was starting at the retreat center, about an hour or so up in the mountains. A *dathun* is a one-month sitting retreat, where you sit from seven in the morning to nine in the evening, do chores, and so on; in short, you get a very thorough introduction to what sitting practice is all about. I honestly didn't believe I could do it, but I decided to go because I just didn't want to go back to hanging around waiting. Even though it was about ten hours a day on the cushion, it was something I could do, and something I could add to my "practice resume." She also gave me a handout that described a more complex meditation than the one I was doing. Developed by a guy named Padma Karpo, it was quite interesting, and I have used it as a main practice through twenty-six years of practice.

I stayed in Boulder for a couple of days, checking out the town and the bars and coffee shops. I still liked doing all that; I just didn't want that to be the only thing I had to do. The leader of the group gave a talk during that time at Naropa, some general thing or another, so I went to Naropa that evening to hear him in person for the first time. He was well known for always being drunk and always womanizing. He was paralyzed on the left side from an accident where his Jaguar had crashed into a joke shop in Scotland. Someone one time had asked rather rudely, "Sir, I understand there were two women in the car when you crashed, and you were drunk." To which he responded, "Sir, you cannot get two women in a Jaguar." In any case, I never found this hypocritical or off-putting; it rather attracted me to the guy, and the fact that he had a problem with his walking on his left side made me think he would be sympathetic to, or understanding of, my situation. I liked women and drinking, had a limp on the left side, and liked Buddhism. At least this guy wouldn't be insisting that we live in the street, meditate, and panhandle for a living or sell incense in airports, which actually was one of my fears of getting more deeply involved. I had a short leg cast and crutches at the time. I arrived a little bit late. Everything was set up like a standard lecture, with folding chairs rather than cushions. I walked in the back a little bit after the talk had started, and he saw me come down the center aisle. As I walked, he kept on with his lecture but stated, "You have to give up your cast and crutches, and show us who you really are." This shocked me. Was this some sort of weird coincidence? Was he being nice? Was he being rude? This also did no good for my raging paranoia, or for my growing knowledge of Tibetans and the Tibetan guru/disciple relationship. I worried—or fantasized—that I might be special or recognized in some way, specifically the sort of thinking that causes the paranoia to rage and the façade to fade. In any case, it was a good lecture; he seemed to be a little drunk, but quite likable. He had guards and attendants, flowers set by his table, and a glass of sake on the table as well. I decided he was just being metaphorical and that I had no idea what he meant, so I just pretended to not have noticed what he'd said.

The scene was quite fascinating and very well developed. The Buddhists were all over the place: a coffee shop, a bookstore, and restaurant were known to be owned by Buddhists, and there were lots of people there to study. The air was abuzz with innuendo, where everyone seemed to be squawking their wisdom at one another. I had never really seen this before, and I didn't like it, knowing how it would infect the mad part of my mind with all kinds of spooked-out spirituality, rather than the calm one I was looking for. I also found it strangely difficult to find anyone to talk to in the atmosphere. I felt isolated and frustrated; I couldn't get through to anyone or find anyone looking for a normal conversation—from my perspective, everything was charged with unnecessary gossip and innuendo and the ever-unpleasant New Age "wisdom."

In any case, after a few days, I left for the *dathun*. The Boulder scene seemed great, and, though there were way too many New Agers for my taste, overall, it seemed there were nice ordinary people involved, and so I thought about moving there. I was having second thoughts about grad school in Milwaukee, because of navigating the snow and cold with my leg. I did it for three years with a full leg cast and crutches, but it was a hassle and potentially dangerous. The doctors had told me that if something happened to my leg again I would likely lose it.

The Rocky Mountain Dharma Center was as good as travel to a foreign country. The residents and staff were mostly ex-hippies but not too burned out, and not too into coke or drugs as far as I could see. There were also a good many mountain types; hillbilly wannabes, you could say. All quite fun. There was a growing trend against drug use, and the Buddhist scene somewhat mitigated against that. Trungpa had said that some of the experiences were genuine, but, as they were drug induced, they were not useful and could not be maintained or regained without drug use.

The land was purchased by some of his original students, and they built little shacks on the land to live in while they developed the retreat center. A group of hippies calling themselves the pygmies were a big part of the earliest students, and they still get regularly referenced when talking about the history of the place.

The thing about this whole group was that the leader, Chogyam Trungpa Rinpoche, had agreed to teach the full range of Tibetan Buddhism, from the basics to the most-advanced practice, which is the rare and dramatic six yogas of Naropa. There was a strict curriculum that had to be followed: first, a lot of sitting, including one one-month *dathun,* a three-month seminary, and then a rigorous introduction to what were called the "preliminary practices." All this happened before you actually got to do deity practice, mantra recitations, and that sort of thing. There were a lot of required classes along the way as well.

The preliminary practices, called *Ngondro,* consisted of one hundred thousand full prostrations, one hundred thousand repetitions of a purifying mantra, one hundred thousand ritualized offerings to the pantheon of gurus and deities, and then one million repetitions of what was called the "guru yoga mantra." After that, would be a series of practices based on deity visualization and mantra repetition. The first was called Vajrayogini, a red, naked female deity that improved the experience of emptiness; the next, called Chakrasamvara, was designed to increase skillfulness. After that, came a protector deity, the six yogas, and a number of other things. It would take years to get to the point of doing the six yogas for anyone that was interested, and that was the reality of the Tibetan system. In 1982, they hadn't taught the six yogas at all. The Tibetans could do it a bit faster in their strict and long-term retreats, but this program was designed for what they called American "householders," rather than monks or yogis. These were Trungpa's students, those who were officially accepted by him were to have jobs and houses, as well as a practice. This I found very attractive; I had some rather odd fears of being forced into some sort of indentured monkhood or hermithood or something if I ever got really interested, but the design of the plan here was quite acceptable, and I thought it would not only help me recoup what I lost in the accident, but also enhance it.

The fact of the matter was that there were very few cultish behaviors or brainwashing coming from the leadership or the system he had designed. Everything was a matter of requesting permission and doing necessary qualifying practices and course work. They even discouraged the rich who just wanted to give money and hang around. It was all about actually doing the practices, and doing them "fully, completely, properly, and thoroughly," as they said. No brainwashing at all; you were encouraged to be skeptical and to just believe what you believed until you understood something differently. Many of the members did exhibit cultish behaviors and tried to introduce some of this into the gossip, but they were unable to influence the basic system; and, if you stayed with the system, with what was written, there was little trouble with the "infiltrators," as I saw them.

In spite of my dislike of the likes of Ram Dass, Rajnish, the Hare Krishnas, and so forth, I found the possibility of involvement with a Tibetan guru quite attractive—the one in Boulder, especially. Everyone there seemed to have a nice attitude toward it all; there was no brainwashing, no selling at airports, none of the odd stuff. It all seemed very sane and logical and fascinating.

The shrine rooms were ornate and beautiful. Overall, the people were fun, joking about it all as much as they were serious: chanting the sides of cereal boxes, making up jokes with a Buddhist theme, rewriting songs with a Buddhist theme, and so on. Ornate Tibetan *tangkas* were everywhere, along with great T-shirts, incense, drums, statuary, and so on. There was a bookstore at RMDC, and another one in town that specialized in all these things—and they were great, lots of toys to decorate a great hobby. A great lifetime commitment to a very inspiring and motivating hobby. I felt I had found a situation I could settle into, had confidence that I would get better—that I would resolve the raging madness, either through meditation or through sorting through it all by learning about the spiritual landscape of Tibetan Buddhism that was so muddled in my head.

The *dathun* was rigorous but fun. The first three days of sitting I had pretty much nothing going on in my head except regret for having signed up, being overwhelmed by hot boredom, sore knees, and so forth. I have never considered myself a particularly good meditator, but I do try. I felt I was talented and motivated, but, given my state of mind, I was not much prone to the very common mistaken belief that one was already enlightened. Whenever I did even entertain such a belief, just as in a prepubescent fantasy, the madness was near enough to remind me that it was nothing more than that. Many people got into thinking they were something, or that had achieved something, even with very little practice. It was evident in the "more enlightened than thou" attitude that was commonplace: a kind of fixed, arrogant, looking-down on others, or emulating gurus with virtually no study or practice background. There were also a lot of normal Americans who kept me interested. They were able to avoid all the arrogance and madness, and seemed to be actually achieving a level of calm and gentility toward their worlds that made everything seem possible and valuable. It was even somewhat reminiscent of the Shingon priest, which was encouraging.

The day at *dathun* was straightforward enough: we got up at around seven; meditation began at eight in the morning, and went until nine or so in the evening. You would sit for a period, and then do walking meditation to stretch your knees. They never really told you how long you would sit before walking meditation began. It could be anywhere from forty-five to ninety minutes, but it usually lasted about an hour. You would then walk formally for five minutes or so, and then go back to sitting. Eating was done in the shrine room as well, in a ritualized Japanese form called *oryoki,* where every movement from setup through cleanup is thoroughly choreographed. This practice I enjoyed particularly. As I was in a cast and on crutches, I never volunteered for serving the food, but each day there was a ninety-minute work period when I would work in the kitchen using my experience from cooking at the Playboy Club. We had a midafternoon tea break, which was restorative. After a few days, I recognized that I was going to be able to make it, and I settled in. We were supposed to observe a thing called "functional talking," where you would only speak if it was absolutely necessary. I was a functional talking failure. I just wanted to socialize too much, so I didn't take that part seriously.

There were chants with each meal, at the opening of the day, before dinner, and again before the finish of each day. These were all very cool, very fun, and accompanied by drumming—also very cool—and so forth. These rituals broke up the day, giving you a better feel for the philosophy and lifestyle of Tibetan Buddhism.

They had all kinds of activities that were woven around the Buddhist practices and the leader's interest in creating a very full monarchical-type situation. He even had a small unarmed army dedicated to peace and gentility, a police force to guard him and other visiting teachers, and so on. During the *dathun,* we learned that his army was having a two-week encampment over the hill. One of the more experienced residents said it was traditional for the *dathun* to raid the encampment. This sounded fun, and, in spite of the danger of running around in the hills and trees with a cast and crutches, I decided to join. It was a riot; we prepared sandwich bags filled with flour to use as bombs, and we snuck up on them. There was a small but steep valley at the bottom of the hill where the encampment was taking place. Their only weapons were Japanese bows and arrows, but even these were not in evidence. They used flour bombs for their own skirmishes, so we were appropriately armed. I wasn't able to run around in the wood s and hills, and, when a bunch of us got captured, not wanting to miss out on the experience and hoping to see or hear the leader, I walked up to the gate and announced that I was one of the raiders. They captured me as well.

We spent the night in a chicken-wire cage as prisoners. First, though, he gave us a Buddhist lecture on war and treating your prisoners like your firstborn, and then he sent down some very nice Port wine for us in the stockade. The next morning, he gave us an empowerment. He called it the "empowerment of all-encompassing commandership," and he administered it by using his red calligraphy seal in the shape of a scorpion to imprint the red scorpion on the back of our left hands.

One guy who was fun and jovial had it placed on his forehead. My first empowerment. I had heard of them, but this was the first I received. I wondered if others were similar. We went back to *dathun* for business as usual, but with a great story to tell. At the *dathun* I noticed I didn't care much that I wasn't drinking. I had been drinking a lot; basically, since after high school, but much more so since the accident. I was pleased to notice that it didn't cause me any distress not to drink. At least, none that I noticed; I had plenty going on, anyway, but nothing directly related to the drinking.

We would also meet with a meditation instructor on a semiregular, almost daily basis, and we learned a few more techniques. One that I liked in particular was called Tong Len, where you would dedicate about twenty minutes to breathe in the negativity of the world—or your world—on the in breath, and breathe out positivity on the out breath. I liked applying this to myself, the accident, and all that it entailed. Nothing really seemed to change the madness, but my ability to live in and maintain the façade was growing. It was more and more like I was two people: the one which I presented to the world, and the one which raged on privately. I was often withdrawn and nonresponsive, even in conversational groups, during times when I needed to sort something through or was a bit overwhelmed. Anything that hinted of failure or mishap was immediately met with a powerful fear of being transported once again into hospitals or homelessness—the loss of everything once again. I couldn't really relate to women, but could manage one-night stands. It seems I would unconsciously undermine anything that even hinted of a possibility of a real relationship. Not that I knew anything of the unconscious in those days. All I had was a growing knowledge of Buddhism and Buddhist psychology, and this doesn't include an unconscious, at least not in the way conceived by Westerners. As usual, I was considered eccentric but likable, and so I was able to meet people and engage in these experiences.

The Tibetan Buddhist system is called Tantric or Vajrayana, the path of deities and mantras. Many people would think there was some sort of weird sex thing going on, which I couldn't stand. There is a thing called tantric sex, which is basically between a man and a woman; it is not at all perverted, and it is only done after many years of regular practice, but oddballs would always think there was something weird going on in the background. I always found this insulting both to me personally and to the Tibetans and to Buddhism, which are all quite wholesome and sound. I was quite put off by even hints of that sort of thing going on, and did not notice much besides a lot of sleeping around in the way that was common in the seventies and eighties. I had no idea how people had come to believe that all that foolishness was part of the system. There was nothing written or said by the instructors and leaders that would do anything but mitigate against such behaviors.

Every morning of the *dathun* we would take five daily vows: to not drink, not kill, not steal, not lie, and not have sex. It was funny the way the room would be at about half volume during the chanting of the vows to not have sex and not drink, as you would know at least the intentions of the people on the cushions near you. All in all, though, everyone seemed serious and motivated. Those who were not were unlikely to turn up for a full thirty days of sitting. It also, I was told, weeded out killers and rapists, as those sorts could not manage to sit. Those who planned to drink or have sex that evening would skip the relevant vows. I was also told that anyone who could follow their breath would be unlikely to go mad. This was reassuring to me, as I still had fears of turning into a complete paranoid psychotic or schizophrenic. This was certainly better than that, but the fact that it could still distract me or overwhelm me on occasion kept me on my guard.

The rest of the *dathun* went uneventfully, and I left feeling like I knew the practice and was no longer a beginner. I even had an empowerment and a couple of other practices as well. I bought some souvenirs, and, instead of going back to Milwaukee, took a volunteer position as a cook there in Boulder in order to maintain my practice and also to get to know the scene and the people better. That was great fun. Lots of drinking and partying around a seriously disciplined situation, bonfires on the hills, mini parties in the little shacks that everyone lived in, and so forth. I even had an opportunity to have a personal interview with Trungpa Rinpoche. The situation was growing quite large, and it was more and more difficult to meet him. There were opportunities to serve in his household. He was creating this huge monarchical situation with himself as king, and all revolving around discipline, meditation, and Buddhist arts, so he organized servants and guards to allow and manage closer contact. He was also teaching a series of Tibetan practices of warriorship associated with the mythical kingdom of Shambhala, sometimes known to us as Shangri-la.

According to him, the place actually existed on earth at one time; but, when the entire population became enlightened, the kingdom rose up, and it now exists in some sort of a heavenly realm. In any case, he was creating a Shambhala kingdom and a Buddhist situation, and everyone there wanted a part of it—and wanted him, or at least to be close to him—so he became harder and harder to get to know. I really had no idea what to ask the guy when I did finally meet him, so I told him about my interest in Japanese arts and Zen Buddhism, asking whether it conflicted with what he was offering. He ended up suggesting that I go back to Japan and follow it up, and then come back again. Not much of a surprise, really, but there was something charged and dramatic in it all, given the atmosphere created around him.

I was deeply impressed, a good bit fascinated, and still convinced that there was something to it all that would resolve my difficulties and lead to a much better quality of life. The constant isolation, the inability to communicate with anyone except in the most superficial terms, and the seemingly unconscious propulsion away from any women who would make appropriate girlfriends. There was also a constant underlying feeling that I not only had to do something for myself but also—for some reason—for my wife as well, and this continued to drive me. I continued to keep trying to participate as much as possible in this newfound scene.

The Shambhala track was the way of the warrior, was based on meditation to develop what Trungpa called the Four Dignities: four stages of achievement along the path of warriorship, symbolized by a tiger, a lion, a garuda (a mythical bird from Asia), and a dragon. Japanese archery was a complementary martial art that he considered quite in keeping with the way of the warrior. All martial arts were encouraged. After a few years, I was able to squeeze in four years of tae kwon do as my bid to keep up with this all. I was too busy to get any farther than the first belt (yellow), but this was fine. I had the four years of martial arts practice, even if I didn't get any advanced belts for it.

I did spend another six months in Japan, but that didn't go too well. I couldn't get a job with a visa, the group of friends had changed a lot, and I didn't like working illegally, even though it was quite common in those days. The following March, I went back to RMDC, hoping there would be an opening for a cook. Japan was uneventful resume-wise; but, paranoia-wise, things had gotten far worse. Japan is not a place to be paranoid in. They live by intuition and communicate so lightly, it almost seems like ESP—something which I did not believe in, but which I could not stop thinking about, given my state of mind. You see samurais and ninjas everywhere in three-piece suits. People whisper about invisible armies run by family-owned corporations, and so forth. I constantly felt like I had fallen into the middle of a battle. The corporate world was battling it out, and this poor American ESL teacher had somehow fallen into the middle of it.

When I returned to the States, it seemed the whole country had gone mad, taken over by New Age madness, perversion, and stupidity. It was even worse than when I'd left. Everyone talked in innuendos and charged their speech with hidden New Age madness and perversion. I couldn't stand it or them. No one could speak without a double or a triple meaning in what they were saying. And the arrogance was palpable, Everyone thought they were something or someone—Buddhas, boddhisattvas, siddhis, saints, witches, and so on—but no one thought they were, or wanted to be, ordinary Americans. The fact that a lot of the Buddhist terminology, and even some Shambhala terms, were squeaking into this madness, bothered me. I couldn't help but think again that Trungpa's students and their nationwide connectedness were somehow largely at fault. Many thought they would be the next Trungpa. And the squawkers all thought that they and their friends were God's gift to Buddhism, and the rest of us were fakirs. Mutual-admiration societies bent on the destruction of all those who would dare to do things as designed.

The pretense, presumption, and delusion with which they approached everyone made it easier to hide mine, but it still drove me nuts. It was almost impossible to have an ordinary conversation with anyone. When I arrived, RMDC did have another cooking job available, with a new head chef who was as demanding as a drill sergeant and as nice as anyone could be—a really odd mix. He was, outside of the kitchen, a very pleasant fellow and a very serious practitioner, the sort who seemed to have pretty much given up thoughts of a career outside of what worked with Tibetan Buddhism, and he was living his life around centers and the practice of Tibetan Buddhism. He was also a very good artist who painted Tibetan *tangkhas* in the original style. He was impressive, and one of the first Americans I got to know who had done a lot of it. I met a bunch more later, but this guy was civil and tame and decent, the way you'd expect an American studying this stuff would be, and, in a way, that reminded me of the Shingon priest in Japan. It gave me some confidence that, in spite of the madness raging in the crowds, there were people who got it, and so it was possible to achieve that sort of demeanor. As time went on, I was lucky enough to be able to meet and become acquainted with some of the original students, those closest to Trungpa. I even met a nun who, years later, would herself become quite well known and the author many popular books on Buddhism. The people I actually met and talked to were quite nice and seemed to be getting a lot out of it. Many were teachers and administrators of the organization.

The Shambhala and Buddhist teachings all emphasized decency and human dignity; but, during that summer of 1984, everyone was caught up in this odd sort of perverted innuendo and witchy tricks and all sorts of New Age craziness, and the most infuriating thing was that they thought the odd behaviors, the indecency, and so on, all were somehow a special and deeper understanding of those philosophies. They seemed and acted crude toward me and everyone else, and there was absolutely no end to the arrogance, pretense, and stupidity. Everyone expected you to understand it and get on board with it. If you didn't get on board with it, you were the target of it. Of particular note was the constant prying into one another's business, the incessant slanderous innuendos, and the constant belief that the ugly behaviors were somehow necessary to enlighten their less-enlightened targets. Through all the crudity, they seemed to think that they were enlightening people; that they were the examples of enlightened behavior, and that their targets saw them in that light.

I couldn't help thinking that some sort of spiritual disease had broken out, not just among the Buddhists but all across America. Either that or some huge wave of cockroach-like invaders were trying to take over and destroy the whole thing through slander, perversion, and stupidity, making it all look like a cultish charade rather than the legitimate life-affirming discipline that it—Buddhism—was. The constant, idiotic, read-between-the-lines squawking at one another, the impulsiveness of it all, the pretending to be some kind of enlightened spontaneity, the crudity of it—it all just seemed like a deliberate slap in the face of what was being taught or some sort of mirror image of the Chinese takeover of Tibet, where perverts were taking over the American Buddhist scene, like a wave of the Chinese army took over Tibet, and trying to destroy it.

On many occasions, I was moved to quit and just give it all up, not because of what was presented but because of the constant stupidity and harassment. And yet, there were people around who got it and did it right, and that was enough to keep me going. That, plus the belief that Buddhism could provide real solutions—and my belief that the stupidity would pass as soon as these books hit the troublemakers where they lived and they actually gave them a try—all that combined to keep me going, and I stuck with Buddhism.

Many would think they had done the real work in a past life, and, for that reason, the two or three books they'd read, and the few hours of practice they had gotten in (in this lifetime, that is), were sufficient to give them license to act in ways that were so contrary to what was being taught at RMDC. I, too, often thought that the leaders of this group were largely oblivious to it all, as they didn't spend that much time in the common areas, and these offensive behaviors would not occur much when the leaders were around formally, and everyone sat on the cushions and was quiet.

What I found personally crushing was when these slander clubs started making me their target of interest, learning about me only to falsify my history, saying I had never been in the Peace Corps, that the death of my wife was a lie, that I had never been to Japan didn't speak Japanese or French, and so forth—all the time saying that I was somehow the perfect target for that sort of treatment. It was completely demoralizing, humiliating, and deeply wounding. I had already become rather deeply committed to following up in the program; I'd applied for the 1985 three-month seminary, with an eye toward getting permission to begin the Vajrayana preliminary practices. But, as I said, the targeting completely demoralized me. No one treated me like a guy who was working through a real-life tragedy and who might have some excuse for a little eccentricity. I *was* a former Peace Corps volunteer who had spent time in Japan. All of these details *were* my authentic personal history—they explained both my existence and my eccentricity, and yet, the slander crowd seemed to take great delight in getting everyone to believe they were false. It became more difficult than ever to make friends. It was infuriating and humiliating. In spite of it all, I did make some friends, as there were those who were not into the madness or who saw the madness for what it was, and, in either case, preferred to get to know people themselves. Little oases of normal socialization in a desert of crudity, all in the midst of this great scene dedicated to decency and sanity.

The crude and insulting behaviors never let up. I didn't get into the 1985 seminary because they said I seemed too angry. I was very definitely angry—angry at the crude, slanderous, and dismissive behaviors—but they didn't seem to get what my anger was about. I had problems with intensity as a result of the accident, and I was not just hurt by but also tremendously angry about the treatment I was receiving, particularly because it was so obviously contrary to anything we had signed up for. I hated it when people didn't understand that I was just generally intense, not angry—and, even more to the point, that the anger was justified in the face of the crude behaviors.

In August of 1984, I moved to Boulder, with an eye toward attending Naropa Institute to take up some further Buddhist studies. The whole town seemed overwhelmed by the madness. Everywhere I went, I was subjected to the innuendos and the pretenses. I even felt that the perverts were trying to make me look like one of them; and, to add insult to injury, they pretended that I *was* one of them. It was impossible to avoid, and absolutely nothing would get through to them. They all insisted that they were the majority—the norm, the mainstream—and everybody else had to deal with them. I did what I could to battle the madness, mainly by getting to know the local baristas and bartenders, letting them clearly see that I was not one of that crowd. This had a strangely polarizing effect, where there now seemed to be not just the perverted innuendo mongers, but a good group as well; and those of us in the good group were out to set the troublemakers straight, in order to get things back to normal and away from the New Age madness. I was again "perfect" for the role on both sides. My leg, now without the cast and crutches but with a limp that was quite noticeable, made me easily identifiable to both the crowds of liars and the crowds trying to set them straight.

People came to RMDC and other centers from all over the country, and, from there, they would go to their home centers, and keep it up some more. I was not the only target, but, for some reason, I was a favorite of some sort. I think this was because my leg made me easily identifiable. I also wondered if my intensity itself was the source of the problem. They harassed me for everything I said and did, and I began to dread every moment among them. Around Christmas of 1984, I moved back to Wisconsin. I'd had enough.

. . .

The Milwaukee center was still basically human, but Milwaukee had become as bad as Boulder. I couldn't help thinking that the national connectedness of all the Trungpa centers, and the size of the crowd he had attracted, made them the main source of the madness—perhaps it was an innocent source, but it still was a source. I applied for the 1986 seminary and was accepted. I guess being outside of RMDC made it difficult for someone to say, "That's that angry guy everybody is slandering and harassing." I then went to Karme Choling, also called the Tail of the Tiger, a Trungpa retreat center in the mountains of Vermont. I sat in another month-long intensive in further preparation for the seminary.

Karme Choling was in a fabulously beautiful area of Vermont, as I said, and the buildings had all the ornate Tibetan and Shambhalian trappings. It was a great place to practice, and I saw a lot of the same faces I had seen in Boulder and at RMDC; unfortunately, the madness was there in Vermont as well, and it didn't take much time for the standard insulting innuendos to get to me again. It was miserably frustrating, and it seemed to be getting worse. There were also the constant innuendos about cults, satanic worship, molestation, sex groups, and so on. Many pretended to be "exploring" in order to weed these out, while others pretended they were in, just to get a rise out of people; still others thought they were helping, and got sucked in. No one seemed to have the twofold necessary and primary skill to prevent all this: ordinary awareness/ordinary conversation. The cults, if they even existed, needed the gossip and innuendos to sustain themselves, and so they fed into it, with their targets as the accused and themselves as the avenging crusaders against it all.

As an example, one guy who sat as timekeeper in front of the room deliberately tried to humiliate me in front of the people sitting. There was a woman I liked sitting next to me. She had a good boyfriend, so I wasn't interested in her except socially; but, one time, in front of the whole room, the timekeeper acted as though I was communicating with him through gestures, indicating that I'd had sex with this woman. Fortunately, she didn't buy any of it; but, in a room dedicated to decency, he was still saying that I'd written her name on the bathroom walls, deliberately trying to compromise me with her and anyone else who was watching. I hardly knew this guy, and I had no idea why he, or any of the people like him, had singled me out for their peculiar attentions. I still just wanted to have ordinary social conversations with ordinary people, talk about Buddhism, and meet some of the leaders.

At this point, I couldn't shake the belief that the world was about to end in a nuclear disaster, and that the gossips had somehow brought me to the attention of the CIA, the Klan, and other such groups who had decided that whatever was wrong with me was serious enough to warrant having me killed. I would scan the hills for snipers, and then meditate rather intensely in an effort to psychically make the entire problem go away—whether it was a delusion or not. I knew these were paranoid delusions, but I could not stop them, and so I felt I had to take them seriously. The socialized part of my mind knew better than to tell anyone about this, but it would occasionally leak out in hints and gestures when I was with people I felt I could trust. My loyalties were more and more with the socialized part of my mind, as that was cheerful and fun, even though a bit childish. The other part was quite miserable, but it often demanded attention, at which times it would either terrify me or entertain me enough to get my attention—when it did get my attention, by whichever means, of course, I was afraid of being overwhelmed by it.

I didn't have a tent or enough money for a room, so I slept at night in the shrine room with the other more impoverished members of the *dathun*. That was more fun than anything else. I was able to continue my reading and improve my understanding of Buddhism. I felt convinced that the higher teachings in seminary would solve my psychological problems utterly, and I intensely prepared myself for that retreat. There were required courses and readings, and I pursued it all quite seriously.

6

Buddhism à la Trungpa Rinpoche, et alii.

... who passed through universities with radiant cool eyes hallucinating Arkansas and Blake-light tragedy among the scholars of war ...

—ALLEN GINSBERG, "HOWL"

The thing that made Trungpa's group so effective and popular was the overt lack of cultishness built into the official system; that, plus the thoroughness of the presentation of Tibetan Buddhism, all of it translated into English by a translation committee run by Chogyam Trungpa and another Tibetan Lama. Thus, when the cultishness emerged, it seemed like an invasion of some sort, perhaps by cultists, perhaps by misguided Christians who wanted to end it all. Whatever the real source, it seemed like cockroach-style invasion of an absolutely beautiful mansion.

The whole of it was based on three paths: the Hinayana, Mahayana, and Vajrayana. The first part was the Hinayana, the path of basic personal discipline, nonviolence, and meditation; it was similar to the Buddhism of Sri Lanka and Thailand. The second part was the Mahayana, which was like Chinese and Japanese Zen; it included more of a component of compassion, reaching out to others, and doing good in the world. The third was the part that was particular to Tibet and neighboring areas, the

Vajrayana—the diamond vehicle—which included the deity practices, the mantra recitations, and, eventually, the six yogas. We were to be introduced to these practices at the end of seminary. It was this last part that I felt would finally allow me to resolve the confusion of the raging part of mind. Through a deeper knowledge of things psychological and spiritual, I felt that I finally would be able to look at what was causing the problem, and then I would be able to resolve it. At the end of seminary, if you passed everything, you could get permission to begin the grueling preliminary practices of prostrations, purifications, and so forth. This was preceded by the mind transmission from Trungpa Rinpoche himself. This was the transfer of the core wisdom of the tradition to the new student through a lecture.

I saw no psychologists or counselors, and rather easily picked up on the vague but popular notion that Buddhism and meditation were somehow better. I didn't want to see any traditional counselors because I was afraid they would drug me, lock me up, or something of that sort—or, worse, that they would bring me to the attention of even more of the innuendo-mongering squawkers who, sadly, were taking over the world.

I identified rather closely with several of the renowned lineage holders of Tibetan history. The line that Chogyam Trungpa belonged to and was teaching was called the Kagyu, which was one of four main lineages of Tibet: the Kagyu, the Gelugpa, the Nyingma, and the Shakpa. The Kagyu were headed by a guy called the Karmapa, who was amazingly cool in this Tibetan genre; the Gelugpa is headed by the Dalai Lama, who is more worldly, more political, and better known the Karmapa. Yet, the Karmapa and the Kagyu are more rooted in full-on spirituality. Here is a list of the leaders of the Kagyu, from the beginning (about the year 1000) to my 1985 seminary: Vajradhara, a primordial Buddha; Tilopa, a monk with visionary experiences who turned to worldly pursuits; Naropa, a renowned scholar; Marpa, a translator; Milarepa, a mountain hermit; Gampopa, a monk who established many monasteries and the core system of Kagyu monasticism; and, finally, Karmapa. They had this system of rebirths, where major teachers were able to reincarnate consciously, and then others of the lineage could find them. The Karmapa is known as the best of all these reincarnating forms, known as *tulkus*. He leaves a letter at the time of each of his deaths, telling people in cryptic, symbolic terms where his next incarnation would be found. At the time of the *dathun* in Vermont there was quite a bit of intrigue, as the sixteenth Karmapa had died, and the letter for the seventeenth had not yet been found; there was quite a bit of concern and turmoil around all that.

The yogi Milarepa had lots of yogic powers, and many miracles were attributed to him. What I found a little odd is that many of the practitioners there would believe that Jesus and Moses had never existed, but that Milarepa and others were real. For me, if any were real, they all seemed more plausible; I found things like walking on water and virgin birth more believable, rather than less, because of the confirmation of such things from another culture. I also found it useful to identify with those major characters of the lineage. When I was feeling poor and isolated, I would think of Milarepa, the mountain yogi; when appreciating my language skills, I would identify with Marpa, the translator; and so forth. I had to be careful doing this, as the delusional part of my mind would want to think of myself as actually being one of those major characters. This was a common delusion/daydream in much of the *sangha,* but it was one I didn't want to indulge too much for fear of making a fool of myself by means of the wilder part of mind taking it on too deeply.

There was no shortage of the deluded, given the timeframe; 1985 was still full of drug fallout from cocaine, LSD, and everything else. Long-term alcoholism was also a growing problem, leading to the confabulation and delusion so common with that. A famous beat poet— one of Allen Ginsberg's friends—one time came up to me, thinking I was some sort of secret guru or reincarnation, and he began looking in my shoe, and then, in what seemed to be an LSD-style delusion, started predicting the future out of my shoe. Many of the beats were a part of the scene, and Naropa Institute in Boulder had the Kerouac studies program headed by Allen Ginsberg.

I had a couple of brief encounters with Allen. One time he borrowed a cigarette from me to give to a friend, and we had other similar encounters. We chatted very briefly when he borrowed the cigarette, and, from that point on, whenever he saw me he was quite cordial and friendly, waving at me like an old friend. I thought perhaps he had mistaken me for an old writing student of his or someone he knew better, but I didn't say anything because it was socially cool to be known by Allen. Besides, I liked him and wouldn't have minded actually getting to know him.

In Buddhism, everything is lists. The four noble truths, the twelve *nidanas*, the eightfold noble path, the six *paramitas*, the five root *kleshas*, *ayatanas*, *dhatus*, *skandhas*; the five these, the seven those, and so on— all with lots of cool-sounding Sanskrit terms. It was a useful device for learning and sorting through the large and complex philosophical system, and it suited my penchant for memorizing things. As meditation experience grows, you get a deeper understanding of the lists and the philosophy, and how it is all a tremendously coordinated full philosophy without internal contradictions. I had occasional tinges of guilt and mixed loyalties, given my Catholic upbringing, but I enjoyed it all too much to give that much thought. I thought the Catholics would be well served setting up month-long and three-month-long retreats, not to mention all these graded practices.

The core of Buddhist enlightenment is based on an understanding and realization of emptiness, which, in its basic outline, is not difficult to understand; to experience it fully and establish some stability in it are the difficult parts. It's a straightforward-enough concept, and it exists in many cultures and philosophies, but often in a somewhat different guise. The core idea is that all things physical or psychological have no lasting existence. Everything is in a state of growth or decay, so nothing can be said to exist in a permanent way, and from that you conclude and that everything is a product of mind. Later, you realize this is true: an empty, clear mind is the source of everything. A friend of mine once quipped that everything does have an existence, it is just a temporary one; this was his one-liner attempt to dismiss the entirety of centuries of argumentation on the subject. Cute as that was, the point of growth and decay, and the fact that nothing is stable and nothing can be counted on permanently, is the basic understanding that you explore to get deeper and deeper understandings of the emptiness, and when you are stabilized in that understanding, your spiritual experience will increase—most important, you can actually reach a point of a stabilized psychology in a state free of suffering. Not too bad, really. It didn't seem like that big of a deal, but the crowds pretty much lived and acted like they would have a life and a following like Trungpa's, and that they could establish their own kingdoms once they made it. I liked that idea myself, but I didn't really think I'd get the deep-level understanding, and, even if I did, I would not get a life like Trungpa's. I was more hoping for a life full of challenge, with money, a wife, and a cool house. It was all a good intellectual challenge, and it fit in well with my Western philosophical and psychological reading.

I kept studying, practicing, and reading. Doing all I could to get the nonsense around me to stop, and to get to the point where these practices would get my life back on track. I reviewed and reviewed some more; I made charts; I read and reread; I compared Western and Eastern, and Eastern with Eastern (different types within it, I mean). I honed my approach to the reading, trying to work with just "root" thinkers in order to streamline my study of the vast corpus of material.

An important aspect of emptiness is the concept of "egolessness." At first, this seems to be a lack of arrogance; but, in reality, it is a psychological triumph in which one actually extinguishes the ego, and lives in a more natural, immediate, and spontaneous way, without all the constant internal checking back and self-talk that ego generates. This was a baffling concept at first. It is actually quite difficult to master, and it is presented as the core of the effort. To be truly egoless is to be enlightened; or, at least, to be a "boddhisattva," which is a kind of Buddhist saint. There are then ten levels of egolessness after that, and traversing them all leads to full enlightenment which is called "Buddhahood." There is also the path of miracles, the path of siddhi, which was something associated with the six yogas and which was not being taught. A person who makes an achievement such as walking on water or walking through walls or flying is called a "siddha." There was a lot of fascination with siddhi and miracles, and the biographies of the major Tibetan saints included many stories of miracles not unlike those of Moses, Jesus, and the Catholic saints—although, by any measure, Moses was the most spectacular.

Emptiness is studied in four stages: the first is basic stability, which is called one-pointedness; the next is simplicity; the third is taste; and the last is nonmeditation. There are detailed descriptions of these states that are achieved through the meditation practices. There is a belief in a purer form of the universe, which can be viewed through attainment of these states. There is even one belief which states that the world is actually constructed of spheres of rainbow light. Very few would be able to see that aspect of the world, but steps toward it can be achieved, such as seeing the disillusionments, which are semihallucinations that characterize the achievement of simplicity. These seem to be reflected in Western mystical paintings in some sense.

The world is also populated by beings which most cannot see, like angels and demons; but, the Tibetans have a very complex worldview in that way. They also see the body as hollow and potentially filled with chakras and channels, rather than organs and muscle. It struck me that the main difference between Eastern and Western thinking in these matters was that we began with the world and worked inward toward wisdom, while they begin with the mind and work outward. Western theories such as the *unus mundus*—the one world so much discussed by Jung and his followers—is just a view of emptiness, so both traditions actually end up in the same discoveries of wisdom, but the starting points are opposed.

As time went on, I learned more and more about Trungpa. He was a writer, a poet, and an artist; world traveled, well educated, and a very good speaker of English. The accident where he crashed his Jag into a joke shop left him paralyzed on the left side, and he walked pretty much like someone who'd had a stroke. He wrote a lot of books on Buddhism, he and was classically trained as a head monk and *tulku* of a monastery in Tibet, where he remained until he escaped to England after the Chinese takeover of Tibet. I pretty much considered all the squawkers and perverts as a reflection of the Chinese takeover, while I thought of the people who could maintain their discipline as the Tibetans. Trungpa's drinking and womanizing were his only apparent deficits, but, as I said, I actually sort of liked this; I didn't see any of it as hypocritical, especially because he was open about it and thought it would help keep the teetotalers out, which it did—at least those who were real crusaders. Buddhism did attract a lot of people who wouldn't smoke or drink at all. Trungpa attracted fewer of those. I learned that he drank from morning to night, and that he pretty much had a different woman most every night. *Very cool,* I thought. I wouldn't have minded a lifestyle like that myself, as I often quipped; but, honestly, I was more interested in a relationship, with dinners, hobbies, careers, and so forth.

Trungpa was married to some member of British royalty or nobility or something of that sort. A very nice, very attractive woman, whom everyone called "Lady Diana," and she was treated as the queen of the monarchy Trungpa was establishing. I often thought that he, too, would have preferred to have a more normal lifestyle—just a life with her, I mean—but there was something in the demands of the situation he was creating that prevented it. I also heard that he was having serious health problems as a result of the lifestyle, and these were complicated by his injury. The party life in the group was quite good. However, due to the nonsense of the squawkers and innuendo mongers, I had a very difficult time making a circle of good friends. I tried to stick as much as possible with the more normal members, but they were often influenced by or afraid of the squawkers themselves, so it was hard to make friends.

I was happy Trungpa was straight. I didn't like the growing awareness I had of a closeted and very unsavory bit of homosexuality in the group. It seemed to be closeted with a spiritual excuse. Those involved seemed predatory, and there were times I thought I noticed hints of pedophilia here and there, something I was and still am quite against. I was horrified to think that anyone could see pedophilia as somehow spiritual, or justified in the Buddhist or any other religious situation—or in any situation at all, for that matter. This was no better than the perverted priests in Catholic scandals.

Trungpa's appointed successor—a guy they called "the Regent"— was a known bisexual, and I heard that Trungpa had told him to give up the gay side of things. I didn't mind open homosexuals—I actually kind of liked them, based on past experiences I've described—but given that this tawdrier form of homosexuality was around, I was glad to hear that Trungpa Rinpoche had taken that stand with his "Regent."

In design and much of the execution, the atmosphere was great. They had formal parties, ballroom dancing, poetry, music, and theater; it was a very full life situation, one that I very much wanted to participate in fully. Most important, I wanted to participate in it *without* the squawkers and innuendo mongers. As time went on, I became more and more aware of the substance of their squawking, and then I became more skillful at stopping it, distracting it, and making fun of it; but, nevertheless, the popularity of the phenomenon was maddening. As soon you straightened out one, ten more would come out of the woodwork, and they would start it all over again. For them, it was a great game of ruining people socially and professionally; and, somehow, they always found some way to justify it as being in keeping with the disciplines they had signed up for and the vows they had taken. The most common excuse was "crazy wisdom." Crazy wisdom was a concept of Tibetan Buddhism that Trungpa talked about a bit, and of which he was considered an example. A wise or enlightened person engaging in eccentric and hard-to-understand behaviors, such as his drinking and womanizing, was thought to be demonstrating outpourings of wisdom in order to resolve complicated situations. Naturally, the more frivolous of the Americans saw everything they did as crazy wisdom: their drinking, their womanizing, their anger, their gossip mongering. As if taking one line from the Bible to justify behaviors that were not allowed elsewhere, they were taking two words from Trungpa and using them to justify everything.

My real goal at this time was to settle in a city with a big center, get the master's and PhD in linguistics I had always wanted, maintain the Buddhist practice, and get a wife. Still, the sense that I had to re-create what I had lost was an underlying theme of everything I did. I lived in constant fear of the whole thing repeating itself, and I saw every mishap as a recurrence of the accident. I couldn't let my guard down for a moment. If I did, the world would come crashing down around me again. The meditation helped my awareness, and I began to think of my time with pain and crutches as a kind of unstructured meditation, because it forced me to stay very alert to the atmosphere and the details of the environment.

Even now, because I don't like to stumble over my limp, I am constantly aware of my feet, a kind of forced walking meditation. If I let go of my awareness of my feet, even to look at a window or eat something, I sway a bit, and then I can stumble. So I kind of saw myself has having a four-and-a-half-year edge on whatever level of practices I had completed.

I also challenged myself on the crutches and cast, with two trips to Europe, the first year in Japan, and a trip on the Siberian Express when I left Japan. The Siberian Express was quite a challenge for the crutches. You had to walk through two cars to get to the dining car for meals. Between the cars, the walkway would shake and sway in a particularly awkward manner, and I had to stand and watch for three or four shakes before I could aim the crutches and make the crutch-aided jump across. Otherwise, the trip was quite nice. We stopped at Lake Baikal, at an icon-covered church in the middle of nowhere, and, finally, in Moscow, with several planned tours and meals there. From there, I went on to Berlin to see John (the friend who'd stayed with me in Wiesbaden), stopping at Warsaw for a couple of nights on the way. The change from Russia to Poland was quite dramatic. In Russia, everyone seemed malnourished and paranoid; but, in Poland, like a change from night to day, everyone seemed healthy and friendly, much better looking, too. The whole trip took about two weeks and was actually quite boring, but with the chatting and joking with the other foreign passengers, things progressed well enough. We had liquor enough to liven it up, too; some sort of sweet wine from the dining car.

Emptiness and impermanence are the only two things you really need to know to get an idea of what the Buddhists are aiming at. Emptiness is the nature of yourself and everything in your environment; and impermanence is the nature of things, in that everything passes away. Awareness, the tool you use to recognize emptiness, is just not being distracted by thought, being fully aware of the five senses, and not reinterpreting everything. By deepening your understanding of these two things, you clarify your mind and your world.

Impermanence was great for me, because it really lessened the blow of the accident. The constant reliving of the trauma, the dreamlike world I was living in, and the constant need to use the practices to make sure I could stay with the five senses and not be swept away into the dark-night journey of the soul, which constantly threatened to take over. I would often think that I had done something in this life that was a source of bad luck, and that I had to keep reinvestigating my life to find out why I was being "punished," with recurrences of the accident, a lingering thought leftover from Catholic school and Catholic guilt. The idea of karma took the pressure off that, as I could relax and just think that there was something in either my or Deb's or both of our past lives that was the source of the problem, and nothing could be done to research it. It had been so many years since the accident that I could not admit to anyone that I still had such difficulties with it. It was embarrassing to be so incapable of coming to grips with it, so I shut it up even more.

As time went on, I picked up a couple of Tibetan names: Jigme Chosang, "fearless good dharma," was the name I got when I first became a Buddhist; and Yeshe Jungnal, "source of wisdom," was the one I got when I took what they call the "Boddhisattva Vow," which is a vow not to get enlightened until everyone else does first. The first name was given to me by the Regent and the second by a very well-known and highly placed Kagyu teacher named Jamgon Kontrol Rinpoche. I had an actual, very cool, spiritual experience when I took that vow, and it seemed to have been precipitated by him. I had a view of what I think was what they call a "pure land," a beautiful, cartoon-like world where everyone was wearing orange. I barely saw it, but I was quite amazed. I also felt he had done it as a nice gesture, because he noticed the nonsense that was occurring around me and my inward turmoil—he sort of was giving me a view to hold onto and stay motivated by as I sorted through my personal and environmental troubles.

After that second *dathun* (the one in Vermont), I went back to Milwaukee to wait for seminary. The problems continued, and I continued to read. During that time, I learned that I was going to get a settlement from the government for the percentage loss of use of my leg. I would be getting a good check every month for five years: just enough time to get a master's and PhD, and just enough money. I was quite pleased, and I applied to one university in Montreal and another in Hawaii. The one in Hawaii accepted me, offering a tuition waiver, so I decided to go there. I would attend seminary in the summer of 1986, and then, as if transported by seminary to paradise, I would move to Hawaii to obtain my degrees.

Seminary itself was marvelous: three months of study and practice of Buddhism, leading up to the "direct mind transmission" from the guru. Everything that came from Trungpa himself seemed right on—and about as cultish as a Catholic High Mass—and yet, none but a few seemed to notice this. They were as high on their cultish pretenses as they were on their drugs during the preceding years; many were still using, which made them think that somehow they had trumped the gurus and the system—adding drugs to the mix obviated the need to actually study and practice. The seminary was divided into three sections: Hinayana, Mahayana, and Vajrayana. What goes on in seminary is basically secret; but, actually, it is the same old Buddhist stuff, just presented a little more directly. When you first sign up you think there'll be classes in auras and all sorts of New Age nonsense, but there isn't actually. Buddhism really emphasizes a straightforward relationship to everyday reality, unlike Hinduism or some of the Western traditions like Rosicrucianism or Theosophism. Each of the three sections of seminary had two weeks of sitting, followed by two weeks of study. It was very satisfying. At the end of it, I and most participants were allowed to take the final transmission; a few were not, and a few changed their minds; and all this, too, was straightforward. There were about 365 of us in all, if I remember correctly. We were all housed in two-person tents. There were shared shower facilities and outhouses, some with plumbing. The mountains were beautiful, and it was a very large retreat center, just a one-hour walk from a beautiful view of the Great Divide.

In thinking about that final moment—the transmission of the wisdom of the lineage, that is—I had this odd fantasy of Trungpa Rinpoche seated on a gilded throne on a mountaintop, with a long line of seminarians walking up to him, one by one, and then bending down to each place their ear to his lips while he said, "Jesus Christ is the one true savior." This struck me as hilarious, and I couldn't shake it; but, transmission actually just turned out to be a lecture with a somewhat pithy tone to it. Nothing shocking or weird, just the same old Buddhism, but the tone of it somehow got to the heart of the matter of emptiness and of having a good relationship with the world. I was very pleased that I did not have to work through my relationship to

Buddhism through some New Age-y weirdness, and also that I was not somehow bound for a monastery or a cave.

Seminary was pretty serious. It was a risk, even in those days, to take three months off from your life to engage in what many thought was a cult experience. There was still no brainwashing. The innuendo mongering and the same stupid harassment, the dismissals, and so forth, all persisted, which hurt my ability to socialize in some sense, but all that was actually more subdued. What was most rankling about it all was that it was so much to the contrary of how things were designed. I made a few friends, but I still felt that everyone except those who actually bothered to talk to me thought I was lying about my entire past—that I was some sort of closeted criminal who really didn't belong. I particularly disliked the implication that I was some sort of New Age weirdo, because that implication was made by those who actually *were* New Age weirdos. They simply couldn't believe that an ordinary American could come to an environment like that, but not be a New Age nut job. The more they harassed me, the more committed I became to not joining that side of things. It just seemed so egotistical, so retarded, and so basically sadistic—all things that do not suit the Buddhist training, and all of which was excused as being some sort of crazy wisdom. That one little phrase was all it took to excuse the most tawdry, insulting behaviors. *Vajra* this and *vajra* that were also good excuses. If a master gets angry, the Tibetans say that it is not regular anger, but *"vajra* anger,"* and therefore justified. All the squawkers naturally deemed their innuendo and gossip mongering to be *"vajra* squawking,"* thereby rationalizing that their slander benefited their targets.

There were also hints that some of them were involved in some sort of sexual practices, none of which were sanctioned by the group, and which I only half believed were going on to the extent hinted at. Most of it seemed more accusatory and exploratory than real; more like people were afraid of such perverts getting into the group, and, in their fear, fell into accusing and blaming each other, constantly testing to make sure what they feared was not there. Others seemed to be genuinely involved; and, as always, the ones who were involved continually targeted the innocent and ignored the guilty. Predictably, they used crazy wisdom, combined with the fact that Trungpa was a womanizer, to excuse their behaviors and to stir up these fears.

One of the strangest excuses for the slander and innuendo—and one of the most common—was that they thought they were somehow protecting Trungpa, the situation, and their targets by slandering them, and also anyone slanderers didn't happen to like. That, somehow, the slander would keep the true weirdos either out of the group or too confused by what went on to do anything truly weird. All this was absolutely opposite of what Trungpa himself did, and what he taught. I think the main reason that Trungpa's behaviors never bothered me was that he never troubled to hide them. He was open about the drinking and the womanizing. If I had heard about these things but been told to help cover them up, I never would have joined. As it was, I saw it as no impediment to what he had to say; he had great books and lectures, and he was creating a very exciting situation.

Those who seemed most genuinely involved in the cultishness and perversion were recognizable through the extremes of arrogance that they paraded around as a kind of mark of their enlightenment; rather than seeing themselves as arrogant, they saw themselves as part of an unspoken, secret cadre supported by the leadership. There was no official sanction for those behaviors, and I saw no covert sanctions, but they saw themselves as an accepted elite sanctioned by the group. They were constantly lording over others. Trungpa Rinpoche was careful to point out that he was the sort of monarch who inspired lordship in others, rather than lording over others, but this didn't get through to the squawkers and those who would have preferred a cult.

Those whose innuendos were more sexually charged were quite unpleasant to deal with, and they seemed to be the ones fueling everyone's fears and perpetuating the innuendo mongering. It was as if they could cover up and hide their own activities by firing up everyone else against targets other than themselves. At one point, Trungpa Rinpoche even saw fit to put out a general directive to "stop the innuendo," but this had little effect. There seemed to be a kind of high associated with it. They were high on their own egos, and on the schadenfreude from engaging in group harassment of strangers, with stories and gossip that a child could recognize as false, or at least exaggerated, but they couldn't lay off it. They were as addicted to the harassment as they had been to alcohol, drugs, and Twelve Step programs in years past; and, even worse, they seemed to be raising their children to be the same way. Of course, these were the crowds, not the officers or the teachers or the people working properly in the environment, and not those who actually understood that the way to learn these things was to actually practice them. The crowds I am referring to are the cockroaches, the infiltrators, the madmen and—women who somehow had come to cloud so much of the atmosphere. It was maddening, never ending, repetitious, and stupid. It went on for years; and yet, none of them made the slightest attempt to question the soi-disant wisdom of their behaviors and those of their mutual admiration societies.

Boulder was full of it as well, and, as I would notice later through giving papers and presentations in linguistics, it was throughout the country, not just in cities with large Trungpa centers. I still somewhat feared that the whole thing might have originated from Trungpa's group, because of the numbers he had attracted, their wide dispersal throughout the country, and their ability to connect and reconnect with everyone at their local centers, retreat centers, and events. Trungpa was there to establish Buddhism and Shambhala in America, but the innuendo mongers seemed to only be interested in creating a world of innuendo mongering. Some even saw the whole thing as an effort to take over America, and maybe even the entire world, with a Buddhist monarchy. Not surprising, given the level of proselytizing built into the culture from Christianity, but it was just such a deviance from the principles of what any religion or philosophy should hold that made it so unbearable. Even with the wild side of my mind, I never saw any of it as a threat to America, just as more of a welcome contribution, with lots of useful and interesting ideas coming from the East and, particularly, Tibet.

The most exotic class they had at seminary was one on the "protector principle," which described the logic behind the fierce deities who served as protectors of both the lineage and the practitioners (those practicing in a genuine way, that is). It was straightforward enough. Protectors were thought to be enlightened beings that were warrior-like and that took a role in protecting the situations that were set up.

They were meant to be terrifying to demons, wrongdoers, and so forth. I wondered if maybe they didn't speak enough English to hear what was going on, given all the innuendo mongering. Strangers to Tibetan Buddhism often mistake these protectors for demons, and accuse Tibetan Buddhists of practicing some unwitting devil worship, but the Tibetans see the protectors as more warrior-like than evil. The evil demons are run off by the protectors.

As seminary came to a close, I had the transmission, and then received permission to begin the Ngondro, which are the preliminary practices required before going on to the more advanced practices of deity visualizations and mantra recitations. This took most people at least a few years. It was meant to weed out the undisciplined, and also to train those who were more disciplined and devoted. Many never completed the first set of the four trainings: the hundred thousand full prostrations to the lineage. These are considered secret practices as well. They are quite nice, contain nothing weird, and provide very good mind training and discipline. As my leg was so mangled, my meditation instructor in Milwaukee—and my doctor—said that I couldn't do the full prostrations, which would put both legs at risk; thus, I was to do a modified version, called "tabletops." This was a relief and also a bit of a shortcut. Rather than being physically draining, it was like light exercise. I figured I could look at my three and a half years on crutches as the physically demanding part. I was given a limit on the number of tabletops I could do each day, and I completed that part of the practice in just a few months. The practice was still somewhat demanding, and, psychologically, it brought up a lot. I thought it was helping with all the madness, but the world continued; and, though I was more and more committed and loyal to my presentational, social mind, the other mind continued to rage in the background. More reading and more instruction in the Buddhist philosophical system also made me better able to sort through it all.

It was somewhat demanding on me as a Westerner raised Catholic to work through the crucial attitude of devotion to a guru—it bumped into thoughts of the one true savior Jesus Christ, and that sort of thing—but, I didn't find this a conflict. I was surprised by how easily I took to the Tibetan style, in fact. I even imagined Jesus Christ as part of the lineage from time to time, which was considered quite appropriate. I also kept up with my study of Christian mysticism, through the interpretations of it by Jung and Jungians.

I was very impressed by Trungpa Rinpoche and his system, and I never felt pressured, sold into, or manipulated by any of it. There was always plenty of room to leave and plenty of challenges to make it difficult to continue. Up to the last point of seminary, anyway; at that point, you take a vow to continue the Vajrayana practices for life. It is considered psychologically dangerous if you stop the practices. Let me reiterate that: the potential psychological danger only concerns the practices; it has nothing at all to do with the slander and innuendo mongering. But, not surprisingly, those who were involved in the innuendo mongering and slander foolishly thought that all of it was part of the system, and so they considered it to be part of what they couldn't—and shouldn't—stop. The more I listened to them, the more moronic they seemed. Putting all their efforts into indiscipline and indulgence, and yet, thinking that the path of discipline and renunciation somehow prevented them from stopping. What balderdash! The only reason I took it seriously in any way was because it could ruin a person socially and professionally, and also because it was growing so rapidly. It was also happening in Hawaii, where there was a very well-developed Buddhist scene. Hawaii had Zen, Tibetan, and Chinese Buddhism—some of it going back to the religions of the original plantation workers from Asia, and a big part of it from the American Buddhism craze of the 1970s and '80s.

At this time, there was plenty of New Age nonsense going on. Rajnish was sponsoring group orgies in auditoriums to "wear out" the excessive sexualization of the time; Koresh was around at that time too, along with plenty of televangelism. There were more gurus and miscellaneous trips than you could count or list exhaustively: rebirthing; satanic worship, like Anton Levy; some interest in Crowley; yoga, which was very big; there were also armed groups of militant Christians in the hills in the West; the group that suicided, thinking a UFO was coming to get them; the Reverend Sun Myung Moon, and the arranged mass marriages of his followers; and on and on.

Zen was pretty much considered respectable, but participation in anything else would be suspect by those who did not like the New

Age movement. At first, I was willing to talk about my involvement in Trungpa's group, but I soon stopped and just said I was doing Zen, because it attracted less innuendo, and I did not want to be labeled a New Age kook while I was trying to seriously pursue a master's and a PhD.

7

Graduate School—Hawaii, 1986

"... who were expelled from the academies for crazy & publishing obscene odes on the windows of the skull ..."

—ALLEN GINSBERG, "HOWL"

Before I arrived in Honolulu, I heard about two centers near the university: Kalu Rinpoche's center, run by Lama Rinchen, a classically trained Tibetan Lama, and a Zen center run by Aitken Roshi. Soon after I arrived, I sought them out and began practicing at their centers, in addition to the practice I did on my own. So, at that time, I had my Ngondro practice, a PhD to pursue, about four hours a week in the Zen center, and a few hours a week at the Kalu Rinpoche center with Lama Rinchen. I was busy enough and enjoyed the practices.

As time went on in Hawaii, I eventually answered about forty of the Zen koans; this took about fifteen years or so. Koans are those enigmatic little puzzles, such as, "What is the sound of one hand clapping?" I wasn't considered particularly good at it, and my answers were not very deep. Aitken Roshi said I was too intellectual, and that was why I was slow and a little superficial. Once in a while, I would get a nice answer, but most of them were sort of plodding. I find it difficult to explain, even to myself, what constitutes a good answer. It seems to come out of a space similar to that of spontaneous writing: you kind of know when you're there, and you kind of know when the answer is there; but, with all the false starts, missteps, and so forth, it is difficult to be fully confident or to write a clear description of the answer or the source of the answer. The full curriculum had about seven hundred koans, and, if you answered them all, you would be qualified to become a Zen teacher. I still did not really have a good grasp of what enlightenment was all about, but I found the practices to be quite grounding, and my knowledge of the intellectual side of things was growing considerably. Aitken Roshi once pointed out, "It took me twenty-five years to answer my first koan, and I have seen some people do it in a few weeks. I am sure you will fall somewhere in between." I found this reassuring about my pace.

Aitken Roshi himself was quite interesting. He originally took up Zen as a prisoner of war in Japan during the World War II. He was captured over there as a civilian employee of some sort just when the war broke out. Because he was not a combatant, he was not treated that badly, and he learned Zen. As the years went by, he became a renowned American Zen master, with full permission as a lineage holder to teach koans and make new teachers. Widely respected in the field, in both America and Japan, he has written about a dozen books on the subject.

Enlightenment fascinated the crowds, particularly the innuendo mongers, many of whom thought that they already were enlightened, or that they had good access to it, and so forth. The Christians all thought they were saved and, thereby, had some divine sanction to participate as they did. I think that may have been the problem for most of them: thinking they were something they were not, I mean. I had the constant nonsense in my mind to reassure me that I had not yet accomplished anything with which to allow me to act like a nuisance at strangers' expense. That nonsense itself would try to assert its own wisdom, still sometimes threatening to overwhelm me, but I was more and more confident of my ability to cut through it, and hoped to calm it all with a bit more practice.

The Zen environment was quite nice, but I still could not make more than superficial friends, because of the charged atmosphere and the constant feeling that they saw me as some kind of New Age weirdo, rather than just an ordinary graduate student, because of my involvement with Tibetan Buddhism. Once people get that in their heads, they no longer see you clearly, and always approach you with caution and accusatory tones and glances. Zen centers, overall, are better from that point of view. They have fewer excuses like crazy wisdom to fall back on, and they stay more with the Mahayana good-heartedness. There is also little to do but sit, and this discourages the weirdoes, who, most often, cannot sit at all. I worried that my association with the Trungpa group would also make people think I was too on board with womanizing and drinking, and this did seem to be a problem sometimes, but Zen centers fall more in the direction of excessive martial-arts–type stoicism than New Age indulgence.

Lama Rinchen ran a tight ship, and, even though it was a Tibetan center, which meant it would attract a lot of the New Age types, he maintained pretty good control over a pretty sloppy dynamic in the culture. I was quite lucky in the timing of my arrival in Hawaii. A very short time after I arrived, Kalu Rinpoche was there to give the Kalachakra empowerment, considered one of the highest of the Tibetan tantras. It was considered a major blessing for the participants, and it actually provided a deity practice to go with it, one that could be done without having first completed the Ngondro practices. It was quite a spectacle, both in the arranging of it and in its execution. A dozen lamas arrived from all over the country and from Asia, and dozens of volunteers were setting up the elaborate mandala and making all the arrangements. People were coming from all over the country to receive the empowerment. I was lucky in that Lama Rinchen saw me as helpful, and so he allowed me to be around the whole thing, even though I had only known him for a short time. I ate with the lamas a few times, did odd jobs, some driving, and so forth. I had very close contact with the Tibetans, which was rare in Boulder.

The Tibetans were all quite nice. Their discipline and training was very impressive, as was their devotion to one another and their respect for the hierarchy of lamas. There was little visible infighting. Instead, they had a cheerful, joking, friendly way of getting along with each other and everyone else. The Americans were obviously very jealous and very competitive, but no one took them to task for it. The Tibetans had a very sweet but masculine style, all of them seeming a little bit boyish and playful, but very serious, nonetheless. They joked around and were happy to give advice, pithy comments on your practice, philosophy, and so forth. They were quite warm toward everyone. Their discipline seemed a lot like a doctor's bedside manner, but with more humor. I took some of them to the beach and for a drive, and so I got to see much of their interactions with one another. They were very spiritual, had a much wider view of the world, and did respond to New Age-y realities, but without the bug eyes and crazy talk. They also did not seem to notice the wilder side of the scene that was around them; or, perhaps, they just ignored it.

They were a bit sexist but still quite warm to the women, not domineering. I heard one say that they have to warn lamas who are knew to America not to tell people they think the world is flat. That amused me, but, rather than seeing them as simple or primitive, I was more impressed by their psychological sophistication and deep maturity, and their very simple, everyday sanity in regard to their approach to the world. There was no hint of New Age craziness about them, and yet, the Americans never seemed to notice that. The Tibetans' tendency to smile and nod at everything that occurred around them made it difficult for the New Agers to think that there was a problem with their behavior or demeanor. I felt that if the Tibetans noticed any of it at all, they were just humoring the Americans. After observing the Tibetans for a while, I even wondered if there wasn't some level on which the flat earth was better.

The Kalachakra empowerment took three days. These empowerments, too, are considered secret, but anyone who has seen a Tibetan-style introduction to the mandala of a particular deity knows how they go. This one is particularly elaborate. I was lucky in that I had a seat in the front row, right in front of Kalu Rinpoche, who presided over the whole thing. He was particularly impressive, even among the Tibetans. A man in his seventies, he had made two twelve-year retreats alone in the mountains of Tibet. Although he was considered particularly enlightened, he was quite humble; at a lecture that preceded the empowerment, he said, "A pretty good empowerment flows through me." In response to someone's question about what constitutes good visualization, he said, "If you can visualize the entire Kalachakra mandala of some seven hundred deities on the tip of your nose, and still see the red veins in their eyes, you are good at visualization."

The point of these empowerments is to get permission to begin visualizing a particular deity as yourself, or in front of you and reciting his or her mantra. The idea is that the deity is a personification of a particular state of mind, and, by visualizing yourself in that form and reciting that mantra, you develop that particular state of mind. The Kalachakra is a personification of a particularly high state of mind. Others would be personifications of compassion, emptiness, wisdom, health and healing, and so forth. There are hundreds of deities likes this in the Tibetan pantheon. The most well-known that don't require the Ngondro practices are Green Tara for general good luck, White Chenreszig for compassion, Manjushri for wisdom, and Medicine Buddha for healing and health. I received the Manjushri empowerment a while after the Kalachakra, and I can't help but feel it helped me earn my master's and PhD.

Trungpa Rinpoche went to great lengths to explain that the deities are not to be taken as external deities, but, rather, as personifications of particular states of mind, and that an excessively theistic orientation toward them could be detrimental. This helped me accept the practices in the face of the First Commandment and my lingering loyalties to, and fears of, my Catholic upbringing. The whole thing was beautiful and exciting, with the Tibetan horns and drums, a *dakini* dance, and hundreds of people from all over the country in attendance.

Afterward I returned to my routine and got down to business working on my PhD. The fact that I had five years of checks coming in and something to do for those five years took a lot of weight off me. I was able to relax a bit and settle in to my practices and my studies. I was quite motivated by the linguistics, and I watched for papers and works on word boundaries to see if anyone else had come up with the theory of word boundaries that I had noticed back when I was an undergrad. As I was in my thirties now and a student, not a guy with a decent paycheck, my access to dating was quite limited. I also felt I still undermined myself in that way because of the accident. Dating took on way too much importance and gravity, and I couldn't approach it in a simple and fun way—and I was unable to adequately hide my feelings on the matter.

Soon after I started my PhD, I became interested in the argument as to whether or not linguistics was really a science. The behaviorists' argument stated that anything that did not deal with physically measurable properties was not a science, thereby dismissing linguistics, other forms of psychology, and all the social sciences as sciences. I kind of resented that, because I saw the theoretical underpinnings of linguistics as quite thoroughly rooted in the scientific method. Chomsky argued that anything that was done within that scientific method was, indeed, a science. I wanted to bring more to bear on this argument. I heard that Jung had argued that analytical psychology was a true science, even though it didn't depend on any physically measurable properties, because, instead of the physically measurable, it used what was predictable in the mind. The fact that mother complexes, father complexes, and so on are found throughout the world is a fact that cannot be denied, and that needs to be accounted for by science. In short, anything that the empirical method could be applied to was a legitimate object of scientific research. I thought linguistics was exceptionally interesting ground in this way, as did many others. This is particularly true of syntax and theoretical grammar: there is no way anyone will ever find physically measurable properties of nouns and verbs and the other parts of speech and parts of the sentence, and yet, there are countless empirical statements and theories that can be made about human syntax.

I began reading Jung to find his comments on this subject, and I soon found myself immersed in a long and complicated read of his entire collection of works. His ideas of archetypes corresponded nicely with the Tibetan view toward deities, and I found I could use Jung and his methods to sort through what was going on in my mind, allowing much more of the imagery to come up, which helped me learn more about it all. Given my practices and linguistics research and classes, I had little time for this, so I read Jung during my morning and evening coffee-shop breaks. I spent an hour each morning and each evening at Coffee Manoa, a very nice and tastefully decorated coffee shop near the university, which attracted a big university crowd. Over the five years it took to get my degree, I read the entire collected works of Jung; I actually read volumes 5 through 13 three times each. I somehow found that the third reading of each of these works was the most elucidating. The vacations during graduate school left me lots of extra time to work on my reading and to take retreats. I also read many of Jung's close followers. Taking a hint from the Tibetans, I decided I would only read him, and the writers he approved of, to be sure I was on track with the approved theory. I read much of von Franz, Edinger, Hillman (not really approved by Jung, but still important), and several others. I became aware of collections of essays and monographs approved by the Jung Society, and I read these avidly as well. I was reading more in this area and in Buddhism than I was in linguistics, even though I was a graduate student in that subject.

I read von Franz with particular zeal. She wrote of alchemy, creation myths, the grail, and dozens of other very pithy and interesting topics in the history of Western psychology. The book on creation myths presented dozens of these myths from around the world, as well as an interpretation of them. I read this book several times. Her and Jung's books on alchemy also attracted me, and I read these several times.

What is most striking about the Jungian theory is that gods and goddesses, even those of the Tibetan pantheon, are taken as archetypes that exist natively in the mind or the brain, and that all cultures relate to various configurations of these archetypes: the mother goddess, the father god, the trickster, and so on are just a few of the many archetypes that are available to any person, anywhere. Like Trungpa Rinpoche, he also took a less theistic approach to them, seeing even the Western God of monotheism as an aspect of one's own mind.

As time went on, I completed the Ngondro, and then I went back to Boulder for the first official empowerment to a deity practice with the Trungpa group. I was able to do the prostrations rather quickly because I did tabletops, and I spent a month in retreat at RMDC doing the purification mantra: one hundred thousand repetitions of a hundred-syllable mantra. I didn't do the solitary retreat, even though they have provisions for that; I preferred to do what they called an "in-house" retreat, in which you are not a part of a group, but, instead do your practices in a shrine rooms set up for that purpose. This allowed me to socialize at meals and in the evenings. I later finished the mandala offerings and guru yoga back in Hawaii.

The preliminary practices come with visualizations as well, but they are still considered introductory. It is a strong belief that these things cannot be done without an official empowerment. There is something about the quality of mind that requires that someone with thorough experience in the matter transmit the ability through the empowerment to the newcomer. I did the rest of the Ngondro—the mandala offerings and guru yoga recitations—in my little studio in Honolulu.

Every time I got to Boulder I would go to the same haunts: Tom's Tavern, the Irish Pub, the Trident Bookstore, the Boulder Bookstore, and so on. I was by now quite an expert on the crowds, and I interpreted everything from a Buddhist and Western psychological point of view, doing whatever I could to deflect it from myself, making fun of it or shooting it down—I did everything except try it. It struck me that anyone who tried it, even a little, became twisted into it, and then couldn't stop. In that way, it was like any other addiction.

The first empowerment in the Trungpa group is of a deity called Vajrayogini, a naked, red goddess who epitomizes emptiness. I received this in Boulder from the Regent. Once you have the empowerment, you are given a long complex ritual practice called a *sadhana,* which focuses on the mantra repetition. You go through about an hour-long ritual buildup, and then you recite the mantra as much as you can, and, finally, you go through a complicated ritual closing of the practice. It takes a couple of hours.

Once you complete one million of these, you do two, ten-day fire rituals in group retreat, and then, after that, you do three hundred thousand more of the mantra recitations. It goes fastest on retreat, because you do not have to go through the entire hour-long ritual to build up to the recitation. Instead, on retreat, you can stay with the recitation for hours, building up your numbers. Of course, you are supposed to be focused on the discipline and wisdom of the practice, not the numbers, but it is hard to ignore that reality. After that, the next empowerment is called Chakrasamvara, which is concerned with skillfulness, a kind of psychological and mental agility for working with diverse people. This is a male deity, seminaked and in union with the original goddess, Vajrayogini. It reminded me a bit of Plato's original man, who was in union before the creation, but then, sometime afterward, split into two parts, male and female.

I wondered if Plato's philosophical eye allowed him to have visions similar to those of the Tibetans. For Plato, the man of highest development has visions unlike other men, and he referred to this as the "philosophical eye." For the crowds, anybody who had hallucinations—whether from long-term drug or alcohol abuse, schizophrenia, or any other cause—was treated as though they had the philosophical eye. Everyone wanted to hallucinate, and it never occurred to anyone that the philosophical eye was a very special phenomenon, far different from these hallucinations; they were oblivious to the fact that attaining the philosophical eye took years of discipline, not years of indiscipline and drug abuse. Many of them had the annoying habit of hallucinating at you or on you, and then seeing you as some unfortunate who needed their assistance to remove the "bugs" that they were hallucinating on you. I liked to think that, rather than the philosopher eyes, they were developing "fly eyes" or "cockroach eyes" or "devil eyes"—similar to those of long-term alcoholics and drug addicts, more pink elephants than Buddhas. But the crowds never made that distinction; any bit of hallucinating was a mark of their wisdom.

The Chakrasamvara recitations have to be done in solitary retreat, and the retreat centers have little cabins set up for this purpose. They even seal the door for a portion of the retreat, similar to Tibetans sealing each other up in caves to do their practices. Again, you do one million recitations of the mantra. There is much more to the practices than just the recitation. There is a long complicated series of ritual practices that you do with the *sadhana,* up to the mantra recitation, so the time to actually recite the mantra is only a portion of the whole thing. It takes a long time. In the traditional three-year retreat, these things can be done much faster; but, for someone with a job and a spouse and so forth, it takes years to complete all these practices. However, the *dathun,* seminary, Ngondro, Vajrayogini, and, finally, Chakrasamvara, all must be completed before advancing to other practices, such as the six yogas of Naropa. I was lucky in that I was not in a relationship—although this was something I otherwise regretted—and I was in graduate school, so

I had much more time than the average, forty-hour workweek, married practitioner.

I made many trips to the mainland to take the other trainings offered by the group on the Shambhala meditation technique. This was mostly on the West Coast—Berkeley, San Francisco, Seattle. I also attended or presented at conferences in linguistics, and this got me around the country a bit as well. I presented at quite a few conferences as the years passed, even doing two on one trip to Europe.

Shambhala meditation is a secular approach to meditation, focused on the development of warriorship, which is the way of the gentle and peaceful warrior. This, too, has a long series of graded practices leading to longer retreats. This is as ornate and beautifully decorated as the other Tibetan Buddhist practices.

It took me until about 1990 to finish the Vajrayogini practices and to get the Chakrasamvara empowerment. I did not complete the last three hundred thousand recitations, but they let me into the empowerment on the provision that I would complete those three hundred thousand before actually doing the retreat practice. My Zen was progressing at that time as well. I had finally begun to get answers to the koans. This was after about three years of working on them.

I did the two fire rituals, which were quite exhilarating. At the end of the first one, I found myself inspired, and sort of spontaneously wrote a poem in the Tibetan style. The purest form of Tibetan poetry is done spontaneously. I had that sort of inspiration and wrote the poem, but then I rewrote it a few times. I am still rather proud of it, even if it wasn't totally spontaneous.

"For the Eyes of the Solitary Warrior Only"

The War was never Begun
The Battle Never Ends
Winning and Losing are Costly Illusions
The Solitary Warrior Knows when to Engage
Make a Good Dinner. Be Sure and Place Flowers.

At a later time, I had another such inspiration to write a poem. This was for the occasion of the retirement of the Zen teacher, Aitken Roshi. I was aware of a famous occasion in Zen history: a poetry battle of sorts had broken out when the Fifth Patriarch of Chinese Zen was looking for a successor. Centuries ago in China, the Fifth Patriarch had instructed his monks to express their wisdom in a poem. Whoever had a true realization of his Buddha nature—his original nature—would become the Sixth Patriarch. The head monk, Shen Hsiu, was also the most learned, and he wrote the following:

> The body is a Bodhi tree,
> the mind a standing mirror bright.
> At all times polish it diligently,
> and let no dust alight.

The poem was praised, but the Fifth Patriarch knew that Shen Hsiu had not yet found his original nature; on the other hand, Hui Neng couldn't even write, so someone had to write down his poem, which read:

> Bodhi originally has no tree.
> The bright mirror also has no stand.
> Fundamentally there is not a single thing.
> Where could dust arise?

> 菩提本無樹,
> 明鏡亦非台;
> 本來無一物,
> 何處惹塵埃?

The Fifth Patriarch acted as though he wasn't impressed with this one, either; but, in the middle of the night, he called for Hui Neng, giving him the insignia of the office, along with the patriarch's robe and bowl. Hui Neng was told to go to the south, and to hide his enlightenment and understanding until the proper time arrives for him to spread the Dharma.

I wrote the following, and, without being seen, put it on the bulletin board at the Zen center for the retirement ceremonies:

> No mirror, no dust
> No robe, no bowl
> What precious teachings flow through the body speech
> and mind of this great teacher.

I thought it was a nice tribute to a retiring teacher, and I enjoyed the whole scenario. When I attended the ceremony, I saw that the poem was still on the bulletin board, but I had no idea really whether he or anyone else had noticed it.

. . .

In April 1988, Trungpa Rinpoche died of liver problems, no doubt aggravated by his drinking. There was a huge ceremony for his cremation at the Vermont retreat center, and people and lamas from around the world came to participate. Everyone was very impressed with what he had done, and we all treated his cremation as a particularly important occasion. I was able to attend and found it quite exciting. Everyone knew Trungpa was dying, but his death still came sooner than most wanted. I always felt he would have stopped drinking if something in the environment had changed. I also wondered if he didn't deliberately drink and womanize himself to death, thereby becoming the master of all drinking and womanizing. Strange thoughts and speculations like that surfaced at the cremation, but no one really knew the whole truth. He was very sorely missed. Everyone knew how ill he had been, but still seemed quite lost in his absence. There were plans, of course, and a successor was set up—the guy called the Regent—but no one knew to what degree that huge, wonderful situation was driven by the living force of Trungpa Rinpoche, and so everyone was afraid it would collapse without his leadership. His son was also seen as a kind of a successor, but it was unclear at that time whether he wanted to take on the role.

People were naturally curious about Trungpa's reincarnation, given the Tibetan beliefs, but the best anyone ever got out of him—at least, as far as members like me, or I myself, heard—was that he would come back as a Japanese scientist who would wander into the situation, have a spontaneous remembrance of his past life, and then take over. That was considered his style of humor, but I am sure there are those keeping one eye open for a Japanese scientist of about the right age to wander in.

They had built an ornate crematorium in the Tibetan style on the grounds of Karme Choling, which would afterward serve as a monument to him personally. Back at RMDC, they were building a beautiful and ornate ritual stupa in the Tibetan style. American artists and Tibetan artists worked together to create an authentic stupa, built to all the rigorous ritual demands that have developed during two thousand years of Buddhism. For instance, the central pole was to be made from a giant cedar tree, that had to face east—thus, throughout the entire process, from the cutting of the tree, through the carving of it, to its installation, the workers had to keep track of which side was facing east in order to ensure that it still faced east when it was installed. They also made thousands of quarter-inch by two-and-a-half-inch miniature poles for the miniature clay stupas—called *tsatsas*—and, with these, too, the workers had to keep track of which side was east. The entire structure was designed and erected to equally exacting ritual standards.

Of particular note, Trungpa Rinpoche decided to have a giant statue of Chakrasamvara and Vajrayogini built into the second floor of the stupa. It was a marvelous room, designed for the practitioners of that practice. The statues were lifelike, and stood about eight feet tall. It was the only innovation included that I am aware of, but it was welcomed by the higher lamas, one of whom even remarked that he wondered why they had never thought of it before. I actually attended the opening ceremony for the stupa, and I felt I was in the presence of a major work of art from Medieval Tibet or Renaissance Europe.

At the actual cremation, a huge, turquoise rainbow appeared in the sky. It was more of a ball than a bow, and it was all in shades of turquoise, but everyone called it a rainbow. I'd never seen anything like it, and it was miraculous enough to be mentioned in the local papers.

The sky was bright and clear, and the turquoise rainbow appeared as the body burned, and everyone marveled at it, seeing it as a confirmation of the value of Trungpa's work.

I volunteered to stay and help with the cleanup, and, for this reason, I received a little envelope with three snippets of hair from Trungpa Rinpoche as a relic. I also received a little jar of salt, from the salt that was used to preserve the body while it was in state waiting for the cremation. I was pleased with these gifts, but I felt a little uneasy, as people who had been around him much more than I had and new him better than I did, did not receive any such gifts.

As part of the ceremonies, Dilgo Khyentse Rinpoche, a Nyingma teacher with strong ties to Trungpa Rinpoche, gave about four days of empowerments, the entire curriculum that Trungpa Rinpoche had intended to teach. I was able to attend these as well. Afterward, he gave that same set of empowerments again in Halifax for those who had not been able to attend the cremation. I got a ride up to Halifax, where I attended these same empowerments again.

Unlike the people who just hung around the scene, thinking they were good at all these things, I had sufficient feedback from the Zen and Tibetan teachers to know that, while I might have had a little talent and was genuinely motivated, I was not a star of any sort, just an American guy doing a lot of Zen and Tibetan practices. I almost felt sorry for the New Age crowd, all of whom thought that the slightest bit of insight or wisdom qualified them to hang out a shingle or pontificate at passing strangers, always in that annoying squawking way of theirs. If only they had the wherewithal to get some feedback from someone besides their mutual admiration society, they might have been able to get out and stay out of the entire addiction.

The Tibetans even warn of the dangers of this mentality. They credit people with having genuine spiritual experiences, which they call *nyams,* but warn them not to make too much of them. There is a danger in thinking you are something you are not, yet few really took this to heart. Perhaps I am being too harsh. The brainless squawking and pontificating that went on was noisy, distracting, and embarrassing to any serious practitioner who noticed, but I do suspect that the larger numbers of practitioners were not engaging it and did see through it all.

As a target of these behaviors, though, it colored my whole perception of the scene, making it extremely difficult for me to participate with the more normal side of the crowd.

A year or so later, the Regent, who was bisexual, as I mentioned, was discovered to have AIDS. That in itself is not a crime, of course, but it was further discovered that he had passed it on to several others, even after he knew that he had it. This caused a huge scandal, creating a schism in the group. He thought he had had some sort of *vajra*-like protection, and so he was incautious. Most people flipped out about this. They could not see how a Buddhist, dedicated to not even squashing the bugs that land on you, could have been so incautious with human life. Many left the group entirely, and a separate pro-Regent group split off and started their own. He even gave a Vajrayogini empowerment on his own to this group. He died of AIDS-related pneumonia a few years later.

In the spring of 1990, I had completed my coursework and comprehensive exams, and I was ready to write my dissertation; sure enough, no one else had addressed the problem of word boundaries in phonology, and so I was going to be able to explore my theory in my dissertation. My preliminary write-up passed as a dissertation proposal. This was the theory that I had come across while an undergraduate almost twenty years earlier. To reward myself for my work, I took a five-week trip to Nepal. I'd heard there were a lot of Tibetan monasteries there, and I wanted to have more one-on-one experiences with genuine lamas.

This trip was also paid for from what I had coming in from the settlement for my leg. I always felt conflicted about this money, as it arose from a tragedy. B I was using it productively and in ways that were consistent with what Deb and I had been doing before the accident—what we had planned to continue doing—and all this made me feel better.

8

Nepal—1990

> . . . who cowered in unshaven rooms in underwear,
> burning their money in wastebaskets and listening to
> the Terror through the wall . . .
>
> —ALLEN GINSBERG, "HOWL"

Nepal turned out to be a nice adventure. I stayed at a well-known, long-term stay hotel in Kathmandu. A place frequented by international mountain climbers, hippies (or ex-hippies), and those seeking out Tibetan teachers. There was a restaurant not far away that showed videos of Western movies every night, so I had a place to stay at night and something to do in the evenings, and I would spend my days seeking out and hanging out with Tibetans and Tibetan hangers-on. It was hot, there were a lot of beggars and poverty, and mostly dirt roads, even in the city. There were a number of bars, but I was not drinking at this time. I'd basically stopped drinking during the summer of 1985, and I stopped smoking after that. It wasn't from any sort of spiritual aspiration; the smoking was too expensive, and the drinking was too out of control. I'd been to a few AA meetings, but I didn't continue to go. It was nice enough; I just found I didn't really need the encouragement of others in order to not drink, so I didn't bother attending. I did the whole master's and PhD program without anything alcoholic. It was refreshing and became quite easy after the first year. Once I had made it through one full year of holidays and other excuses to drink, I had the confidence that it wouldn't bother me. The urge to drink didn't much plague me; mostly, I just had memories of fun times.

In Nepal, found that Chokyi Nyima Rinpoche was teaching foreigners in English, so I started going to his monastery to listen. Good talks, very pithy, a lot of the same old Buddhist stuff; but it is difficult material, and hearing about the same thing a number of times from different teachers is quite helpful. I found the hangers-around a little arrogant and hard to relate to. There was an elephant ride in a park nearby that I wanted to go to, but I couldn't find anyone to go with me, because everyone was too jaded. That was too uncool and touristy, so I went on my own. I had gotten quite good at traveling alone and grown quite comfortable with my own company, but, at the same time, I felt a deep need to share my experiences with someone—and I would've preferred that someone to be a girlfriend or a wife.

I spent nine days in India before I returned home for the remainder of the summer, after which I planned to pick up graduate school again. While in graduate school, I started seeing a therapist a bit; I didn't talk about the accident much, just about troubles I was having with people—the crowds, and so forth. I found it very difficult to articulate what I was seeing with the crowds, and I worried that I would be labeled as paranoid, so I didn't go into it too much. I was also trying, as much as possible, to do everything with just meditation, no meds, and not too much therapy. The therapist I was seeing was a Jungian, and she helped me with dream exploration and interpretation, which I found very motivating. During that time, I talked about my inability to get into a relationship, even though it had already been twelve years since Deb's death. The therapist said that this was undoubtedly still a problem, and that I was most likely unconsciously undermining my chances at a relationship.

She recommended a book called *Widower,* which I read. It gave me a satisfactory explanation for the problem, but it did not really offer any solution. The premise of the book is that men who lose their wives usually end up in one of two situations: either they enter into a very dependent relationship right away, or they end up virtually homeless and ruined—with the latter being the more common of the two. I felt that the latter described my situation, and I couldn't imagine what things would have been like without the workers' compensation. Without the support of the workers' comp, and the constant need to repress everything to maintain my leg, I suspect I would have been pretty bad off, and, given the complications of the accident, perhaps even more so than other widowers. That money was fueling my practices and studies, which kept that wilder part of my mind at bay.

The thing the book explained about the psychological dynamic of the widower was that most men tend to rely on their wives as their emotional regulators: most men do not have much access to or awareness of their feelings, so they use their wives' abilities in that arena to keep them in tune. When the wife dies, both the source of the pain and the potential emotional regulator are lost; the widower goes into a tailspin, where he can access neither the regulator nor the loss. I am still like that in many ways. I even like to call women friends and ask them about what I want to do, because I am not sure enough of my feelings on the matter. All the meditation and psychological work in this area helped a lot.

Aitken Roshi recommended a book called *Focusing,* which offered a technique on how to access and pinpoint feelings. It was new to me that merely accurately labeling a feeling could have a strong, pacifying effect. Once I learned the technique I got better at that, but even with this growing mountain of knowledge and practice, I was still quite mad. The madness still overwhelmed on occasion, and I would have to struggle for a few days to get myself out of it. I found that being present in public would help a lot, as I was more afraid of the public humiliation of an outburst than I was entertained—or seduced—by the dynamic. I was more likely to be overwhelmed by it when I was home alone.

At RMDC during the summer of 1984, I'd found a book entitled, *The Seduction of Madness,* written by one of the Naropa teachers. It made the same point I had been making to myself about how the madness had an entertaining, seductive quality to it that was quite difficult to resist. I held back on relating my experiences of this part of my mind to therapists and meditation instructors, afraid that they would label me psychotic, schizophrenic, or something of that nature. Another book making the rounds in Buddhist circles at that time: *How to Be a Help*

Rather Than a Nuisance. I thought that should be mandatory reading for the squawkers, as I saw most of the group dynamic as a nuisance, but I never actually read the book myself. The title itself was enough for me to see it as good mandatory reading for them.

While in Nepal I asked Chokyi Nyima Rinpoche if he knew of a situation where I could do some Vajrayogini practice. I told him that I was a student of Trungpa Rinpoche and had done all the required preliminary practices. The Tibetans all respected Trungpa and the situation he had set up, and they liked to encourage those who had actually done the whole Ngondro. They ignored his drinking and womanizing, encouraging people not to look at him as if he'd been an ordinary drinker and womanizer, and implying that something much deeper had been going on. They also complimented him on the seriousness, thoroughness, and depth of the things he taught and the overall situation he created.

Chokyi Nyima told me his mother ran a retreat center in Parphing, and I was welcome to go up there to do a few days of Vajrayogini practice. The place was built around a famous cave where a tenth-century Tibetan guru named Padmasambhava had practiced. I thought that was way cool, and I wanted to do a little of the practice in that cave. There was also a spring nearby, which was sacred to Vajrayogini, and I looked forward to visiting this as well. I don't know why but he gave me a little present: a three-sided miniature dagger with a Tibetan protector on the handle. I was quite pleased, and the childish part of my countenance was ecstatic. I had the good sense to hide that, though.

The trip was only a few hours, and I got a ride with some Tibetans, but I can't remember how. The place was amazing—small and simple, yet beautiful. What was most amazing about it was that the only way to get up the hill was to ascend steep paths. There were no roads. It was a big block of mountain on top of a larger mountain. I couldn't, for the life of me, imagine how they'd built a monastery up there. Lugging the cement blocks and materials up the steep paths of the cliff seemed as impossible as the building of the pyramids. In any case, I had arrived; I introduced myself, and then I was brought to meet Chokyi Nyima's mother. She was very ill with gallbladder problems, which caused her tremendous pain. I was told that she never took pain medication because she was trying to wear off the karma of the disease. She was sweet, welcoming, and motherly. I was in the habit of telling every one of the higher lamas and such about the death of my wife, thinking it would give Deb's karma a boost, no matter what had happened to her. I told Chokyi Nyima's mother about it as well, and she was quite moved. She thought it quite sad that such a tragedy had happened to two young people who were trying to help others. Because Deb was concerned about me and her students at the time of her death, I figured she'd had a good rebirth, but wanted to commemorate her through telling the lamas.

I was then shown the cave where Padmasambhava had practiced. They proudly pointed out a handprint in the rock, which Padmasambhava had made one thousand years before, through the power of his mastery over the material world. He merely placed his hand against the rock, and it left an imprint. I put my hand in it. I sat in the cave for a bit. It definitely felt good, powerful and spiritual—not in a Star Wars Jedi– type way, but in a very genuine, and far less adolescent, way. While I was up there, I was able to do my morning chants every day in the cave, and this gave me a wonderful feeling of connectedness and togetherness. I wouldn't have minded a miraculous cure for the flip side of my mind, but this didn't come. It probably was possible in principle, but it didn't happen.

I was also able to visit the spring that was sacred to Vajrayogini. This was a small little grotto with a square little spring, about five feet long by six feet wide by four feet deep. I took a drink from it, thinking that there was little likelihood of catching something from a sacred spring. There was a sense of empowerment in this as well. I never really trusted those feelings, but I never really ignored them either. I didn't want to turn into a flaming New Ager, and I didn't want to feed the wild side of my mind too much, but I did enjoy the feelings, nonetheless.

There was a small cave at the base of the hill below the little monastery, and I was told that inside there was a statue of the goddess Green Tara growing out of the wall. I went to look and was quite surprised to see this little miracle. The statue was just a few inches tall, but it didn't seem at all carved. It definitely seemed to be coming out of the wall on its own. One of the nuns at the monastery said that another nun was doing it sort of deliberately. At least, I think that's what she said; there was a big language barrier.

After returning from Parphing, I decided to take a trip to India to visit various Buddhist sacred sites. I went to Saranath, Bodhgaya, Nalanda, and then to Darjeeling and Surmong, the seat of the Karmapa, who had still not been found. I had a book of Hillman with me, so I kept my knowledge of Jungian psychology present and fresh. In Surmong, I met Jomgon Kongtrol Rinpoche. He was a very high Tibetan lama, but still quite easily accessible to the passing American Tibetan wannabe. I had a short interview with him, which was quite nice. A few years earlier he was teaching in Honolulu, and I'd had the opportunity to sponsor a Medicine Buddha empowerment by him. I paid a price I'd arranged with Lama Rinchen, and gave monetary gifts to him and the presiding monks. A rich guy would've given much more, but they were pleased with and grateful for the gifts I could afford. I dedicated the empowerment to the health and well-being of my parents. As the sponsor, I went to a dinner with this very highly placed lama and some of his monks. I sat next to him and was able to tell him, too, about my wife and the accident. I also tried to give him my impression of the madness in the centers and the New Age. He seemed quite interested, and I wondered if no one was telling these guys about the madness going around in all the centers and in the country. I was getting better at articulating the problem and explaining it to others. I really wondered how much in the dark these leaders were, as it was significantly less prevalent when they were physically present. I no longer felt I was imaging it; rather, I was confident that I had discovered a significant problem in the culture, not unlike the mass hysteria that had characterized Nazi Germany. However, the New Age stuff was not hysteria, either. There was something different about it, something more contemporary, and I was determined to find someone who'd written about it. I read a few books on Hitler, and one by Frankl—I think that one was on mass psychology.

I remember many occasions when I tried to tell lamas or others about the phenomenon, but it was hard to describe, and I was not sure if they would merely think that I was nuts and imagining things, or that I was pointing out something obvious that they were themselves working on. I had even tried to signal Trungpa and others that I thought they were not getting a good impression of what Americans were really like, as they were getting a very skewed crowd, ex-hippies, New Agers, and so forth, but only a few who were what I considered to be average Americans.

The whole of the New Age madness was so contrary to everything the Tibetans were teaching, and so contrary to ordinary Western manners and decency, that I couldn't believe the lamas even knew about it. The crudeness, the perversion, the constant idiotic commentary squawked at passing strangers. Did the Tibetans think that this was ordinary for America? They didn't watch television and didn't go to movies, so their view of Americans was limited to the crowds they were attracting.

The trip to India was good and uneventful. I went to Bodhgaya and visited the temple under the bodhi tree, the place where the original Buddha had his enlightenment some twenty-five hundred years ago. There is a temple and a wall built around it. I grabbed one of the leaves as a souvenir. I gave some beggars a little change, and, suddenly, dozens of them surround me, and I had to hop into a passing rickshaw to get away from them. I saw some more temples there, and then I went on to Nalanda where I saw the remains of the famous Buddhist university that had been there about one thousand years ago. It was all quite impressive, and it gave me a deep sense of history and connectedness to Buddhism and to all the practices I was doing.

9

PhD Matriculation and Running a Business—1991

. . . who got busted in their pubic beards returning through Laredo with a belt of marijuana for New York . . .

—ALLEN GINSBERG, "HOWL"

I returned home, and, in about six months, wrote my dissertation: "X-Bar Theory and Morphological Juncture." It turned out well and was about two hundred pages. When I finished it, I told the head of my committee, a very well-known linguist named Derek Bickerton, that I thought the theory would also work for a theory of syntax similar to Chomsky's. He thought that that was a bit nuts, but he was interested. He said he would read something if I wrote it up, so I wrote about forty pages on the subject. After he read it, he suggested that we write a paper together and work out all the details. He had some ideas of his own, but the core ideas were mine, and so he offered to put my name first on the paper.

My five-year settlement was about up, and so it was time for me to start working again. I worried a bit about my ability to deal with the demands of a real job after all this time and given all the difficulties I had with people at the university, but, mostly, I looked forward to it. I got a job as an ESL Instructor at Hawaii Pacific University, and I was able to continue the work on the theory. The theory actually took five years to complete, as it was a part-time effort for both of us. Derek said he'd had ideas like this for years; he really wanted to work them out, and having me to do a lot of the leg work allowed him to work on other more pressing projects. He had twenty-five years of significant experience with theoretical syntax, and, without that, I never could have done it. When we finally finished it, I had the benefit of all that experience, and so I was fully capable of working with syntax in its entirety. By the time it was over, it was unclear to me who had done the most work—or, at least, the most significant work. Certainly, Derek's contribution was the most important from the point of view of the necessary preliminary knowledge, but the original idea and many of the working principles were mine. He made one very necessary breakthrough, along with some others. At one point, he wanted to change it to "Bickerton and Bralich," and rewrite it for publication. That would have been more marketable, as he was widely published and he was the senior linguist, but I said I'd like to keep it as it was. Early on in the project, I told him it was possible to write the theory so that every aspect of it could be programmed in a computer language, and, for that reason, we worked in secret so that we could eventually create and patent the software. So, rather than trying to publish my dissertation theory, I focused on developing it further into a fully programmable theory of syntax.

Given that I was working at a university, I was still able to find time and money for occasional retreats, either with the Trungpa centers or at the sesshins at the local Zen center. Sesshins are ten-day Zen practice intensives focused on sitting practice and answering koans. I generally would just do the morning sessions, but I think I did one full sesshin. These were a bit hard on my leg, as there were more rigorous demands for a stricter posture in Zen than there were with the Trungpa centers.

The work with the theory was progressing, and I was getting more experience in ESL, focusing as much as I could on the teaching of grammar, but I also taught essay and research writing. The grammar teaching kept me very fluid in things that I needed to work out in the theory.

At this time, I met a Japanese woman who would become my best friend for many years. We met in one of my classes. Yumi was a shy and cute Japanese girl taking my intermediate grammar class. We didn't socialize at that point, but she was a real treat, bright and enthusiastic and cute and fun, always helping her classmates and working very hard to get A's. She didn't want to miss the slightest question or a single comma. In spite of her shy and cute demeanor, she had a real samurai fighting spirit about succeeding in English and going on to an American university. She had a baby face, so she looked the same age as most of the students, but she actually was a bit older. Some of her friends were in the same class, and they all helped set a nice tone. Teaching ESL in Hawaii at that time meant teaching mostly Asian students who were trying to improve their English skills enough to get into American universities. The program was rigorous and effective. The students really drove the effectiveness, though. Unlike American students, who can be lazy and resistant, the Asian students were hardworking and constantly trying to raise the bar to get into college as soon and as effectively as they could. They were cooperative with the teachers and each other, and even asked for more homework if they thought that what they were getting was not sufficient. It was a great teaching environment.

As I said, it took five years to work out the theory with Derek, and, by this time, I was running a small college-prep ESL program at a different local ESL school. I had time and a bit of money, and so I was able to continue the practices. When the theory was finally finished, I was able to hire a programmer. I raised a few thousand here, a few thousand there—some by borrowing, some by getting investors, in a clumsy but slowly effective way. I did not have the business connections or the necessary confidence to get a big investment without any proof that the secret theory could actually be programmed. We had to program it first to get a proof of concept, because if we showed anyone the actual theory, we could compromise our ability to get a patent on it. After a few months, we had small demo programs that made it possible to raise more money. Derek was on board, but only as long as he was not in any financial jeopardy. He was nearing retirement, and so he didn't want any business fiascoes cluttering up his life. I was anxious for this, as the I/T boom was in full tilt, and many garage ideas were hitting it big. As the ability to program human grammar would significantly improve computers' ability to "speak," I thought I had a sure hit on my hands.

During this time, the crowds didn't change much. Everywhere you went, the air was still charged with innuendo and slander, and everyone thought it was just the greatest high to harass passing strangers with their pretenses to wisdom. Anyone sitting alone was the best target. What was most important was that there was no chance of feedback from the targets. The crowds must have understood that, on some level, they were dead wrong—or merely destructive—so they had to make sure the targets could not respond. There was no escaping it, and I was always an inevitable target. Whenever I landed anywhere for any length of time, the same idiotic storylines would follow me around. They generally were of two kinds: either wildly perverted or wildly focused on pretenses to enlightenment, spirituality, and/or psychology. I tried to use my growing knowledge of these subjects to mollify the crowds, or to correct them, but this mainly seemed to inflame them even more. For every one person I quieted, at least one more would turn up.

As the years passed, the madness in the crowds spread, eventually taking on a life and a dynamic of its own. All real American socialization had been replaced by the targeting. The information carried by the crowds was almost always mistaken and slanderous, but no one bothered to notice or care. Many seemed to even know that it was slanderous, but they still thought it the greatest thing in the world to prove their skills at the social ruin of their fellows. Pretense, presumption, and delusion were all they had, and all they wanted. They would often state that the delusion was real, and reality was not—that the delusion was somehow magical and effective, while reality was flat and ineffective. It seemed that no one socialized anymore on the basis of being with people they liked, but solely for the purpose of harassing those they didn't. It seemed ordinary socialization was over in America, and people had totally lost the ability to talk to their friends without a target; and, when they did talk, they would only talk about the targets. Huge squawk fests would break out, where different tables would take turns joining in with each other to harass agreed-upon targets. The targets were invariably considered bad, and the mobs, good. The targets were accused of anything and everything; and, the more heinous it was—the more embarrassing it was to the targets—the more it was considered to be true.

Little by little, my company was growing. At its height, we had five employees and made some very respectable software. We also got the patent for a universal parser of human grammar. We actually patented human grammar! That has always entertained me: a universal parsing system for human grammar. Software that could do things that Microsoft, IBM, and the large universities couldn't, but we never were able to market it. We had raised five hundred thousand dollars and made five pieces of working software, but it went nowhere. I took it to the last moment, going without pay for weeks at a time, finally ending with not a dime to my name—some tickets for driving without insurance, which I couldn't pay, and late rent. Yumi, as always, was supportive, but I was quite embarrassed. I also wondered whether the curse that had haunted the back of my mind since the accident was affecting my company, and I sought some sort of solution.

I was living at Lama Rinchen's center at the time, and had been for a couple of years. Our relationship was not the usual guru/disciple type of thing, but more like that of ordinary friends, one of whom happened to be American, and the other, Tibetan. He had about twenty years on me in age, and about fifty years on me in practice, so I always treated him with respect, but Trungpa's attitude toward maintaining one major guru always prevented me from really joining in too closely as an official student of Lama Rinchen, or taking up with his other students. I treated him as a respected older gentleman—and as a lama and a monk—and he treated me like a friend. I would occasionally ask him advice, but it was usually not about practice, more about daily life and living, and so forth. He didn't really encourage people to treat him as a guru, but more as a representative of one, and as the head of the center he ran. He was always just a simple monk, and he didn't make an effort to assume any of the more exotic trappings.

He actually had a very impressive background. He had been a monk from a very early age, and at sixteen was selected to undergo the three-year retreat that would qualify him to be a lama. This was in the 1940s, I guess, maybe earlier. He escaped from Tibet during the Chinese takeover in 1959, went to India, made a living selling sweaters, and even had a girlfriend until the Tibetans were sufficiently established in India, and then he went back to being a monk. He was originally one of Karmapa's monks, but now he was in the monastery with Kalu Rinpoche at the head. So, he was a classically trained Tibetan lama, but he was never recognized as one of the reincarnating leaders that characterized much of the hierarchy of Tibetan Buddhism. He was always very pleasant and very accepting of everyone, as all the lamas were, and it took several years of knowing him before he would give a tougher message, if one was needed. I remember he told me that you need to know someone for a couple of years before you can really know and understand him. He was also a lot of fun. It was just pleasant to be around him, and the scene around him was interesting and disciplined. Most of the people who lived at the center were his students, but, occasionally, someone like me, from a different group, would stay there.

By this time, Yumi and I had been friends for about ten years. She had gotten herself through the ESL program, and then through preliminary psych courses at Hawaii Pacific University, and finally received a master's in psychology from Chaminade University—all very impressive, really. When she arrived in Hawaii, she had only a low-intermediate level of English and a bachelor's degree from a university in Japan. After the master's, she went on to get a PhD from Pacifica Graduate Institute of Jungian Psychology in California. All her studies were great for me, because I would study with her. At first, she often had trouble with difficult passages, sometimes even an entire chapter; but then, I would read them, and we would discuss them until she was satisfied that she understood. She worked twice as hard as the native speakers, because of the demands of the second language, but she always insisted on a very deep level of understanding. I was her sounding board throughout her whole education in psychology, so I got to see firsthand and in great detail what a master's and PhD in clinical psychology entailed, but I only had to do a little bit of work. I read quite avidly from her materials, as well as from my own. That is where I began to understand Freud, Freudians, and object relations theory, and that changed the direction of my reading a bit. I still found it more effective to read just the masters and their appointed followers, but I read much of her books as well. There was too much bickering among theorists if you drifted away from the recognized masters of a theory, and then you couldn't really get a good sense of the original writer's full theories. All the bickering was just distracting, I felt.

Yumi and I had a relationship of mutual dependency where we were each other's support. She would prevent me from whining and complaining, and I would keep her thinking on track when the reading was rough until she got through it. I also read and edited all her papers, so she never had all the misplaced "a"s and "the"s that so characterize Asian writing. Even at her advanced level, there were still a lot of small mistakes in grammar that I was able to correct for her. We discussed writing for graduate school in general, and specifically in linguistics and psychology, so I got a lot out of it.

I later worked on a master's in counseling myself, getting about halfway through it before the demands of my company made it impossible to finish. In spite of all this, and all the practice, I still couldn't get to that part of my mind that raged and constantly threatened to take over. The façade was much stronger and always cheerful, but the background was still miserable and mad. I learned about a disorder called Post-Traumatic Stress Disorder (PTSD), and a related one called Prolonged Traumatic Stress Disorder, and settled on this as the cause of all my problems. I was relieved to know that I was not psychotic, paranoid, or schizophrenic. What I read about these disorders also seemed to indicate that the darker part of my mind would not take over; it would just constantly distract me. Just knowing that didn't change things much, but it did help me sharpen the focus of my reading and practice. I needed to find out exactly the dynamic was and how it operated in my mind, and I felt that if I did, everything would clear, and I would be back to normal—that is, back to where I was in 1978 before the accident and tragedy, and that none of it would recur, and the jinx/curse would be broken.

The impetus for all this was not just the fact that these things needed attention but also that they all seemed to impact the physical realities of my life. My inability to get on without that constant distraction of the nonsense, paranoia, and fantasy. The impact on my life was one of constant crisis. It was more than just panic or stress, it was physically observable obstacles to my life situation that all seemed like repetitions of the original accident. The parallels were always unmistakable, and it was always happening. I would lose jobs, lose all my friends, lose relationships—everything always seemed to be coming crashing down, and I had to be on constant alert to prevent as much of it as I could. I was constantly scanning my world and my environment for potential disaster. If I let down my guard, things would repeat costing me jobs, friends, and a home; if I kept my guard up, I could prevent a lot of it. So, no matter what anyone said about my letting go in a Buddhist sense—or dropping it, or whatever—I could not, because it would all repeat; and, when it did, things got worse, and then the darker side of my mind threatened to take over again. The constant focus on it was the only way I could manage it.

It also seemed to me that the reason I was such a great target for the squawkers had something to do with the PTSD itself—something to do with the intensity and the scanning that made me an easy target. I couldn't stop it, and the crowds simply weren't sympathetic. They needed and wanted targets, and I suspect the best ones were those with PTSD.

Nothing I did ever erupted in violence or mayhem, but it still worried me. I think the Buddhist training, more than anything else, prevented me from having violent outbursts. One time, near the beginning of my Buddhist training, I did punch a guy a few times. This was shortly after a poorly planned and wild-minded attempt at marriage with the massage therapist, which ended in a fiasco, where, yet again, I lost all my friends and saw the whole world collapsing back into the scenario of the original accident. She walked out on me, saying, "This thing is fraught with death"—not exactly what you expect to hear from your intended. As I've said, I thought about the possibility of all of this being the result of some sort of curse from Africa; as though I had naively angered someone, and then had a spell thrown on me that ruined my life and any attempts to reconnect with it. The feeling of dread at the initial purchase of the motorcycle, the drowned scorpion I'd seen in the water supply just before the accident, and things of that sort, all fed this sort of thinking. Even the odd behaviors of the construction volunteers around Deb made me think this way. I preferred to think in terms of PTSD, but it was hard to avoid this other kind of thinking. I didn't want to accuse someone of murder by witchcraft just because of my paranoid delusions. Such a thing could be taken quite seriously in Africa, and I didn't want innocent people getting caught up in it, so I kept it all to myself. However, in the time I spent watching cop shows on TV I learned of the concept of closure: that the real criminal has to be found in order for the survivors to have closure. Because I continued to relive the accident, I began to wonder even more if there hadn't been an aspect of murder to it, causing it to remain "open" for me as long as the culprit was undiscovered. This gave me reason to think about who had actually done it, which only made the curse seem more real. Again, I didn't want to accuse anyone falsely, and I had no idea who would have or could have done such a thing, but my need for closure kept it on my mind.

The guy I hit was basically pushing my buttons on a sensitive issue, but he didn't know that; and then, out of nowhere, I found myself slugging him. This was very uncharacteristic of me, and it frightened me tremendously. The odd thing was that no one took me to task for it. It happened in a bar, but they continued to let me in, and no one really said anything about it. A mutual friend said that the guy I hit "probably had it coming." I didn't know if he really meant that or was just trying to reassure a troubled friend—just saying the sort of thing that you say in those situations—but I did find it reassuring and pacifying too. Immediately after striking the guy, I had a particularly bizarre experience, where I seemed to have stepped into a world of red and green streaks in a field of black. I wondered if I had fallen into some sort of Carlos Castaneda experience that I wouldn't be able to get out of. This lasted for about a two-block walk, and it also scared me. I redoubled my efforts at Buddhism and meditation, resolved to be watchful of any impulse or thoughts toward violence, and basically calmed down.

10

Ergo Linguistic Technologies
—1995-2000

"... who ate fire in paint hotels or drank turpentine
in Paradise Alley, death, or purgatoried their torsos
night after night ..."

—ALLEN GINSBERG, "HOWL"

Having discovered PTSD, I read every mention of it that I could
find. There was not much on it. Freud talked about it a bit, but
more as an incomplete bit of his theory than as something he had solved.
Object relations talked about it as well. The only problem was how to
unlock the twist or the clump or whatever it was that came from the
original accident. I had heard about drugs for these things, but I'd also
heard that they only treat the symptoms, and the underlying problem
never gets addressed. As I had come this far, I decided not to try them,
because I really preferred to unlock and undo the entire thing.

At this time, I liked Freud but preferred Jung, and so I kept most of
my reading in that area, though object relations theory was a growing
interest. I then read Alfred Adler's books—four or five of them, anyway.
I heard somewhere that Adler's theory was an extroverted version of
Freud's introverted theory, and this interested me. A few years later, I
would read all of Melanie Klein's books a few times each.

Of all the reading of Adler, one thing stuck out in particular. I had always had trouble with the term, "narcissism". I just couldn't figure out what it was, how it differed from arrogance and pride, and so forth. However, when Adler called it "pretensions to godlikeness" I finally got it. That whole dimension of myself and the crowds of harassers who thought they were enlightened or special or gods or whatever was just that: pretensions to godlikeness. It was all narcissism. I felt threatened by it, and the crowds had been overwhelmed by it. I was then able to separate that from ordinary arrogance and pride, as they did not have that dimension of godlike pretense to them, and then I was able to see the dynamic in myself and the crowds much better.

The crowds and the people around me were still the same: the harassment, the innuendo, the slander, the pretense, presumption, and delusion. I wondered why they never even once stopped to question what they were doing; some confusion between enlightened spontaneity and confused impulsiveness, I guessed. I supposed that, as my own narcissism was hard to see in myself, it must have been equally difficult for the crowds to see it in themselves. My skills at deflecting it were growing, but these were skills I didn't really want. I just wanted to have an ordinary social life without the New Age harassment and gossip. I also thought that engaging in it all could always make it worse, as people would become jealous or angry or feel insulted if you didn't take their inanities as God's pure and unadulterated truth.

The crowds had shifted somewhat from coke-addicted, sex-obsessed lunatics to Twelve Step, sex-obsessed lunatics. The New Age undertones were gone—or, at least, going—but there also seemed to be a backlash against it now, as the crowds sought to seek out and destroy hippies, drug addicts, New Agers, and anything that was not mainstream or right wing. The mainstream, and belonging to it, was now the next big thing. In some sense, this might actually have been better, as the crowd was seemingly looking for a more normal life, but I was always mistaken as an appropriate target for their deluded strivings. And, even though, the underpinnings of it all still had a New Age ring and "wisdom" to it, it was becoming more and more antiNew Age and even more Christian.

All the bars seemed to change to sports bars, and everyone in them seemed to be sports fans running out all but the sports fans. Fern bars and singles bars were gone. I imagined this was due to the years of drug abuse and New Age nonsense, as well as the fact that people couldn't stand to look at themselves anymore; they could only look at targets, and felt guilty about it. Watching sports has the ability to completely obviate the need for self-examination. Obsessive sports watching would be on the menu for anyone who had totally lost the ability or the nerve to introspect.

Yumi missed an awful lot of this; in general, people who don't speak English natively missed it too. I wondered how much the Tibetans could have understood, and how much of it seemed to be centered on mistaken beliefs about Tibetan Buddhism, particularly by the perverts who thought their perversions were part of the Tibetan thing. Everything was done with innuendo and vague allusions, and much of it required a rather significant knowledge of the culture—of movies, literature, and television—as references of these sorts were used to make comparisons and accusations: Star Wars allusions, Tolkien allusions, and things of that sort. I don't know how much Yumi actually understood. When we were out in public together, things seemed to go better, and she actually seemed helpful but really gave little hint that she was getting much of it.

I still had the underlying fear that it was coming largely from the Trungpa Rinpoche group, as a result of their large numbers and ongoing national connectedness through all the visiting and frequent meetings at different national and local centers. Also, they attracted a large number of the New Agers, given the mystical reputation of Tibetan Buddhism. I worried about it because the situation, as designed, was so beautiful, and I really loved it. I saw the perverts and the New Agers more as a kind of invasion of cockroaches, which the Tibetans, monks, and lamas in their vows to do no harm would not destroy. I also worried that all the invaders thought the monks and lamas were actually accepting their behaviors in a kind of "nothing can be done" attitude. There is nothing written in Buddhist, Shambhala, or even Christian texts that would do anything but mitigate against such behaviors and perversions; but, still, the perverts and New Agers insisted it all was "spiritual."

Sure "spiritual"—spiritual with a red tail, maybe! I thought to myself. I really couldn't stand it, and people kept insisting that I was somehow a part of that side of things, which I found insulting, humiliating, and infuriating. I constantly had to sort these feelings through the sieve of Buddhism in order to get to my original goal of just trying to work through that weird double personality I had developed.

What was particularly disturbing was the indignity that they would subject themselves and others to. Constantly digging in their pants, their crotches, their noses—and doing it *at* people, and then acting as though the objects of their grotesque attentions somehow needed, wanted, or deserved these grotesque attentions. They were also masters of the backward bow. People they respected or feared were treated with deference, while everyone else received a pants-on moon—that is, the backward bow. They saw this also as a kind of mark of distinction, and, rather than looking at their own jealousies, pettiness, and passive-aggressive hostilities as the source of their behaviors, they saw it is a mark of their being members of some sort of unspoken elite, and of their targets as somehow deserving the malicious treatment and drawing it out of them. They also seemed to have a hallucinatory experience along with it that somehow further justified the behaviors.

Everything they said was based on confabulation and delusion, but they pretended it was wisdom and enlightenment for their targets. Spontaneity was confused with impulsiveness, and they blurted out whatever came into their heads in the name of "spontaneity." They wanted everyone to join them so that they, too, could be members of the grotesque elite. The obese, both male and female—and the grotesquely obese even more so—were the most likely to indulge these behaviors. No one would address it, no one would call them to task, and no one made any attempt to dissuade them from the behaviors or to direct them toward the dignities they were supposedly masters of. It was a huge, hypocritical farce. People were afraid of getting that sort of treatment themselves, and so they kept silent.

They all acted from the superstitions of medieval peasants, rather than nobles, and yet, they saw themselves as nobles and elite. Few, if any, would oppose the behaviors; and all, with a rather typical rape mentality, blamed the victims—that is, those who wanted to do things correctly—for attracting the attention. The targets were at fault for being too good at what they did, for making others jealous, or, as in a pubescent masturbatory fantasy, for having some sort of "special" disease that could only be cured in this manner. It struck me as an aspect of a "rape mentality," a growing culture of rape in the larger culture, where pimp behaviors replaced dating behaviors. Blaming the victim is the mark of that mentality, and, in my reading, I have encountered the reference to these cultures as rape cultures. Some of the younger men actually used these behaviors as a means of capturing women and dominating them; unable to attract a woman, they turned to these behaviors in order to steal one.

At one time in Honolulu, Yumi and I underwent the training to become suicide-hotline counselors. I did it for about a year. Yumi, at the last minute, changed her mind. I think this was because she was worried about the many dialects spoken in Hawaii, which might lead to possible confusions on the phone. Based on this experience, years later, I would take the training to become a rape-hotline counselor. The training confirmed my beliefs about the dynamic and how problematic it is for a culture. I did this for six months or so, but then I drifted away from it. I never got many calls, and I thought there were others better suited for the job than I was.

Many of the grotesques either were hallucinating or pretending to be; over and above that, they acted as though their hallucinations, rather than being further evidence of their derangement, were somehow a mark of their progress toward enlightenment. The Tibetans, the lamas, and the monks never engaged in these behaviors and never encouraged them. Everything that was taught and written in all the traditions spoke loudly against such behaviors; but, in the spirit of "*vajra* this" and "*vajra* that," this was "*vajra* indignity," and it was proof of their wisdom, not their folly. It spread like wildfire, and it seemed to make them high in some sense. A lot of the New Agers, many of them ex-addicts, were engaged in and high on it. It was tawdry, despicable, and infuriating, but incredibly popular. The indignity and grotesqueness was also mirrored in the perverted nature of their gossip and innuendos.

What was so beautiful in design and so dignified in its manner had been invaded by an army of grotesques bobbing their heads, grinning their shit-eating grins, and treating everyone to the gift of their incredibly ugly attentions. I wanted to be known as an associate and student of the beauty and dignity of the situation, and I was horrified and embarrassed by and for the grotesques.

After my company closed, I again fell into the belief that my whole life was falling apart, and the darker part of my mind began standing up a bit more. I was also convinced that it was the PTSD that had prevented the success of the company. I was a finalist for a $1.3 million government grant, but I lost it during the interview stage, and I thought this was because of my intensity. There were other successes as well: a $50,000 job from a company in Japan, a $25,000 job from Sandia National Labs, a $75,000 grant from the SBIR, and a best-technology award from an international conference in Japan. I gave a few papers and presentations on it as well, all of which were very well received. All these achievements were reasons for self-confidence, but nothing ever came of any of them.

After the company failed, I became a bit manic, was completely broke, and was out of touch with the overcrowded ESL teaching positions. I needed money desperately, and so I went online to see what I could find. I lucked out in finding an eighty-thousand-dollar-a-year job as a technical writer in Silicon Valley. I worried that I would be abandoning Yumi in a time of need, as she was nearing the time to write her dissertation. I also wanted to be a part of that process, but I had no money and was in serious financial trouble.

I had always wanted to be a professor and teach graduate students, but the ten-year sidetrack of the theory and the company didn't take me in that direction. I wanted to see Yumi go through the process, and I wanted to help with the reading when and if necessary. By this time, her English was so good, as were her knowledge of psychology and the vocabulary of psychology, that I wasn't all that necessary, except for the commonly confused "a"s and "the"s that I described earlier. But I was so broke, there really was nothing I could do, and that large paycheck would certainly help. I figured I could do the job, maybe sell the software in California, and be back in a year to help Yumi—and I could do a lot by phone and e-mail to help her as well.

Silicon Valley was good, and the job was good; I liked the money and the access to the I/T crowd. There was a Tibetan Center in Berkeley that I was aware of. It was Shakya lineage center, a little less known than the Kagyu and Gelugpa. It was run by Lama Kunga, who specialized in making treasure vases. I had had some small contact with him when I was doing some karma yoga, buying treasures and vases as presents for various centers I had been to. I even presented one that got buried at the Zen center, and, in a nice ceremony, Aitken Roshi had it buried on the grounds of the new temple they were building.

When I visited the Shakya center, I found they had a much more open idea about giving empowerments than the Trungpa group. There would be about three or four a month, and they would offer a wide variety of the different deities of the Tibetan pantheon. Over the next year or, so I took more than a dozen of these.

Berkeley and San Francisco both had Trungpa Rinpoche centers, and I would visit these when I could as well. Not much Zen during these days. I had been practicing, on average, about fifteen hours a week: an hour and a half in the mornings, and an hour at night. The realities of my schedule made it imperfect, of course, but I was pretty much always able to maintain a morning and evening practice.

The San Francisco and Berkeley centers were particularly overwhelmed by the squawking and delusions, and I had a very difficult time getting along with the people there. It finally devolved to where they asked me not to return, rather than confronting the troublemakers. Their membership was largely made of those with this mentality, so it was probably the only decision they could make. At the time, I was also embattled with members of Trungpa's group e-mail list. They had a discussion group online, and, every time I wrote something, there were those who would jump all over it, thinking that whatever I said was some sort of threat to their desire to dominate. They would rage at me and not be held accountable for it, and, if I responded or complained, I was the one taken to task. I felt it a kind of duty to my PhD to respond and try to straighten these things out, but the bullies always dominated. They never won, as far as I could see, but they always prevailed. It was a bit like Rush Limbaugh, a man who, in his entire life, has never made an argument and has never won one, and yet, he has gotten through by shouting over every legitimate disputation of his views. The members of the Trungpa groups in the area and online were the same: they never made an argument, and they never won one. They just merely ganged up and shouted over any intelligent voice that would dare to step in their way.

After about a year, Yumi decided to move to San Jose for a year to be near me while she wrote her dissertation. I found her a nice studio that was about a twenty-minute drive from my house in Sunnyvale. The studio was a nice little bungalow owned by an American guy and his Japanese wife. I was very excited: I had a great job; Yumi was moving to the area, and she had a fun project that I could help her with a bit; plus, life in the valley still held some promise of selling my software. On the day she arrived, from out of nowhere, even after just receiving a large venture-capital fund, the company I worked for laid off about thirty employees, including me. There was no warning. I felt as if it had been deliberate, and, as I passed the office of the lawyers, I heard one of them say, though as part of a different conversation, "We have to retraumatize him"; this made the whole thing seem like some cruel setup designed to break hearts as much as watch the bottom line.

The atmosphere of the corporate world seemed as tainted by the New Age nonsense as anywhere else, but here it had a business tint to it, and the dynamic seemed to be one of dominance versus skills, where the least qualified and the least motivated ganged up on anyone who dared to defy them with hard work and good motivation and good ideas. There also seemed to be a fair amount of deliberate targeting of individuals in the office, and, naturally, they chose me as the target. My boss, though a little odd himself, was supportive. He liked the fact that I worked well and quickly, that I could be counted on to get things done on schedule, and that I was willing to pick up emergency projects without complaining. A few years later, the corporate targeting was made clear to me by a co-worker who unapologetically informed me that I was a target, saying, "Once you make one person the pariah, it takes the pressure off everyone else"—as though there were nothing that I could do about it, and nothing that anyone else would do.

With the layoff, I was crestfallen. Yumi was in her studio for the first day, and I had to tell her I'd been laid off. I wanted to cry out but didn't; I was just so embarrassed. All the boasting of a good job and a good paycheck to have fun with while she wrote her dissertation was suddenly taken away. It seemed like the scenario of the accident repeating itself all over again. Every time something seemed to be getting good, the rug got pulled out from under it, and I was left with nothing. The curse, or jinx, from Africa was active again. Yumi was very nice about it, and quite understanding and encouraging, as she always was. I would be able to get unemployment to pay my rent and all, but it was significantly less than I had been earning, and it dashed my promises to her of fun times by means of my big paycheck.

This was at least the third time I saw a major breakdown in my environment that paralleled the original accident—the marriage fiasco with the massage therapist; the fall of my company; and, now, the loss of my job on the day of Yumi's arrival. Everything that went wrong I viewed through the lens of the accident, and all of it reminded me to push back the wilder side of mind, to steel my social presentation, and to maintain the hypervigilance.

I was driving with a Hawaii driver's license—because I didn't want the California DMV to confiscate it for the fifteen hundred dollars or so that I had in fines in Hawaii—and, naturally, right at the time that I'd been laid off, I got a letter from Hawaii telling me that my Hawaii license would be canceled. Another vehicle-related dead end that would potentially make it more difficult to visit Yumi.

As I said, Yumi was quite nice about everything, and, as time went on, I settled into my new life. The dot-com blowout was in full bloom: now, instead, of hundreds of tech-writing jobs, there were none. I found myself working at a local Barnes and Noble when the unemployment ran out.

Yumi's dissertation was based on a very fascinating idea, and it provided me with a great source of knowledge of Japan and Japanese mythology. She was going to write a Jungian interpretation of recent behaviors of modern Japanese women in terms of the ancient Japanese goddess Amaterasu Omikami. As a big part of the Jungian psychology has to do with the flip side of your psychology—female for men, and male for women—I would have access to all the latest and greatest Jungian work on the feminine, and then I would be able to look at my soul, my feminine side. Yumi would write her dissertation, and I would be able to address the accident in terms of my anima, the feminine soul of a male.

In this case, I more than just read and rephrased passages she found confusing: I read much of the work she had gathered as research: books and dissertations on Japanese mythology, sociology, psychology, and feminism. It was not a feminist dissertation, but it dealt with those issues. The book grounding the whole thing was entitled, *The Feminine in Jungian Psychology,* and the author, Claire, was Yumi's dissertation professor. Claire was a well-known, widely read, classically trained clinical psychologist and Jungian. Yumi also had the classical sources of Japanese mythology, as well as a lot of miscellaneous papers and books, all as components of her research. This was not only great for my knowledge of Japan and things Japanese, but it also provided me tremendous insight into the minds of modern Japanese, and, particularly, modern Japanese women.

Yumi's main contention was that the women of modern Japan are involved in a large and silent protest—in fact, some writers call it the Silent Revolution—but, rather than this being a modern feminist protest parallel to that of the West, she argued that it is quite within the bounds of Japanese tradition for women to lead large societal changes while the men stay within their traditional roles. At one time bound to samurai lords, the men of Japan now were bound to corporate leaders. The daimyos had been replaced by CEOs of still largely family owned companies, and the women were still the masterminds of cultural change. She demonstrated how the original queen of Japan, Queen Himiko, was a woman who ruled with her brother. Himiko had ruled in an open way; her brother, from the background. Yumi further pointed out in her argument, as others had, that Japan was basically a feminine culture—not a matriarchy, not a patriarchy, and not a masculine culture, but a feminine culture, where the egos of the culture were feminine, whereas the Western culture's egos were masculine.

Those who originally put forth this idea also argued that Buddhism has basically a feminine ego as well. Something quite different from what we have in the West. I began to think of the Jewish tradition as patriarchy based on the father, and the Christian tradition as masculine also, but based on the son more than the father. I thought of India as a matriarchy, and Japan as a feminine culture in a similar way.

I read dozens of books on Japanese culture and psychology, and Yumi and I would discuss them over dinner as she crafted her dissertation over the course of two years. Except for my financial difficulties and inner turmoil, it was a wonderful time. Yumi seemed to be aware of my inner turmoil at times, but she never mentioned it, except perhaps to direct my reading in certain directions. I always suspected that her insistence on a very repetitive rereading of Melanie Klein and others was not because she could not understand it, but to ensure that I understood it properly—and yet, she always insisted in the guise that she didn't understand. I, of course, never let on much, but my stress levels were obvious. In her very Japanese way, she would never do anything directly. Even though she was very fond of America and wanted to stay for the rest of her life, Yumi always was, and still is, very Japanese. This is typical of many Japanese residents in America: they like the country and the culture, but they remain very formal, pleasant, and Japanese, embracing the culture but not enculturating.

Shortly after Yumi and I started spending time together in Hawaii back in 1991, I decided to start drinking again. I didn't want to fall back into the excesses of alcohol consumption of my past, so I took a slow and considered approach to it, having one drink on Thanksgiving, one the following Christmas, and then one a month, and then one a week. I wanted to make it through a whole year or more in this manner, so that I could see all the holidays and drinking excuses again, but with an extreme form of moderation. The Buddhist sitting practice helped a lot, too, and I was afterward able to have two or three drinks at a time, two or three times a week. Once in a while, Yumi and I would stay up all night watching videos and drinking, but this only happened about twice a year; it was quite enjoyable falling asleep on the floor and waking up in the morning still sitting against the couch.

We read and reread books on Japanese culture, mythology, and psychology. Yumi reported to her dissertation professor regularly. I always admired her courage in writing, as she would have seventy to a hundred pages finished, and then just throw it all out and redo the whole thing from scratch—her perfectionism wouldn't allow her to accept anything less than her best. I liked to think that my reading and our talks contributed to it in some ways, but it came out very Japanese in its essence, although it was in the American academic tradition.

Her argument was convincing and elegant, and I felt that the whole thing would qualify as a popular book among readers of Jung. Yumi pointed out that the goddess Amaterasu's decision to withdraw from society until certain social change is effected drew a parallel to the behavior of modern Japanese women.

We came to a deeper understanding of the Japanese focus on things sweet and cute as a byproduct of their main form of relationship: the *amae* relationship, which is a particular form of dependency, much like that of a young girl using sweetness and cuteness to get her way. In the West, relationships are based on love; in Buddhism, on compassion; but, in Japan, they are based on *amae*—cuteness and dependency.

Japanese social interactions were also further understood by a sociologist's view of the three aspects of the Japanese mind: social self, personal self, and higher self. The social self was the one that was determined by the strict cultural and social demands of Japan; the personal self held all the true feelings of the person, shared only with their in-group of family and friends; and the higher self was that of Zen enlightenment. With that understanding, I was much better able to relate to the Japanese and to understand the experiences I'd had there. Of course, intuitively, people come to an understanding of all that; but, having it spelled out in a soundly worked-out theory was very helpful to me. I also was able to see my PTSD mind in that scenario, where my hidden, personal self was deranged, but everything else was going smoothly.

At one point, I suggested that Yumi include some Freudian interpretation of the Japanese myth, but she rejected that rather haughtily, making me think I had insulted the culture or some such thing. She insisted there was nothing Freudian in it, and that it was quite different. Her dissertation came to an end, and she went back to Hawaii; but not before we both were able to attend her graduation ceremony. She was very proud, and I was very proud of her. It was a beautiful little ceremony on the school's campus in the hills just outside Santa Barbara. I was particularly impressed because of the years of effort

Yumi had put into both learning English and studying psychology. She had started as a low-intermediate ESL student and made it through to a PhD in clinical psychology, in English.

I was very sad to see her go, but I could not afford to move back to Honolulu, and she could not afford to stay in California. Besides, culturally, Hawaii was much better for her: she had a large circle of friends and a much better chance of getting a job there. I was stuck working at the Barnes and Noble bookstore. Nothing was happening in the I/T world, except for those who had a lot of money. Even showing my software to people was difficult without joining clubs with ten-thousand-dollar sign-up fees, and everyone seemed quite predatory and quite dedicated to the "get the inventor out" mentality.

Without Yumi around on a regular basis, the wilder part of mind asserted itself more, but things seemed much more manageable than they had been in the past. I began a very serious reading of Freud while working at Barnes and Noble. I read a dozen or so of his books, several times each. This reading interest would last for years. I wanted to undergo a full Freudian analysis, but had no money to do so. I had difficulty with Freud at first, as he was focused on a level of sexuality that was quite disturbing; but, as I got used to it and applied to myself, I found it more and more acceptable. I also saw tremendous parallels to Buddhism. This was surprising and a bit fishy at first, but, as time went on, it became clear to me that both theories were dealing with the same truth. I came to think of human wisdom as something discoverable, and as one thing that all cultures were working with and seeking to understand. The world of psychology was equally as fixed and determined as the world of science; it was just that psychology was subtler and more complex, and so it was more difficult to formulate the one true theory of the mind.

I took an approach to Freud that I'd originally discovered when learning about how to approach Chomsky. Rather than nitpicking or getting turned off and distracted at every point that seems off to you, you give the theory and the theorist the courtesy of hearing him all the way through before making a decision. I took this approach with Freud, read "The Ego and the Id," and several other works that gave good overviews of his system, and, little by little, I was sold on it. I never got caught up in the one-liners, such as, "Freud is a pervert" or "Freud was disproven" or "Freud had a mother problem". One of the most challenging and easily dismissed parts of his theory is the castration complex in boys and penis envy in girls. I found, though, that Freud's discussion of it was quite acceptable, and it made a coherent and important point. Most people tend to take these parts of the theory far too literally, not seeing them as coming from incipient sexual attitudes rather than frank sexual thoughts, and then they tend to reject them as impossible and to see Freud as off his rocker. I read dozens of books by him and his immediate circle; some of them I read three or more times. As time went on, I got to know the names of others in his inner circle, reading as much of them as I could as well. I also discovered Anna Freud, who explored ego psychology in some depth, and I read most of her books.

I developed several simplistic overviews of Freud's theory, seeing neurosis as just three things: hysteria, which was mostly for women; obsession, which was mostly for men; and paranoia. At one point, Freud argued that hysteria was a failure of art, obsession a failure of religion, and paranoia a failure of philosophy; I saw the Buddhist system, and, particularly, the situation created by Trungpa Rinpoche, as addressing all three through art, study, and religion, and I further saw sitting meditation as a grounding factor underlying the whole thing. I also looked at the entirety of psychological pathology in a three-step way: the worst was psychosis, which implied that you could not handle life requirements and had lost track of both physical and psychological reality; next came personality disorders, which are characterized by narcissism and being a problem for others; and the least debilitating was neurosis, which would cause problems for you rather than others, and which was also the most easily cured of the three. I took the entirety of the crowd phenomenon to be one of personality disorder. I couldn't figure quite where PTSD fit in.

In an age where many people ostensibly have given up religious beliefs and have no confidence in psychology, they still have lots of magical thinking, and many ideas about how to "hold" their psychology in order to influence others, to improve themselves, to gain wealth, and so on. In spite of dismissals of religion, afterlife, psychology, and, conversely, an insistence on science and logic and life decisions based on science, almost everyone has opinions on the secrets to achieving wealth and success, all of which are necessarily psychological, and many of which are shared via innuendos and insinuations among friends. They dismiss heaven and the afterlife as myths that cannot be proved, and yet they maintain their magical thinking. Often, they maintain a belief in demons or devils or ghosts or UFOs, even while they dismiss heaven and hell and any gods. However, this pretends that people like Jung and Freud, or priests and ministers, or doctors and lawyers have never thought of these things, are no good at these things, or simply are not enlightened enough to notice these things, even while the average joe and his pals, who have studied little other than gossip, are experts. The espousal of psychology or religion is seen as mistaken, and it is implied that they will cost you your wealth and influence rather than improve them. I have heard people dismiss doctors, lawyers, and psychologists as not knowing the level of reality on which they are working and of being totally unaware of it.

Of course Freud himself, his followers, other doctors, and so forth are not unaware of these things, and they have even detailed and examined many of the common beliefs in this area, only to conclude that most of these beliefs were not effective, and, in fact, were neurotic cover-ups for failures of understanding in these areas. Freud pointed out that it was common for someone to think that his magic, his influence, and his psychology were correct when things were going well, but that the same things all were somehow damaged when things were going badly; thus, taking credit when things go well and blaming oneself when things go badly. Dismissals of psychologists and others were merely neurotic resistances to a better understanding of these things. It seemed to me that the crowds tenaciously stuck to the primitive, magical thinking of the masses, while dismissing the knowledge of the experts—that is, the people who actually took the time to look at all the variations, think them through, and find a description of the states of mind that actually improve one's relation to reality and to other people.

The fact of the matter is, any degree of influence or magic or religion meant to influence the world is, at its base, just psychology: the meeting place of body and reality. For Freud, the meeting place of body and reality in psychology was driven by instincts, and a healthy relation to the instincts was required in order to have an effective relationship to the world. He basically proposed that there were only two instincts: one, toward life and activity in the world, which he called Eros, or the hunger/love instinct; and, the other, toward stasis and inactivity, which he called Thanatos, or the death instinct/nirvana principle. His early theory was focused solely on the life instincts—the hunger/love instincts of Eros—and it was not until after many years of research that he began to speak of the death instincts of Thanatos, which led to stasis or peaceful repose of the entire organism.

By reviewing, rereading, and making charts on Freud's materials, I began to have a sense that he did, indeed, have a solution to the problem of PTSD. It was not overtly stated as his theory on this matter; what he called "shell shock" was incomplete at the time of his death. His other unfinished theory was on addiction, and it struck me that the two were very closely related. I needed to summarize the entirety of his theory so that I could keep it all in line and in an easy-to-work-with form, and I constantly found myself simplifying and summarizing. In particular, I felt that the solution lay in Thanatos, the death instinct, which ends in a state of quiescence, the same state that the Buddhists seem to strive for in attaining nirvana. However, the PTSD and addiction aspect each are some sort of a miscarriage of that process.

The death instincts interested me, as they seemed to be the basis of Buddhism, and of much Eastern thought in general, all of which seeks to achieve a state of quiescence through renunciation and discipline, rather than through the training of or experience with the life instincts. In fact, it seems that Freud and Buddhism are the same in many respects; both focus on Thanatos, but the one does so through the withdrawal of libido from the world, while the other does so by working with the world and focusing on maturity. Freud's "normal" is Buddhism's "enlightenment"; the former arrived at through a proper relation to one's Eros (hunger and love); the latter, through a relationship to one's Thanatos (death or quiescence).

Freud's theory is based on an understanding of instincts and the instinctual drives that underlie one's psychological makeup. For him, instincts are the meeting place between body and reality, which, in essence, is psychology. The instinct of hunger leads to a psychology that seeks food, and the instinct for love leads to a psychology that seeks a person in the outer world. For Freud, there are only these two prime life instincts: hunger and love. Hunger is for personal survival, and it can also be called the survival instinct; love is for the survival of the species. Other writers talked about "need" and "want"; survival instincts are matters of need, and cannot be put off for too long without damage to the physical well-being of the individual. The love instinct is also a matter of need; but it will not damage the physical apparatus if it is not met, though damage can be done to the psychological system. His famous sexual theories are derived from the variations in development that result in the maturation of the individual around issues of this instinct for love.

For Freud, these were the only true pure life instincts; any others that might be posited would be derivative of these two instincts: hunger and love. The herd instinct was one possibility that interested me, as it seemed to describe the crowd mentality; but, Freud addresses it only once in all that I have seen of his writing, and he dismisses it as mere rivalry. Thus, for him, the entirety of the phenomenon in the crowds was nothing more than rivalry. Not that he ever commented on the crowds as I saw them, but he dismissed the herd mentality so similar to the crowds as rivalry; I could now see the crowd phenomenon for what it was, a pretense to social graces and friendship covering up rivalries in passive-aggressive pretenses to socialization. I also assumed that what he meant was untreated sibling rivalry, resulting in projections of the original family dynamic onto other persons and situations. Rivalry in the Buddhist sense would just be envy.

Freud's theory begins with infancy, and then it proceeds to look at the development of hunger and love through all the periods of life; primarily, it focuses on this development within the family of origin, before individuals leave home and go out on their own. The actual energy of these instincts Freud called "libido," which exists throughout the body, and the varieties in the means of its dispersal create various psychological states. When everything is in proper balance, the libido creates a state of well-being and satiety; when things are out of balance, a state of neurosis sets in. In particularly disrupted forms, psychosis is the result. He uses the term "need" to refer to the instincts, but he recognizes that they are not absolute needs, as they can be put off or displaced as the requirements of reality dictate. One can forgo hunger and love if circumstances are not perfect, but this will result in frustrations exhibited as anxiety. One can also forgo hunger and love for ascetic purposes.

In infancy, the needs for hunger and love are met entirely by outside forces, and, as the child develops, he becomes more and more capable of recognizing those needs and providing for himself. Freud's sexual theories are the most controversial, but they are not quite as bizarre as his detractors might pretend. If you look at what he actually said about these things, you will see that they are quite reasonable; more than that, you will see them in yourself and others, as they are operative realities that cannot be ignored.

According to Freud, there are three major developmental hurdles on the way to achieving, in reality, a mature relationship with survival objects and love objects. These three are weaning, toilet training, and the Oedipus complex, the last being the most challenging to the reader of Freud. Obstacles to, or difficulties, in these three stages can lead to identifiable problems later in life, which will persist if they are not met and resolved in some way. Problems in these developmental stages leave memory traces in the unconscious, which constantly pressure the individual to act on the infantile wishes or push them out of reality. It's a lot like miscellaneous memories from childhood that are excessively potent or energized or compelling, and that become particularly distracting during times of stress and anxiety.

From infancy, the child has needs for hunger and love, and has a mind that does not separate dream/hallucination and reality very well; but, as he tries to satisfy his needs, he begins to learn that his dreams/hallucinations do not actually fulfill his needs, whereas reality does. And, in this way, he slowly develops a sense of himself, fantasy and reality, reality being divided into those things that satisfy his needs, as well as those people that do. In this way, he also develops his ego, his dream world, and his reality sense, and he learns to relate to his body and his world in a way that will satisfy his needs. Thus, he is already a tripartite individual: instinctual need, self, and reality; or, "ego, id, and reality," as they are called in Freudian psychology. In German, ego and id were simply called, "*Ich*" and "*es*"—"I" and "it." Why the translators saw fit to dig up the Latin words "ego" and "id" will always baffle me, particularly as it seems to confuse the issue by forcing the reader to look for something other than "I" and "it" as the meanings of "ego" and "id"; but, nevertheless, ego and id are the terms known to English-speaking readers of Freud. It just seems a lot more self-explanatory to say the child is developing a sense of himself—his "I" (needs), his "it" (self), and his "reality" (world)—than to use some Latin terms that make the reader think a deeper definition than "I" and "it" will be necessary.

As the child grows, his desires for hunger and love are oftentimes frustrated, but, if they are met frequently enough, and if the infant is soothed with sufficient frequency, he will develop along normal lines. At the times of weaning and toilet training, the child is forced into a stage of development that he resists; and, if this resistance is not handled well, it can lead to neurosis in later life: oral fixations, and anal-aggressive or anal-retentive character traits, all of which are rather well known in everyday modern parlance, and all of which arise from infantile frustrations during this stage. Frustrations during this stage result in anxiety, and the training has to do with learning the new skills and coping with the anxiety along the way. If there are problems, memory traces of the anxiety-producing events are left in the unconscious, and they can become activated later in life through similar anxiety-producing events. A child with an anxiety-producing memory trace from weaning may react to anxiety later in life, either with oral fixations or more complicated neuroses.

Freud's theory of sexuality in the infant is not so much about sexuality in the sense that we think of it in adults, but more a development of the energy of the survival (hunger) and love instincts in various primitive stages. At first, the organ of the love instinct is the lips, for breast feeding, which weaning impacts. Later on, the love instinct localizes in the anal cavity, for the necessary awareness to accomplish toilet training. After that, it moves to the genitals, where it becomes a more easily recognizable sexual instinct that develops through the Oedipus complex, eventually progressing to more normal love objects. In any case, it is clear he is not talking about sexual desire in the postpubescent sense. "I want to marry you mommy" is as far as it goes for most boys, for example, with a concomitant jealous aggression toward the father.

Difficulties in development, particularly at the main stages of training, can lead to relatively permanent wounds, called "fixations," frozen memory traces at the particular points in development, which are very difficult to resolve later in life, and which can result in the development of neuroses. These may be known to an individual as persistent memories from childhood, even from infancy; they may be unexplained, but they will likely persist with some tenacity, particularly during times of frustration.

"Repression," a particularly important concept to Freud, can be described as a miscarriage of the process of maturity, in which the individual forces the painful or frustrating memories out of consciousness and into the unconscious, where they will remain until something forces them back into conscious memory. The focus of the libido is the source of release of instinctual tensions. When these instinctual tensions are met with resolution, pleasure results; conversely, when these instinctual tensions are not resolved, anxiety or pain results. When the weaning, toilet training, or even the dismissal of early oedipal strivings leads to frustrations, repressed memory traces can result.

A repressed instinct still wants to have its aim met, but consciousness is expending energy to prevent it from coming up. This expenditure of energy weakens the overall system. In addition, the repressed content still tries to surface, and so it tricks consciousness by forming symbolic but difficult-to-identify fantasies and habits in consciousness. Thus, an oral fixation like smoking can be the result of a repressed, frustrated memory from weaning that expresses itself in consciousness as the smoking habit. The memory traces from childhood are used by Freudians to trace and undo the fixations.

Freud's psychotherapy developed a method that can undo the original fixations, thus leading to a resolution of neurosis and a better relation to reality. Just understanding Freud's theory can be sufficient for many people. His psychoanalysis involved lying on the couch while talking with the therapist, which allowed the person to develop the ability to say whatever came to mind without the censorship of the superego (the conscience). As this skill develops, the repressions are weakened, and dreams and spoken reports of the patient begin to show the therapist the underlying difficulty, which is then explained to the patient. The patient at first resists the analysis as being untrue, gross, odd, and so forth; but then, as he comes to recognize the truth of the matter, the fixation is released, and he is freed from the neurotic symptoms associated with the interpreted material.

Interestingly, the Tibetan Buddhist practices seem to work on id, ego, and superego, without ever requiring the practitioner to look closely at or analyze the material that is being released. Rather, after long experience with sitting practice, the practitioner has trained himself not to fixate on or lend too much weight to any thoughts or ideas that come out, but, instead, to let them all lead naturally into the state of quiescence. Tibetan practices, where one visualizes the guru on the head, work with the superego; those in which the practitioner visualizes himself as a deity work with the ego; and those that work with the internal chakras and such work on the id. The unconscious as a whole, which Tibetans call the *alaya,* is purified as a whole, without ever looking at its content. As Buddhism posits a long string of past lives as sources of the problem, and, as one can generally only know the past of this life, looking at this life alone may be seen as a little shortsighted. However, they do believe that any one rebirth is emblematic of all past lives, so it may be that looking at the past of this life is sufficient to see the whole of the "seeds of the alaya"; thus, Freud's theory can be seen as one that allows an individual to look closely at the seeds of his unconscious and transform them directly. Which is better or faster or more correct is impossible for me to discern.

The Oedipus complex is somewhat challenging for most people. In this, Freud argued that children around the ages of five to eight develop a primitive sense of sexuality in the genital organ, and then they get a somewhat sexualized attraction to the parent of the opposite sex and a simultaneous rivalry with the parent of the same sex, in a sort of symbolic "I wanna marry mommy/daddy" love triangle. This results in a disappointment that leads to a freeze in the development of the love instinct. The frustration is a combination of fear, disappointment, and anger. The period that follows is called the latency period, and the development of the love instinct remains pretty much frozen until puberty. This frustration causes the child to turn away from the love triangle with his parents, internalizing their authority, which results in the creation of a conscience—the superego, which Freud originally called the "Uberich," (literally, the "over I," or the "big I" that watches over the "little I"). The superego is both an ideal for the ego to live up to, and a source of authority and punishment for the ego that does not meet the ideals which the superego has set up. The setting up of the conscience through the frustrations of the Oedipus complex leads to heightened guilt, as well as heightened responsibility. Those without guilt would be those without a conscience, or those who had not properly met the Oedipus complex.

The creation of the superego, through the internalization of parental authority, is the result of the fear associated with the Oedipus complex. The fear—and this is the one that gets everyone so upset—is the fear of castration. A young boy tugs at his pants too much, has a slightly precocious sexuality, and he is yelled at for not behaving in a more mannerly way; and then, supposedly, on an unconscious level, this translates into the fear of actually losing the organ. In Freud's time, it was common to yell at children of that age, threatening that the father or the doctor would actually cut off the appendage, or the hand; however, Freud quite explicitly said that the child would come to the same conclusions even without the overt threats. Like the ball or stick taken away from the child who does not listen, the organ itself (or the hand) was at risk. He further stipulated that these are not necessarily overt thoughts but relatively nonverbal conclusions that are drawn by the child in the course of maturation and training, and which have necessary, natural consequences—in this case, the development of a conscience.

The superego, which represents parental authority, as well as the ideals of the child, is further modified later in life through the influence of teachers, priests or ministers, older siblings, and so forth. In the Tibetan system, this is also modified by gurus and vows taken to the religion, and also by individual gurus who supersede the authority of the parents, replacing it with the tenets and goals of the Buddhist system.

Freud describes three basic types of neuroses that develop because of frustrations resulting from the realization of the child's needs, which lead to a conflict between: (1) the child and reality; (2) the child and his instincts; (3) the child and his internalized parental authority.

As time goes by, the basic instincts and the facts of reality come into conflict, which leads to just three types of neuroses if the conflicts are not resolved. The needs of hunger and the needs of love also contend with each other: Love for the species/ego for the individual

Id/ego/superego conflicts (in the above)

Ego libido/object libido

Of crucial importance to understanding Freud is the recognition of the unconscious. Many people today grant this to a certain degree, but they still have difficulties accepting that as much is contained there as Freud contends. Everyone agrees that everything in our mind that could be conscious is not always there; we selectively choose what we focus on, leaving other things out as a kind of latent consciousness. This, for Freud, is unconscious too—or, better yet, what he called the "preconscious," which is anything that is potentially conscious. However, he includes much, much more, such as all the memory traces from childhood, latent talents and intentions, instinctual drives, and so on—all of which require certain cues from the ego or the real world to become conscious again. And, most important, the unconscious is the container of the raw instinctual drives.

Another crucial concept that you must understand in order to understand Freud's theory as a whole is his theory of repression, which is a process that prevents painful feelings and memories and unacceptable thoughts and desires from entering consciousness. These concepts were new at the time of Freud's writing, but, nowadays, the idea that we repress, that we refuse to let certain concepts into consciousness, is widely accepted. For Freud, this was the main source of psychopathology: anxiety-producing memory traces are forced out of consciousness by repression, which then vigorously prevents them from entering consciousness. These repressions are what need to be released in order to discover the underlying memory trace that is causing the anxiety and the resultant neurosis. His whole process of analysis was to get at these memory traces by lifting the repressions.

Repressing is the opposite of giving something attention. We get a pleasant idea from the unconscious or the outer world, and we welcome it and act on it. However, if an unpleasant and anxiety-producing memory is triggered, we force it back rather than focus our attention on it. The same force that attaches attention to an idea also forces it back, but this forcing back is an expenditure of energy that produces anxiety rather than pleasure. The effort to push back, to repress, takes away from the energy of consciousness, keeping one a bit distracted, and then the anxiety produced takes away from pleasurable or relaxing states.

The thing repressed wants to come to consciousness, but the forces of repression are pushing it back. Thus, there is a conflict between the forces in the unconscious and those in consciousness. Out of frustration, the unconscious finds ways to release the impulse from the unconscious by using dream processes to confuse consciousness and let the repressed memory traces out in disguised ways. This is seen in dreams and in the fantasies of neurotic people, where dream content and fantasy content can be analyzed in order to reveal the underlying anxiety-producing memory trace. There are two main devices that the unconscious has to disguise the repressed content and allow it into consciousness: turning it into its opposite and pushing it out, or projecting it onto someone else. In the first device, such an idea as anger at a parent is taken as anger at oneself, blaming oneself for the faults of the parent or reversing it into excessive expressions of love. In the second device, the repressed idea is seen as belonging to someone else rather than to the self. Projection and reversal into the opposite are the typical means by which repressed content reappears in consciousness in a disguised way, thereby tricking the conscious censor that sought to repress it in the first place.

Much depression and moral anxiety, even moral masochism, is the result of a repressed idea being reversed and put on oneself. Instead of the individual being angry at his parent, siblings, or others, he blames himself in exactly the way he would have liked to see the parents or siblings blamed.

An important aspect of the Eros, the hunger/love instinct (libido), is its differentiation into an energy of survival and an energy of love. Early in life, a part of the libido attaches to the individual's body and ego, and provides a sense of self: the primary narcissism. As the child matures, much of this libido is also shared with objects in the world. Unlike the love libido, this is more physical, and it attaches to physical objects.

In severe psychoneuroses like psychosis and paranoia, the individual withdraws his libido from the world out of frustration, and it then attaches to the ego in megalomaniacal states. This then becomes the secondary narcissism: the libido that is proper to objects is withdrawn to the more appropriate primary narcissism, swelling that with the libido proper to objects. This addition to the primary narcissism results in the megalomaniacal form of it that is characteristic of paranoia, schizophrenia, and, in post-Freudian versions of the theory, of the various personality disorders. The heightened narcissism makes the individual feel powerful, godlike, indestructible, and wealthy; but, in reality, he has withdrawn his connections to the world and only "owns" his connection to things, not the things themselves.

The confusion of the object libido with the primary narcissism in secondary narcissism makes it extremely difficult to see and to separate, but it also leaves the individual without a path back to the reality of his object world. The personality disorders and paranoia are very difficult to cure, as all of them are marked by this secondary narcissism, which is visible to everyone else but not to the individual. However, the worst cases are those of psychosis and schizophrenia, as, in addition to the withdrawal of object libido onto the primary narcissism, there is no effort to reconstruct the world, such as happens in the conspiracy theories of the paranoiac or the godlike pretenses of the personality disordered. In the more serious paraphrenias, the victory lies with repression, and the combination of withdrawal of object libido and the victory of repression; there is little room for a cure and little sense of the possibility of one.

In the confused rush to understand emptiness and nonthought, many aficionados of Buddhism discovered an extreme form of repression of all thought, which they see as "enlightenment," and then they end up living in a fantasy world of Dungeons and Dragons–style bickering and fantasy, that includes rivalry with one another and within their world.

Proper dispersal of the object libido is achieved when the primary narcissism, that which proper to good self-esteem and even vanity, is not overwritten by the libido proper to objects in the world. It is seen most clearly in love, where the primary narcissism overvalues a loved one or a loved object. The good self-esteem is maintained by the return of love or by the usefulness of the object that is overestimated. Disappointments and loss lead to the withdrawal of this libido and to the potential for the development of secondary narcissism, if there is not a new object or a release of the frustration.

End-of-the-world thinking, utopian thinking, and the conspiracy theories of the paranoiac represent reconstruction efforts by the individual who has withdrawn his love—his libido—from the world.

By now I had become a fluid and educated reader of psychology. I never took any classes after the half a counseling degree, and I never wrote papers, participated in discussions, or took tests on the subject, but I felt I had read more on the subject—and within a more selective framework—than many who actually worked in the field.

I read other things, too, of course: a number of books about Hitler that focused on his mysticism; I also paged through *Mein Kampf* a few times. It seemed jinxed to me, so I didn't like reading it and never bought it, but I stood alongside the shelf while working at Barnes and Noble, and I read a few of pages here and there. A couple of things stood out for me. In particular, he stated that the secret to getting the votes he needed was to concentrate on the one-issue voter, and the one issue he offered them was the threat of the Jews. This was both his great lie—one that was too big to be disproved—and his strategy for attracting the one-issue voter. I also noted a comment by Jung at the time. He had diagnosed Hitler as a hysteric, a problem more typical of women; but Hitler was proof that men could get it as well.

It was also interesting to note that Hitler's mysticism was much like that of the crowds, largely unarticulated and mostly hinted at, nothing that he'd worked out or thought through. All of which made me feel that my reactions to the innuendo and slander were justified. Look where it could lead if left unchecked.

11

Barnes and Noble and More Freud—2003

> ... with dreams, with drugs, with waking nightmares, alcohol and cock and endless balls . . .
>
> —ALLEN GINSBERG, "HOWL"

I enjoyed working at Barnes and Noble but felt trapped. I also felt I was outside my field and, therefore, outside a better pay scale. I was the lead bookseller for about a quarter of the store and for the departments I stocked, managed, and sold from. My sections included Christianity, Buddhism, New Age, philosophy, history, placement tests, and foreign-language books. I enjoyed keeping up with and exploring all the sections, particularly the New Age section, which gave me a chance to see what people were reading in that area and what was available, overall, on the subject. I read a few here and there, paged through a bunch, and got to know the popular titles and authors.

One day, while still working at the bookstore, I saw a job offering for an English teacher at the Defense Language Institute in Monterey, California, perhaps the world's most famous language school. I applied, got an interview, felt I had nailed it, and then, after literally months of waiting, finally got a job in my field. I was hired as an Assistant Professor, a good position where I would prepare members of the military for language learning.

My program was to provide a two-week training course in English grammar, language-learning skills, and study skills to get the students fresh from boot camp ready for language study. The military teaches only the languages from the hot spots of the world, so Arabic was big, Russian was getting smaller, the languages of Afghanistan and the surrounding area were growing, and so forth. It was a good job with good support. My boss was an air force master sergeant. The student body was easy to teach. The sergeants in the room kept order, so there was no need to consider discipline or behavior in the classroom. Basically, I would teach to the lowest rank, let the sergeants handle the atmosphere and discipline, and treat the officers like guests.

Things there were going quite well: good committee appointments, good student reports, and I was getting a few publications and presentations to add to my resume. I was even able to present in DC on two occasions. I also applied and was accepted to be one of the readers for the AP English Composition exam. The AP (advanced placement) is a series of tests high-school students can take to test out of required introductory-level college courses. The English Composition exam requires that they write several essays to demonstrate writing ability sufficient to place out of that required course. Naturally, the exam has to be graded, so the AP program gathers about eight hundred writing teachers from around the country, and they spend eight hours a day for seven days grading exams. I saw this as a good resume builder, as well as a chance to see what was going on with teachers in this country. I was not surprised to see that much of the squawking mentality existed there as well; that is to say, I expected it but was still disappointed. I did the AP grading every other year for six years, heartened by the fact that, each time I did it, the crowd mentality improved.

I also presented at TESOL, a very important conference for teachers of ESL, and I saw this as a good resume builder as well. I actually filled the room with my little talk on teaching grammar, and, afterward, more than the average share of attendees approached me, looking for printouts of my slide show. Grammar teaching had fallen out of fashion during the twenty-five years prior to my talk, and instructors were hard-pressed to see it as easy to teach. I received many requests for my slide show, and so I felt very good about the whole thing.

A particularly good resume builder came along with the 2006 accreditation drive at DLI. A self-study of the entire school has to be done every six years in order to maintain accreditation. The man in charge of accreditation was overwhelmed with work—the position of Chairman was vacant, so he was Acting Chairman at the time while they sought to fill that position, and he was having difficulty fitting in accreditation along with everything else on his schedule. I went to his office to volunteer for one of the committees, and, while I was there, I mentioned to him that I had once gotten a small ESL school accredited. With this background, he gave me the position of Editor and Coordinator of the Self-Study. I would drive the whole thing, and, when I finished, he would polish it up and produce the final product. I was all over DLI, and my other boss let me go on half-time duty so that I would be able to spearhead the self-study. With four large committees and around thirty contributors involved in the self-study, I was able to become known around the school as an effective and pleasant person. I knew the Deans, the Provost, and the Vice Chancellors, and, as the point person in charge of keeping everything on track, I provided a valuable service to all concerned. I had the Acting Chairman's support as "muscle" but never really needed to ask him to step in for anything. The self-study took about a year to complete. I knew the school system forward and backward, and I made a lot of valuable contacts around the school. When the accreditation team finally came through, we ended up with a very strong report, and I was credited, at least by the Acting Chairman, with having saved the 2006 accreditation. I did experience targeting and harassment, but it seemed to be within relatively normal levels of competitiveness among academics.

During this time, I generally called Yumi twice a day and was able to make several trips to Hawaii to visit her. She made one trip to California to visit me, which was also quite fun. I moved into military housing when I took the job at DLI. The master sergeant was promoted to Chief, and then he moved on to another assignment. He was replaced by an air force captain who was amazingly sharp and amazingly interesting. The guy had worked himself up to captain from an enlisted rank, was a part of special forces, and had two black belts—one in karate and one in Japanese swordsmanship. He had done tours in both Afghanistan and Iraq.

While at Barnes and Noble, I had become a Freemason. I had learned about the Freemasons from the works of Jung and others, and I'd had a growing interest in Freemasonry for years. With Yumi gone, I had time for a new hobby, so I joined the Santa Clara lodge, went through the initiations, and became an active member, adding books on Freemasonry and secret societies to my reading interests. I even read one on the Skull and Bones society of Yale. This was quite a good read, and it really filled in a lot of gaps in my knowledge of the Western world and Western mysticism.

I also joined the Rosicrucians at this time and began working on the long series of monographs that they provided. This place was particularly well known for having Walt Disney as a member. He had completed all their studies, which included much of Western and Eastern mysticism. I wondered to what degree his mysticism contributed to his work, if perhaps Mickey Mouse was a kind of Western deity. I had often thought of American cartoons as a kind of Western, nascent Vajrayana. Rosicrucianism was a little different from Tibetan Buddhism, but I began to notice many parallels between the Western and Eastern mystical traditions and psychology. All this made me think, more and more, that human wisdom was a fixed and knowable thing, not some esoteric unknowable that was as easily dismissed as it was embraced, and not something that was owned by one tradition. I studied Rosicrucianism and Freemasonry for the next six years or so.

The Rosicrucians have a well-known temple in San Jose. It is a model of a pyramid from Egypt, and it serves as a museum of Egyptian antiquity, as well as a meeting place and library for classes on Rosicrucian mysticism. The people were basically quite nice, but there was a fair amount of the UFO and New Age crowd who hung around; however, the availability of a large curriculum made it difficult for them to go off with the one book they had ever read on the subject. The Rosicrucian training lacks the highly developed sitting practice of Buddhism, but it does have a core sitting discipline as well: one sits in a chair in front of a mirror, but it is nothing like the ten—or thirty-day intensives of Buddhism.

Yumi had gotten her green card after years of living, studying, and working in the US. This was an important accomplishment for her; she never wanted to do anything illegal and didn't want to get a green card through marriage. She wanted to earn her green card, and, after fifteen years of living in the country, obtaining a PhD, and becoming an autism counselor, she did earn that green card. Naturally, I was very impressed—and also very relieved. It would have been very difficult for her to get a decent job in Japan after all the years she'd lived in the US, and her knowledge of psychology was almost entirely in English, so she would have found it difficult to even work in her field in Japan. She also had some residual frustration about living in Japan, really preferring the United States.

I always worried that Yumi would distance herself from me because of the harassment I received. I worried that it would attach to her, but she never let on that she even noticed it. The language gap around vague references may have made it seem much less to her. I was not prone to letting on, but she saw me as being excessively dismissive toward people in the world, perhaps not knowing just what it was that I tried to shoo away. The stupidity of the harassment always seemed self-evident to me, and I always suspected the source of it had something to do with the PTSD. Certainly, the intensity is often confused with rage, and the withdrawal is often confused with arrogance; however, the total inability of the harassers to even question their own behaviors, or stop them, made me think there was something else going on as well. What was it about PTSD that made these lunatics so stuck on me? Why was I "perfect" or "the best one" for this hideous and foolish treatment? The energy of Thanatos seemed to offer some possible explanation, but it was still outside my grasp. My working with these crowds and my inner search had become very closely intermingled through the years, and my dedication to stopping it once and for all—either by stopping them or by finding something in myself—was now a kind of driving force in my life.

The gossip crowds actually prided themselves on their ability to negatively influence people's lives with their slander, threatening the lives and families and jobs of their targets, which always seemed quite low and fascist to me. They were trying to replace the targets' life choices with theirs—which, of course, would be choices that confirmed their deluded beliefs about their targets—fat girls and minimum-wage jobs for the competent. Meanwhile, the good women and jobs would go to the slanderers. Many even seemed to want to get rid of dating and love relationships utterly, and replace them solely with relationships and jobs that came out of the din of the constant squawking. It all spoke of a deeply entrenched peasant mentality—something like a Maoist peasant revolution, where the peasants were in the palaces, and the nobles were in the huts. Sometimes they admitted to their slander, implying that they would continue to slander until you participated in the perversion—sort of like you would be accused of perverted crimes until such time as you actually participated, and then you would be left off the hook. This was done with an attitude intimating that the perversions were either unavoidable life realities or part of some sort of secret wisdom.

I found this similar to the fascism of Nazi Germany—or communism—and saw much of the movement as a growing fascist mentality in the US and Europe, and I worried about a resurgence of totalitarianism. Many of the squawkers were overtly racist, particularly those in bars, especially sports bars. History repeats itself, they say. Hegel, the philosopher who also wrote on the philosophy of history, said that history repeats, but it repeats as a farce. I saw the right wing— the squawkers, the New Age mentality, and so forth—as the repetition of fascism as a tragic farce. Hitler was the Antichrist, and George Bush—or Jerry Falwell or Rush Limbaugh or someone like that—was the tragic farce repetition of that dynamic. Seeing all this as a tragic farce repetition of fascism was somewhat heartening, in that it meant the dynamic would come to an end when it exhausted itself, or when it was addressed completely and thoroughly.

While in the valley, I also read a few books on kabbalah. I wondered now if I wasn't as obsessed as the New Agers, but at least I did the reading. In some ways it was to defend myself, to know what the crowds were referring to and actually a great hobby. I used Western psychology of Jung and Freud and Tibetan and Japanese Buddhism as the core organizational principles in my reading and thinking and reading everything helped sort through it all. I stayed away from most of the purely New Age stuff as paging through it was generally enough. Most of it was clearly driven by selfishness, greed, and puffing people up with the thought that they too could be an overnight, New Age millionaire or guru with book deals, followers and a lecture tour. I wanted to have a full and thorough knowledge of all these subjects but still had no interest in such crowds.

Over the years, I had been all over America, giving presentations at conferences or attending conferences for myself or for school, both for academic and work purposes. This resulted in a total of about twenty-five trips. In the course of my life up to that point, I had made cross-country drives several times, twice in the late 1990s, which gave me an opportunity to see the madness on a much wider scale. The first of these drives was across America; the second, across Europe (that would be cross-continental, I guess). The American trip happened while I was running my software company. I had a couple of meetings set up in California, and a five-day presentation of my software at the National Association for Computational Linguistics yearly meeting in DC. I decided to drive from California to DC. It was quite fun but more than a little frantic. On the way, I stopped at RMDC and several other spots of interest. I topped the trip to Washington off with a trip to New York to see the Letterman show. I had a seat on the first floor, about twenty rows back and just in front of Letterman. I was always a big fan of his, shouting "Dave" whenever he appeared in a commercial, so this was quite nice.

At one point, Yumi and I had conferences at the same time in Los Angeles, and we took some time off to go to Bill Maher's *Politically Incorrect,* which turned out to be a great date. We saw Debbie Harry, Tupac Shakur, and a couple of others. We also got to see two shows, because we went on a Thursday, and that is when they film both the Thursday and Friday episodes.

About a year after the trip across America, I made a similar trip across Europe. I hadn't really planned it that way, but I had a paper to give in Dundee, Scotland, a paper to give in Bonn, Germany, and about two weeks in between them, which I planned to spend in Paris for old times' sake. After giving the paper in Dundee, at the last minute, I decided to drive rather than fly; I rented a car to drive to Paris, hang out for a bit, and then drive to Bonn. I took the Chunnel on the way over and the ferry on the way back. I drove to Paris and was having fun, but then I decided to drive to Rome, as I had never seen the Vatican—particularly, the Sistine Chapel. I drove 120 miles an hour, and made it to Rome. I would be able to spend about two days there. I knew I was presenting in Bonn, but I didn't know when my paper was scheduled—whether it was on the first or the last day—so I couldn't be late. I was able to tour the Vatican and the Sistine Chapel, and I drove to Bonn from Rome. Both the Vatican and the Sistine Chapel were eye-opening experiences into the depth and reality of Christian mysticism. The Sistine actually seemed like a doorway to heaven, and the Vatican was deeply inspiring. I inquired whether the pope might be doing one of those mass blessings, or something of that sort, but was informed that he was out of town. I made it to Bonn in time for the conference, soon discovering that my hotel was just a few blocks from the house where Beethoven was born. I went down to have a look, but it was closed, and I was too busy to get back during the short hours it was open. All in all, though, it was a fun and fascinating trip.

In Monterey, while working for DLI, I'd found a great little cigar store and while endeavoring once more to read Hegel's *Phenomenology of Spirit,* which in many ways is quite dry, I got in the habit of going there at lunch and at dinner to have a cigar and work through the book. I did this for almost two years, getting to know the family who owned the shop during that time. I had done a similar thing while in Sunnyvale, reading the book for about a year and half during my morning and evening coffee shop stops.

It's a marvelous book that provides a theory of the development of philosophical thought and truth in man through the history of Western philosophy. It got me interested in reading others who discussed the history of the Western world in terms of psychology or philosophy. Goethe's *Faust* has a similar role in literature, in that it retraces poetic forms going back to antiquity, so I studied that for a while. Jung and Jungians do that a lot. Freud's last few books do that as well. I was quite pleased with my growing knowledge of the history of the Western world through psychological and philosophical eyes. A classically trained Jungian wrote a book called *The Passion of the Western Mind,* which details the history of the Judeo-Christian world through the eyes of Jungian psychology. This one I have read several times.

I was quite pleased with my practice at the time, but now somewhat suspicious of it. I wondered if I somehow had done something to trap myself in the split aspect of mind, where one part was mad, while the other was quite civilized and educated. I didn't stop and was somewhat obsessive about it, but, overall, I felt it was good for me. I also saw it is a defense against the repetition of the traumas of the original accident. I still saw impending doom around every corner, and so I had to constantly watch for and steel myself against possible tragedy. I practiced for about an hour and a half every morning and an hour every evening. I had dozens of practices that I had gathered over the years; some of them I used as the times dictated, but I had two or three main practices that I did every day, no matter what. The morning and the evening session each included a half hour of "just sitting."

I had finished all but the last three hundred thousand repetitions of my Vajrayogini practice and had the empowerment for the Chakrasamvara practice, but I could not find the time or money to do the required retreats. At this time, Shambhala International—the new name for the Trungpa group, which was now run by his son—offered the first four of the six yogas of Naropa to those who had at least the Chakrasamvara empowerment. I was quite motivated by this, had some vacation time from DLI, and was able to attend the empowerment and training. I was quite elated. After twenty or so years of practice, I was to be initiated into the highest teachings of the Tibetans. I had to remind myself that this in itself was not a confirmation of any sort of wisdom or enlightenment, just more practices that a person qualified for as a result of getting through the required previous commitments, but I did feel way cool. I was a little disappointed in the crowd at the training, in that many of them were still engaging in the grotesque behaviors, but this was more subdued than it had been during previous years. I enjoyed the training, and, overall, I was quite pleased to be a practitioner of the six yogas; it was almost a kind of reward after twenty-five years of practice.

Over the years, my reading had included a fair amount on shamanism: mostly Eliade and Campbell, but also a few others. The six yogas were actually a concise, insightful, and fully developed training in basic shamanistic techniques: traveling in dreams, warming the body with mystic heat, and so on. The training never mentioned that these were the core shamanistic techniques, but I recognized that they were from my reading. I anticipated, based on my previous experience, that I would find the techniques elucidating, and that I would have at least minor and occasional success with them. Over the next year of practicing them, I found my dreams became cooler, and I would get enough of a sense of warmth in my belly to know the techniques really did work. In general, it is in long-term retreats that people get genuine successes with these techniques, but I was more determined to a have a full life with a practice than to become a mountain yogi in a cave somewhere, so I was satisfied with my level of success. I also had some hope that this would lead to the resolution of the difficulties I was still having, helping me to be able to go about my life without constant fear of impending doom—and without having to constantly fend off real tragedy. I also had some hope that the noise from the crowds would die out. The six yogas are the techniques that actually result in miraculous abilities, but achieving these would require the years of solitary retreat. I was just hoping for a little "magical" assistance with ordinary daily life.

Around this time, Yumi came to visit me. We discussed the possibility of marriage in brief, somewhat abstract terms. After she left, I worried that that discussion might have invoked the curse or jinx that I had been dreading for the past twenty-nine years. And, regardless of whether it did invoke it, from that point on, my relationships with the captain and others in the department, and with the whole of DLI, took a severe turn for the worse. I no longer had the implicit support of the Acting Chairman, as the self-study was essentially done, and the accreditation team visit was scheduled. However, there was some warning from others. Three other civilian employees seemed to have been pushed out by the captain. Nothing was said and nothing was apparent, but something was going on. Whenever I talked about how much I enjoyed the captain's tenure there, the ones who were pushed out would warn me about a darker side of the captain, which I had not seen. At one point he confided in me that he had been hired to fire people. I watched my acquaintances around the facility, and I soon noticed that a lot were being run out; there were many EEO complaints and so forth. It actually looked like they were purging liberals—something again reminiscent of communist or fascist thinking, purging those who might pose a growing political threat. It also seemed they were purging the targets.

Although DLI is a US Army installation, the teachers are mostly civilians, and the civilian American employees are far outnumbered by the foreign ones; and, as these are all from oppressed parts of the world, a mentality of oppression and collective thinking actually went further than one of freedom and individualism. As the students were bound for positions in foreign countries and in intelligence, a lot of people played spy. Basically, there was a lot of room for learning about the cultures in the hot spots of the world, and the security checks would weed out any true spies, but it still seemed that the culture at DLI was tinged with a lot of spy mentality., Instead of playing New Age or Klan or whatnot, they were all playing spy. I didn't like the mentality much, and, to some degree, it seemed the military preferred the civilians not play those games, but it was difficult to get along if you didn't indulge it at least a little bit.

By the time the captain shifted his attitude toward me, I had again become a target for a lot of people. This was when a co-worker told me, "Once you make someone the pariah, it takes the pressure off everyone else." A truly gutless attitude for my money, but there was no stopping it. I did have growing skills to combat it, but nothing that could permanently or effectively stop it. I did discover that, for some reason, they could not get a complaint about it and could not be called on for it. They had to keep everything on a passive-aggressive level to make complaints difficult to lodge. More than complaints to themselves, they especially feared complaints over their heads—and, more than anything, written complaints over their heads. However, written complaints done too often or too hard could backfire; they were most effective as a kind of revenge if you ever got laid off.

So, after six months of a positive relationship with captain—during which time, I could do no wrong—things changed to a situation where I could do no right. Outside his office things were still good, but behind closed doors he would suddenly turned on me, acting and sounding like a drill sergeant upbraiding a new recruit during basic training.

The most telling example of the whole situation was a circumstance where I was scheduled to give a one-day workshop on learning styles at the California Foreign Language Teachers Convention. It was a very nice addition to my resume, and I was anxious to go; however, the official nod from the Director's office had not yet arrived, and some of those who were scheduled, particularly those who were not presenting, would not be funded to go. Two days before the convention and one day before I was to give my workshop, the workshops being a day earlier, the Commandant and the Director finally met to make their decision. I went to the captain to get some guidance on what to do. I met with him and his female, civilian assistant. The meeting was almost eerie. It had all the qualities of a corporate meeting where someone gets laid off. The air was thick with that sort of intensity, and it was clear I was a target of some sort. Whether they wanted me to go or not was completely unclear. I had gone through all the ropes and was waiting for final permission to attend the conference, which I had not yet received. I explained that I could not wait until the following day, as that was the day I was scheduled to present (in the morning, to be specific). We were near the end of the day, and everyone was waiting. He said I should just go without permission, but I suspected that if I did he would not support me. He would say someone else found out and forced him to write me up, or something of that nature. I left with the feeling that whether I went or not, with or without permission, the captain would turn it into some major offense. If I didn't go, he would say I was wasting money; if I did go without permission, he would say he was forced to take disciplinary action—and even if I went with permission, he would make trouble.

I called the union, thinking they might have some inside information on the matter, as they were following the situation closely and would be the first to know. They told me to check with the Provost's secretary. This was at five, and everyone was leaving for the day. They told me to talk to the Provost. He was an acquaintance of mine from accreditation, and I felt I could stop by easily enough. I went to his office but didn't find him, and so I went home. That evening, I called the sergeant who did the scheduling for our department and explained my dilemma. He suggested that I go up to San Jose in the morning and check directly from there, where the convention was being held. If they said no, I would just be an hour or so late for work, but with a good explanation. I doubted that it would be that free of complaint; but I didn't want to miss the convention if I did have permission, and I didn't want to give the presentation if I did not have permission. So, with my stress levels at the highest they'd been in a long time, I went to San Jose. I called in the morning and was cleared to give my workshop. I thought this would be the end of it, but, sure enough, the fact that I had checked around to find out if I could go turned out to be a major offense.

I saw my job falling apart around this push to get me out, so I went to the EEO office and to the union to see if they could help me; and also to prevent a wrongful termination, or to start building a case for one. These were supposed to be confidential exploratory meetings, but, somehow, the captain found out and was furious. Officially, he was not allowed to be furious, as these were ordinary offices available to all employees, but he was furious. Through the union, I brokered a deal with the captain: I would see a counselor and take some courses in getting along with others, and, to get him to ease up, and I began to complete these.

A few months more went by, and, on the day of my contract renewal, I was let go; no negatives on the notice, but I was let go. I felt that the accident was repeating again and that it was because I'd had the temerity to discuss marriage with Yumi, which had invoked the curse. That was the only thing that could explain the recent chain of events. Within a few months, I was near homeless; I couldn't find work, my unemployment was running out, and I was all wrapped up in the intensity, paranoia, and darkness of the flip side of my psychology. I was somewhat limited in the jobs that I could apply for because of my leg, but there still were jobs that I could, and did, apply for; nevertheless, no one e-mailed or called in response. I send out resumes, but nothing happened.

To top it all off, I was sick. Shortly before leaving DLI, I had volunteered to give blood at one of their blood drives, and I found out that I had hepatitis, both B and C. Over the past ten years, I had been feeling weak and had other miscellaneous symptoms, but I had attributed it all to stress and age. I learned what the symptoms were, soon discovering that the symptoms of hep C were worsening. I had a biopsy, blood work, and other tests, and soon found that I was quite ill. I could hardly work more than a few hours a day, but I could not determine whether it was the hep C or some kind of a depression or meltdown. The DLI layoff had been kind of the last straw. I really felt that nothing was to any avail—that whatever I had that worked or that was appropriate for me would end up in ruin, and the squawkers were happy to take credit for my troubles, seeing me as somehow deserving of ill treatment.

After the layoff, I did lodge formal complaints with the EEO and the union, eventually mailing these to two senators and one congressman. I even sent one to the local office of Leon Panetta, who became Director of the CIA in 2009 and Secretary of Defense in 2011. He'd been a congressman from this area years ago and was always known as a friend of the DLI. My theory that written complaints would bust up the dynamic was the main reason for writing the letters. I had no money for a lawyer and was forced to represent myself, which did not end well. I got a formal hearing; but, when I got there, I quickly noticed that I had no ability whatsoever to cross-examine the captain or anyone else, so I lost. Cross-examination is just not a skill that comes up very much in academia.

As a part of my research for the complaint, I looked up websites that are working with a dynamic in the culture called "mobbing and bullying," not just for children but in the workplace as well. In this research I discovered a growing awareness of the targeting mentality in the US, Canada, and Europe, as well as attempts to pass legislation to attack the problem, making supervisors and employers financially responsible for careers that are ruined because of this mentality. These are very difficult cases to prove, as most of the mobbing and bullying is done with passive-aggressive innuendos, rather than with traceable attacks, but there is more and more success in the area. Some of the websites seem quite paranoid, but many of them are responsible, offering clear descriptions of the problem and possible solutions.

After the complaint, I was able to continue my morning and evening practice until I actually did lose my apartment. I was able to stay in the same place for a while, because I found roommates; but, when they left, I couldn't replace them, and so I couldn't make the rent. By this time, with the failure of my business and my growing financial problems, I had a credit problem that made it difficult to find a place to rent. At the last minute, I remembered that the owner of the cigar shop's mother-in-law rented out rooms and asked if she had one available. Fortunately, she did, and I found a nice, inexpensive place to stay, without needing to go through a credit check.

I continued to get weaker. I wondered if the knowledge of the hep C was making it worse, or if the progression was just something normal that happened to be occurring at the worst possible time. I had no insurance now, no money for medicine, and the doctor I'd been going to wouldn't see me anymore because I had a balance on my account.

I could hardly do anything. I got resumes out and applied for jobs, but I was devastated by the whole experience. The job at DLI, which had been the best job I'd ever had turned into a nightmare. It was the Peace Corps and the accident all over again. Now I worried about losing my car, my apartment, and everything else.

I found some work doing medical transcription but was barely able to survive; I lived like a college student or a hippie. I still called Yumi twice daily, worried that she would see me as a tramp or a bum, but this never happened. She was always supportive and cheerful. She even loaned me a little money a couple of times when I almost lost my car or something of that sort, but she was not exactly wealthy herself.

I took a few months now to begin a more serious study of Dante's *Divine Comedy*. I also took some time to read the Cliffs Notes for Milton's *Paradise Lost,* and found this to be an answer to the question of why Jesus Christ was the "one and only" savior. I had never really understood that, but the Cliffs Notes made the point that original sin—the sin of Adam and Eve—had to be purified. The Jungians pointed out that, as the act in the garden was an act of man, it could only be redeemed through a human sacrifice, and it would have to be a sacrifice of the son of God, as he alone was not tainted with original sin. God couldn't take back the gift of free will and just fix it all, because we would all dissolve back into him, so he sent His son instead to fix it, thereby preserving free will. Thus, I imagined that the entirety of the Western world—the Judeo-Christian world as we knew it today—arose out of that sacrifice, and, once that was done, there was no need for any further sacrifice: the sin was purged, and there would be no need to repeat. We wouldn't necessarily get things as good as the Garden of Eden, but the progress of the Western world, so largely based on at least the first eighteen hundred years of Christianity, would be better.

I was quite fascinated by the *Divine Comedy,* this early fourteenth-century work, because Dante had based it on a review of the Catholic church's literature of hell, purgatory, and heaven as it appeared at that time. More than its just being a poetic rephrasing of this material, I couldn't shake the idea that it was a genuine experience—something more than a dream; rather, an actual experience of the states of mind that one enters after death, but as configured by membership in the Catholic church. I saw it as a sort of Tibetan Book of the Dead for Catholics. I didn't read the poem itself at first, I just pored over the notes and introductions in the Penguin edition; though, at one point, I did force myself to read the entire poems at one point. The notes included maps and drawings of the various realms, and this was quite elucidating. I read these through several times, making notes and trying to memorize the major parts of the journey and the characters therein—not so much the historical figures, but the angels and demons that populate each area.

I also noticed some remarkable parallels between Dante's trip to heaven and the Tibetan views of ascents to heaven via the six yogas. In the dream yoga, it is possible for a well-trained and experienced master of these teachings to visit heavens, hells, and so forth, and, in order to make the journey, they go through a series of semihallucinatory steps to reach the heavens. These semihallucinatory steps matched Dante's heavens in many ways, so I was a bit more convinced that Dante was not just a Catholic historian but somewhat of a Catholic yogi or shaman. I made a chart to look at these things side by side to test my theory. I included a few extra categories to help my study.

The Tibetans call the first level of stability achieved in basic sitting meditation "one-pointedness." After achieving this level, you advance to a stage called "simplicity," which is marked by the appearance of these semihallucinations. The first of these is that called "mirage," where the world seems shiny and sharp edged, and you see a kind of a hazy, little lake of blue in front of you. Next, the world is filled with a kind of grayish/whitish smoke; after that, you see fireflies, then a flame, then a white light coming toward you, then a red light surrounding you; and, finally, you experience clarity and vast emptiness. I was reminded also of many of the paintings and drawings of Freemasonry, which seemed to try to depict this same sort of experience, with paintings of altars in particular atmospheres that matched these semihallucinatory stages. I had enough experience of my own to know that the semihallucinations were real, and, with some practice, I could view them myself—I was not able to do this with the degree of clarity of someone who spends years in a cave, but I did it convincingly enough.

In addition to the Freemasonry images, I noticed that Renaissance and Baroque art seemed to be focused on the presentation of not just the personalities of Christianity, but instruction in these sorts of states as well. I didn't exactly get any Dante–type views, but I did get enough to convince me that there was something real in the images, perhaps just not as in-depth an experience as his poem offered.

Dante's trip to heaven is similar. You begin with transhumanization, and then you advance to the smoky-white of the moon and the pale faces there; from there, you travel to the countless lights of Mercury, the joyful lights of Venus, the yellow of the sun, the red of Mars, the white of Jupiter, with the corresponding display in front, and then to the darker hue of Saturn. After that, you reach the sparkling lights of the fixed stars, the nine orders of angels, and, finally, the clear light of the highest heaven, the empyrean.

I was actually a bit paranoid about talking about these things, as they are part of the secret teachings; but, as I am aware of books in print which discuss them—and, as I am also aware of the parallel with Dante—I felt it was safe to discuss them in these limited contexts. With all that I got from the secret teachings, I was always careful to be sure there was something in print in the Western view, and then I would talk about these things from the Western perspective. I took the Tibetan protectors seriously and didn't want to invoke their wrath.

I first noticed the parallel with Dante when I considered the first step in his trip to heaven—his "transhumanization"—as a complex and detailed immersion in the first semihallucination of the Tibetans, the "mirage." After that, the parallels all lined up pretty well, and I became convinced that Dante was telling of a journey similar to the ones told by the Tibetans of their travels to hells and Buddhalands. There is a need to split the flame of the Tibetans into yellow and red in order to accommodate both the sun and Mars of Dante, but everything else lined up very well. This was such a minute and plausible division that I found it acceptable, and certainly not a theory killer. There is a book currently available on this sort of travel by the Tibetans. It is entitled *Delog,* and it details the journeys of a young woman who goes into a semiconscious, sleeplike state for ten days. During that time, she travels to many heavens and hells, and the book chronicles her adventures and relates descriptions of those places.

Once I actually "saw," in correct sequence, the hallucinations described by Dante. This was semidirected by me, but it was quite real, just sort of sitting there in my room, a kind of half-real and half-dream hallucination. This gave me more confidence in my belief that Dante had some very real and very deep experience of these things, and that the Tibetans and the Catholics were not merely telling stories to entertain and control peasants, and also that the Catholics and the Tibetans were not that different from one another. On other occasions, to get this hallucination to repeat, but I only experienced it that one time. Much later, I did have two dreams on two successive nights that seemed to be a lesser view of what Dante had seen. The first actually did not happen while I was at home and sleeping. I was in a filling-station waiting room getting my car smogged, and I fell asleep; as I awoke in that last hypnagogic state before full wakefulness, I saw thousands of faces in a deep-yellow haze, which I figured was either Venus or the progression from Venus to the sun. The second dream did happen while I was asleep in bed the following night: I was standing in front of a stadium full of saintly authorities, and I explained my situation to them, sort of reporting to them the odd world I was living in and "telling on" the crowds and the crowd mentality. I saw this as a light version of

Dante's white rose. I remember myself very confidently saying, "Thank you for listening," as I walked on.

As far as I can tell, the Tibetans don't linger at the lower heavens the way Dante does. Instead, they go straight to the empyrean, where they look around, get instructions, and then meet with saints and Buddhas. I would love to have had such an experience myself, but I am unwilling—and unable—to do the years of solitary retreat that are required in order to build up the necessary state of mind. I also wouldn't mind having more of an experience of Dante's worlds, but, other than the one experience of seeing the "visions" in my room, and the two dreams, nothing that dramatic has occurred again. It seems that I must be working on both my meditation and study of the books in order to achieve that sort of experience.

Like the Tibetan's, Dante's universe is based on a flat earth. Dante's earth is surrounded by nine spheres. Hell is below the earth; under hell, is the bottom of the ocean, from which the mountain/island of purgatory arises. It is a little globe-like, as the ocean extends below the earth and below hell, but the countries are all on the surface. With the Copernican view of the universe, it becomes impossible to ascend to anywhere other than more and more physical planets; there can be no escape to heaven, and no experience of the spheres.

I was able to include Dante's worldview with my scientific Western training by taking the flat earth to include every place I had ever been—my own personal flat earth—and then seeing the moon, the planets, and so forth as providing a direct route to heaven. When you look up, it is easy to see the sky as a sphere encompassing your individual experience, and then to see the stars and constellations as a final spherical "roof," on the other side of which is heaven, with the spheres of the planets located "below" the constellations. The ancients actually viewed stars as "holes" in that final sphere, allowing the brightness of heaven to shine through. The planets delineate the intermediate spheres; so, for instance, if you ascend to the level of Mars, you have reached the fourth heavenly sphere, and then you can meet the residents there.

The nine spheres correspond to the different levels of heaven, and to specific celestial bodies, in this order: the moon, Mercury, Venus, the sun, Mars, Jupiter, Saturn, the fixed stars, and, finally, the empyrean, which is the residence of God and also the resting place of the most-developed souls. After the experience of transhumanization—or, in the Tibetan view, the establishment of some degree of stability with simplicity or mirage—you begin to ascend, and each level of Dante's heaven corresponds quite nicely with the semihallucinations of the Tibetans; however, Dante lingers at each level, including the lower ones.

With the mirage, you ascend to the moon, where you experience the same whitish smoke as the Tibetans do; but, with Dante, it is much more detailed and explored to a much greater degree. You look more deeply into the smoke, seeing pale faces within it, and, in Dante's case, actually meet and talk to the residents there. This is the first level of heaven, which is for those who broke vows in their earthly existence. The next stage is the fireflies; again, in Dante's view, this level is expanded and looked into more deeply, seeing the countless souls of the heavenly sphere of Mercury, as well as the residents.

I was now able to explore Dante's hell and purgatory with more confidence and more determination, in order to get the sense of the organization of the whole thing. I am not aware of anything in the standard canon of Vajrayana Buddhism that would equate with the Western concept of purgatory, but I did once hear a lama refer to a "good hell," which certainly fits the bill, as it described a hell that was cleansing rather than merely punitive. Purgatory was easier to understand than heaven or hell, which was hardest to work out an understanding of. Only heaven matches up with the semihallucinations, as far as I could tell. Hell is accessed in a different way, more like a descent into a bad dream than an ascent; and a view of purgatory requires the trip through hell. You have to go under the earth, pass through hell, and then get to the bottom of the ocean, where the mountain/island of purgatory rises up, upside down from the point of view of the earth.

What I found particularly interesting about the whole thing was that it all involved a flat-earth theory of the universe, and it even mitigated against Galileo, Copernicus, and others, as their theories would not ascent through the heavens. Their theories merely expand the earth to an unnecessary degree. I became more of a flat-earth believer, thinking of Galileo's world as looking into the dirt, and, furthermore, thinking the Catholics had good reason to be angry about what Galileo had been doing.

I also saw a microcosm/macrocosm parallel in my body with that of the world I exist in. The flat earth was at my heart; hell was underneath and equivalent to digestion; and the conical shape of purgatory I saw mirrored in my legs, making the garden of Eden at the top of purgatory actually located upside down at my feet, thereby requiring the trip through hell and purgatory to get there.

Purgatory is organized according to the seven deadly sins, where each of the seven primary levels purges you of those sins until you arrive at the highest and final level, breaking through to arrive once again at the garden of Eden, the earthly paradise. I considered a deepening connection with all this and with what would eventually improve my current situation—and which, of course, would be good for anything that happens after death. Each of the seven levels has a sin, a virtue, a benediction, an angel, and a standard punishment. As I looked at them, thinking of them in terms of Jungian psychology, I began to see that there was a psychological logic to all of it as well; and so, I decided that, along with Freud and Tibetan Buddhism, Dante would remain a lifetime study.

Pride, the first and most difficult of the levels in purgatory, struck me as the same as the narcissism that is so popular today—and that so characterizes the crowd mentality that exists today. However, as the crowds are not willing to look into their pride, I suspected they are more likely bound for hell than purgatory. The pride of purgatory must include some awareness of it, some effort to work on it, or at least the recognition of it as a vice rather than a boon.

I had originally read *Purgatory* while working at the Barnes and Noble. After completing it, I had a dream that very closely paralleled the pageant of the seven maidens. My dream had a gargoyle-like monster pulling a wagon, just as in Dante's story. This gave me a feeling that I had properly read the poem and made it through the initiation it contained. I hoped this would improve my life circumstances. Perhaps the job in Monterey was a positive transformation that came from that reading. I had also hoped for a complete clearing of the stress, panic, and darker side of my mind, but this clearing never occurred.

Hell, while perhaps the most fascinating, is the most complicated and the hardest to get a handle on in a daily-life, practical-psychology way. However, when I first noticed that the first level—the foyer of hell—consisted of people running back and forth, constantly chasing a whirling, changing banner, I realized that this was exactly the same spin as the crowds of squawkers. With that realization, I began to understand. Just as the squawking will follow any banner that presents itself as the mainstream, even if it contradicts itself on almost a daily basis, the first level of hell represents that crowd mentality. The organization of the hells into circles seemed to me to represent the tendency the squawkers have to form "circles," and to believe they are part of elite circles. I began to see them as future denizens of the particular circles of hell. In looking at the crowds of troublemakers as denizens of hell, I was able to see Dante's picture much more clearly, and I wondered if he wasn't having a similar experience to mine in his daily life while writing the poem. Alternatively, perhaps he and I both just experienced the same inescapable realities of life on earth, which would regularly manifest in lesser or greater forms, such as the hell of Nazi Germany or the tragic farce repetition of it in today's crowd mentality.

There are demon-like guardians for each of the major sections of hell. One of these is guarded by the Minotaur, a creature with a bull's head and a human body. In order to get by him, it was necessary for Virgil, Dante's guide through hell, to shout an insult at the Minotaur. I took the Minotaur to be a representative of the anal-aggressive fat white guy, and, as I was walking to the cigar store to work on my memoir, I saw one of them in front of me grabbing himself as though he were doing me some sort of favor. I shouted, "Cut it out, you fat pig!" I seemed to be free of that sort of dynamic in my life.

Hell is basically broken up into three sections, each with numerous subsections. The main division into three is the easiest to follow. These are the sins of youth, which involve incontinence, and which are called the sins of the leopard; the sins of middle age, or violence, which are called the sins of the lion; and the sins of old age, or malice or fraud, and which are called the sins of the she-wolf. I could see some aspect of the crowds illustrated in each section.

At this time, I had to rest after doing everything; but, somehow, I still managed to get to the cigar store about twice a day, and I began writing. Just walking two or three blocks or going grocery shopping required a rest of an hour or more. I didn't know it if was the hep C or a relapse of the PTSD of some sort, as I said; but, in any case, I was weak, and my muscles were atrophying, which is symptomatic of hep C.

On the daily trips to the cigar store, I wrote three screenplays, and now I am working on this memoir. I can get in about two hours a day, fit in between medical transcription and constant resting. Everything I do requires a rest of equal or longer duration. I also managed to market the screenplays a bit, receiving a few requests to read them, which encouraged me.

In the upper levels of hell, there are those punished for lust, greed, gluttony, and so forth. I found that "seeing" the people around me as representing those particular levels would actually modify their behaviors a bit. The fact that they all seemed to belong to circles of friends that participated in similar ways in the world made me think that the circles of hell represented just that aspect of the dynamic.

The deepest hell, where Satan himself is present, is a hell of ice, not fire. The prisoners there are actually embedded in ice. This is the place reserved for those who were traitors against family, neighbors, country, and God. I immediately saw molestation as an action that leads to the deepest level of hell, as molesters are traitors to family and neighbors, and their coldhearted violence against their victims is aptly represented in the ice.

Satan himself is portrayed in a rather typical form, but he has three heads: the first is Judas, the second is Cassius, and the third is Brutus. Judas represented traitors to God; Cassius and Brutus, traitors to country. I thought this left a gap, in that traitors to family and neighbors was missing; so, for the image of hell that I held in my mind, I modified it, keeping Judas in the front mouth, Cassius and Brutus together in the right, and then adding Hitler, Stalin, and Mao in the left mouth as traitors to family and neighbors—or as traitors to the people (the peasants). Naturally, I worried that I would rot in hell for the arrogance of co-opting Dante's design, but I still enjoyed the new image I'd created, and I felt it completed the picture. Satan is chewing on their upper halves and tearing the flesh of their bottom halves with his fingernails.

I was enjoying this study immensely, making charts and musing over it, trying to see the semihallucinations of heaven, and so forth. It also helped with my practice of four of the six yogas. It deepened my understanding of the crowds, even heightening my compassion for them. This compassion was something I lacked in many ways. The crowds were so intrusive, embarrassing, and infuriating that it was very difficult to be compassionate toward them, especially as they were all educated, and so they all should have known better. They were not medieval peasants, and their superstitious behaviors betrayed their education. I could muster neither a Christian attitude of love nor a Buddhist sense of compassion for any of them, except perhaps those in the groups who were open to curing the dynamic rather than just indulging it.

While all this improved my understanding and education, nothing really touched the constant sense of impending doom, the darker side of my mind, and the fact that my life really did constantly relive the accident in lost jobs, lost friends, and potential loss of everything.

Freud agrees that trauma repeats, but he never finished his theory on it. I wondered about the possibility of ego libido being the source of the problem. Most of Freud's theory talks about life traumas causing a regression of the object libido to unresolved fixations of infantile life. In later years, he separated libido into two forms: ego libido and object libido. Object libido was that which attached to other people in your life, and it was involved with love, friendship, and sexuality, and traumas of early life caused unconscious fixations that you would regress to when similar things happened.

Ego libido, that which attaches to things, was essentially narcissistic; a part of it attached appropriately to oneself as good self-esteem, and another part attached to objects. I assumed here that he meant physical objects—things—because he argues that object libido is a product of the instinct for love, and ego libido arises from the instinct for hunger and survival. Love attaches to other people, and hunger attaches to things.

From the point of view of object libido—love—a trauma will cause a regression, and that will, in turn, return to points of fixation of early life. So, if you had traumas in early life, the regression will cause things to be re-experienced in a similar way. In my case, I had a pretty good sense of regression and fixation points, but I was unsure of the results for ego libido. Because the ego libido develops out of object libido as the individual matures, I thought it reasonable to suspect that ego libido would undergo similar processes as the object libido, but not necessarily identical. It struck me that the fixations and regressions in the ego libido would have effects in the physical world; in short, would work like PTSD.

Ego libido doesn't exist until the ego develops, and it is attached partially to the self and partially to objects. However, Freud never said this, but it seemed to me that a trauma which occurs in the adult may also leave an imprint or a fixation in the ego libido that then repeats in the same way a fixation of the object libido causes repetitions in a regressive form. A trauma will then cause a double regression and fixation: one within the object libido and one within the ego libido, the latter being the one that accounts for PTSD. When similar circumstances to a trauma recur in daily life, I suspected one would regress to the original trauma of conscious life via the ego libido and to the original, unconscious trauma of infantile life via the object libido, leaving a person tense and childish. Thus, the problem of PTSD would be that of a freezing or fixation of the object libido in a manner reminiscent of the original trauma, and this is what needs to be repaired or "unfixated."

Finding this explanation satisfying, I tried to look at narcissism from this new point of view, where traumas of adult life both cause a regression to the fixations of the object libido, as well as to the fixations of the ego libido, each one causing its own repetitions—one in the sphere of psychic life and one in the sphere of reality, the world of things. It seemed also to explain the dual nature of my mind, where real or seeming repetitions of the circumstances of the accident would cause the object libido to regress to a place of previous fixation, and the ego libido would regress to the actual accident, where all the assorted assaults on my life and person would recur. So, any time real life circumstances threatened, the dual nature of the original trauma would be reinforced causing the repetitions in the ego libido through re-enactment of the adult scenario of the original trauma and the regression in the object libido, which caused repetitions of the fixations from early life and the family of origin.

With this in mind, I needed to look at the narcissism that is proper to myself (that is, normal self-esteem) and the narcissism that is proper to objects and gets withdrawn in the face of trauma, reattaching with excessive narcissism onto the ego libido proper to oneself. I had to now figure out how to untwist the ego libido, to undo the fixation from the original trauma, and to get it back, in a normal way, onto the objects of my life. I concluded that the withdrawal of libido in the face of the repetitions causes the narcissism, as Freud said, but also reattaches onto the self-esteem that is damaged by the original traumas; good self-esteem in the face of impending doom would then be the only defense. It would keep the object libido from withdrawing and attaching to the "shape" of the original trauma imprinted on the primary narcissism. The shape of the original trauma would be the self-esteem of that original trauma—the self-image, the shocked self-esteem. Good self-esteem lets the object libido proper to objects return to objects in a positive way; panic, worry, fear, and anxiety in the face of impending trauma then pulls in the object libido, resulting in both narcissism and a repeat of the original trauma.

I then revisited all the major scenes of the original trauma, perhaps better termed the long line of connected traumas: the decision to cross the bridge; the moment of the accident and calling out Deb's name; the inability to see her or help her; the sight of my leg; the original feeling of shock; the ride in the back of the truck; and so forth. Touching in with each of them, I tried to master the anxiety of the original moments, and also to disentangle both the object libido pushing me to infantile psychology and the ego libido causing the traumas to repeat.

For years, I revisited a moment in the hospital in Wiesbaden that was particularly distressing. It was when I suddenly remembered that I had not had insurance at the time of the accident and had not yet transferred my international driver's license into a local one. I became extremely frightened and overwhelmed, thinking that everything would be blamed on me, and that I would be in no end of trouble for it—even worrying that the Togolese police might be the next to walk through the door. I thought about this again in 2010, but this time recognized it as a displacement of all my feelings of regret and fear at having been the driver of the vehicle that caused Deb's death, a displacement of all the survivor guilt, and then the repression of it. All the feelings surrounding that were displaced onto the incidentals of the license and insurance. In recognizing this, I had a feeling of tremendous relief, and I felt that this was the way to undo the fixations in ego libido. I once more began revisiting all the major points of the accident, working to undo the fixations and the twists and turns of it all. I began to see the characters in the frozen part of my imagination as reversals of something. The frozen image of Deb being angry at me, for example, I took, instead, as my being angry at her, and then this loosened. Unlike the fixations in object libido, which are largely unconscious, these fixations were all conscious, and so I could look at them more directly. The only blocks were twists like that of the displacement of feelings of responsibility for Deb's death onto something trivial, such as the license or insurance.

It was also necessary to interpret each scene correctly. To use the same example, by recognizing that the fear of not having insurance and no local driver's license was in reality a displacement of the feelings of responsibility for having been the driver when Deb had died, I was able to undo that fixation. It was necessary to undo any displacements, or reversals of intent, in order to get to the true feeling, which, in turn enabled me to undo it in the ego libido.

And, amazingly, it began to work. It was depressing and enlightening and liberating. Each moment was important and had to be revisited. Of particular importance was the shouting of Deb's name as we flew through the air. For years, I had no idea what the underlying feeling was; but, when I saw it as a feeling similar to a little boy who had just dropped the baby he was holding, I recognized the feeling. The last thing Deb's father had said to me before we left was, "take care of my daughter." The feeling and the shouting had to do with "Oh my God, she'll be hurt or worse!" I had dropped the baby and was afraid for her; I felt responsible and at fault, all at once, and I called out her name out of that feeling. Discovering this was extremely liberating, and the ego libido—the good self-esteem, or "vanity"—seemed to return, while the ego libido of secondary narcissism seemed to release itself from of me and go back to the world. I had met the original feeling and mastered the anxiety, thereby returning a good bit of myself to myself, and a good bit of my world to my world.

The squawkers, in trying to slight others, are seeking to damage self-esteem, to push their victims to withdraw their effective object libido onto themselves, causing the repetition of their victims' traumas. However, in order to do this, they need to withdraw their object libido onto their lowered self-esteem, and, thereby, trauma repeats for them as well; and then, once again, they blame their targets, creating a never-ending cycle of abuse and blame.

The Buddhist concept of egolessness always struck me as a major problem for Westerners; not that it was just difficult, but that it conflicted rather dramatically with Western concepts of ego in a way that just leads to confusion, which further leads to the particular confusion of the crowd mentality. The healthy ego and good self-esteem that constitute Western ego is far more like egolessness than the Buddhist sense of ego, and it seemed to me people were turning up in centers anxious to learn the Buddhist concept of egolessness; but, rather than working with ego clinging, they were undermining healthy ego and good self-esteem, confusing that with what they had to let go of and looking for something to replace it with.

Ego clinging seems much more in line with Freud's concept of secondary narcissism: the pretenses to godlikeness that were causing such troubles. Having been raised in a culture where healthy ego and good self-esteem are what everyone is trained to think of as ego, they mistakenly tried to let go of that, and then they settled on the secondary narcissism as the Buddhist enlightenment, a complete reversal in the two cultures: what we call "ego," they call "enlightenment"; and what we call "narcissism," they call "ego" (or, perhaps, "ego clinging"). And then, out of confusion and an interest in enlightenment and egolessness, they take the pretenses to godlikeness as wisdom, and the healthy ego as neurosis.

Obviously, this is a complete reversal, and the source of much of the confusion, where the pretense, presumption, and delusion of narcissism is taken as enlightenment, and the narcissism itself is more than happy to see itself as enlightened. This explained a lot to me, but it seemed to be a problem that was almost without a resolution, as everyone is still being raised with this reverse terminology used to describe particularly subtle states of mind. With the countless books and Buddhism and Western psychology all being deeply established in the culture, and with no one addressing this issue, it seemed that Western Buddhism was destined to go on creating narcissists in the name of enlightenment and egolessness, promoting the worst and blaming the best, all in an honest and heartfelt effort to cure neurosis.

The first truth of Buddhism is the truth of suffering, recognizing there is a problem of suffering to be addressed. The second is the source of suffering, and this is ego clinging. However, I think it may be safer to say it is secondary narcissism. The good self-esteem (or "vanity") of ego, primary narcissism, is just fine, but clinging to a sense of self, clinging to ego, is the result of withdrawing ego libido from the world and onto the primary narcissism as secondary narcissism, and then the world no longer works: trauma repeats, and pretenses to godlikeness—or sainthood, or siddhi, and so forth—prevail. The problem is that the secondary narcissism thinks it is getting things and influencing the world, when, in fact, it is doing just the opposite.

The Vajrayana practices also work in a Freudian kind of way. I saw the internal visualizations of the Chakrasamvara practice as replacing fixations of the object libido with pictures that would untwist them. Most of the Freudian fixations seemed to me to exist at the level of what they call the "secret place," which is the area below the navel. The brightly colored, uplifted visualizations would then be counter measures to the fixations of early life, obviating the need to go through the entirety of the Freudian process to find and undo them. In my case, I was doing both, and so I did not know why I was so bad at the visualizations that I could not have forgone the entirety of my study of psychology with the practices. Not that I regretted the study, it was a great hobby, but if the visualizations were working on the same sort of thing without the need for all the analysis, why did I need all the analysis-like study? While I saw how the Tibetan practices worked on object libido, I did not see how they worked on the ego libido. The efforts at egolessness were perhaps the place to see this, but it is difficult to see how egolessness would correspond with good self-esteem.

I saw Vajrayogini practice, which includes a visualization at the level of the navel, as one that was designed to free up this sort of fixation of the object libido. I did not immediately see anything that would work on the level of the ego fixations, but I endeavored to find something of this nature as well.

Given the abuses of the Chinese—the murder, imprisonment, and torture of monks, lamas and nuns; the destruction of temples—everything else that they have forced on the Tibetan people for the last fifty-plus years had undoubtedly caused tremendous problems of this nature for the Tibetan culture. I saw the Chinese as inhabitants of the circles of Dante's hell, and the Tibetans as sufferers of PTSD. However, I have only heard one Tibetan Buddhist description of what PTSD is. In this explanation, the trauma causes the lower winds to rise up, and this creates the difficulties.

For the Tibetans, the body is run by five primary winds that conduct the functions of daily life: the life wind of the breath; the upper wind, which manages speech; the lower wind, which manages sexuality and excretion; the middle wind, which handles digestion; and the all-pervading wind, which handles muscle function. The lower wind, which separates good from bad in terms of excretion, is the one that rises up and causes the problems of PTSD.

This explanation was satisfying in some sense, but I couldn't connect it directly with the ego libido, and I also wasn't aware of what to do to prevent the difficulty. I also had little to no direct experience of what these winds would be. Perhaps the five winds taken together were what constituted ego libido: when they are functioning correctly, you have good self-esteem and a good relation to your world; when disrupted, they cause symptoms of dis-ease.

After the fiasco at DLI, I was able to manage to see a therapist for a while. She was quite nice, as they all usually are, and quite helpful. She convinced me after a while to get some prescriptions from my doctor to manage my stress. Like the yogis of medieval Tibet or Chokyi Nyima's mother in Parphing, Nepal, I was trying to do everything without drugs, trying to wear out the karma so that these things would never recur in this life or in future lives. I also was afraid I was merely burying the real issue under a drug-induced haze—or, even worse, that I might turn into one of the squawking crowd, most of whom I assumed were all on these kinds of drugs. However, she argued that PTSD and shock were the result of physiological processes that also had to be addressed. I agreed to try. I mentioned this to Lama Rinchen, wondering what he might think, and he warned that I could get an addiction.

I was given Prozac and Klonopin at first. Both were good in the beginning, but they later became quite debilitating, so I stopped taking them. I then tried Wellbutrin, with similar results: at first it made me feel better, but then it became debilitating. The whole time I was on Wellbutrin, I was unsure about whether I was just being foolishly incautious—that the traumas were going to repeat without my seeing them coming, in which case, they would be far worse, and so I tapered off that as well. Soon I was back to my familiar self.

Through my ongoing practice, there were occasionally moments of clarity and emptiness like that discussed by the Buddhist teachers and books, but these were short-lived, and my life never seemed to turn around from one of constant promise and a good buildup followed by complete loss, particularly around issues of relationships, home, and work—all of which seemed to parallel the basic outline of the Peace Corps experience, where everything built to a strong beginning, but then would come crashing down.

So, the pretensions to godlikeness that would come over me in the face of social slights and genuine disappointments in life had to be seen as the withdrawn libido, to the sticking point of the original trauma; and, somehow, it needed to be released or untwisted or disentangled—or something. This also seemed to explain the split in my mind. Letting go, in principle, is a very simple thing to do. Just drop what you are doing and reconnect with five-senses experience; but, in reality, this was easier said than done., The wilder part of my mind was the fixation of the object libido, and the calmer part was connected with the ego libido. Both had to be "untwisted" before I could go about in a more normal manner. I was also able to see it as the lower wind rising up and getting stuck. The stuck place was now seen as the fixations in ego libido. I wondered if there wasn't some sort of fix that I wouldn't even notice, where the lower winds would just stay low, and the stuck places would unstick.

Freud also speculated that the way to recover from a trauma was to master the anxiety that overwhelmed the individual at the time of the original trauma. Looking at my life on the couch now as a repetition of the hospital, and my two trips a day to the cigar store as a repetition of my getting through to lunch and dinner in the hospital, I tried to reinvestigate the accident again. Only this time, I wanted to "see" it from the point of view of the withdrawal of ego libido and the concomitant narcissism, and then try to let go of the pretensions to godlikeness so that I could let the good self-esteem stay with me and everything else go to objects. I returned to more dream yoga as well, hoping to get a helpful dream on the matter.

I had met over the years a number of men who had lost their wives or girlfriends, and, true to form, they all saw it as a life-ruining event from which they never really recovered, living without much of a social life or any deep relationships, and always feeling constant threats to their security.

I was able to see a psychiatrist for the PTSD, once the Peace Corps insurance agreed my condition was caused by the accident. He wanted me to try drugs, and he recommended one specifically used to treat PTSD—a drug called Perphrenazine, which is an antipsychotic, but, which, in very low doses, works well for PTSD. I agreed to try that, as well as Cymbalta, hoping to find a magic cocktail of modern drugs that could take care of any physiological aspects of the disorder, and, after two or three months, it actually began to seem that way.

I was continuing my reading, but my practice was way off due mostly to the fatigue of the hep C, and I was now receiving treatment for that as well. I also felt the drugs were becoming debilitating, and they further hurt my ability to practice.

One morning, I was lying on the couch just sort of daydreaming, and it occurred to me that I felt very much like I was lying on the couch in the house in Lama Kara; on several occasions, I could have sworn I saw Deb in the crowds in the city or on the road as I drove past, but, this time, rather than being angry, she was smiling and cheerful, sort of checking in with me.

Having made the new discoveries about PTSD, the recognition of the need to revisit all the points of the trauma from the point of view of accurately representing the feelings that underlay them all, I also decided to revisit the entirety of my knowledge of myself from the point of view of Freudian psychology, so that I could revisit this as I revisited the trauma. Rather than seeming off-putting or daunting, the endeavor seemed to more and more streamlined and more and more effective. I self-diagnosed myself with the following: bits of paranoia; moral masochism; melancholia(depression); PTSD; and paraphrenia. I addressed these, in turn, by: noticing a minor repressed stream of infantile homosexuality; regarding my family of origin in terms of both love and hate, rather than a vacillation between the two; revisiting the trauma points; and, finally, not letting the forces of repression have the upper hand.

12

Blaming Japhy Rider—2010

... incomparable blind streets of shuddering cloud and lightning in the mind leaping toward poles of Canada & Paterson, illuminating all the motionless world of Time between ...

—ALLEN GINSBERG, "HOWL"

In about 1990 or so, I had the temerity to write a letter to Allen Ginsberg, enclosing a sample of my poetry and asking if he wouldn't mind reviewing it. To my surprise, he answered, writing his review of my work on the back of the letter I had written him. In his own hand, he commented that my writing was a "head trip," and that I should read more Kerouac. He also told me that Trungpa's poetry had been positively influenced by discussions with Allen and some of the other beats. I was quite pleased to have heard from him at all and made a mental note to read more Kerouac. I never wrote that much poetry, anyway; but, as I was writing somewhat in the Tibetan style, I was curious about Allen's take on it—on anyone's take on it, actually. I suspected that Allen just wasn't sure if he knew me or not, and so he'd responded "just in case."

It took me quite a number of years to actually get to reading Kerouac as Allen suggested, and, at around the same time, I decided to write this memoir. I read Kerouac with Allen's advice in mind, and also with an eye toward getting some sense of how to write a memoir. My writing experience was limited to lots of academic material and a couple of screenplays, so I needed some idea of what to do with a memoir.

While in Monterey I would frequent a bar that was an old Steinbeck haunt, just up the street from Cannery Row. I wondered if Kerouac had been there. Big Sur, a place he had visited and a title of one his memoirs, was just forty-five minutes away, and he may have stopped in, looking to chat with Steinbeck. I checked around a bit and found out the 102-year-old owner of the bar remembered Steinbeck but had never liked him. Steinbeck was a bit of a drunk, according to her, and would often mooch drinks from people. I thought about asking her directly about Kerouac, but her daughter and caretaker told me that her memory was failing, and so I didn't want to bother her. What was really interesting to me was that the woman was still able to come down, which she did on Thursdays, when she would have a few drinks. On her 102nd birthday, she actually had eight drinks and left a bit drunk.

Steinbeck and his friends also had a habit of scooping up drinks deserted by exiting patrons, mixing the leftovers into a cocktail, and then drinking that to save money. I checked around some more, and a couple of guys in their nineties said the pictures I had printed out looked very familiar, but they couldn't say for sure if they knew him. In his memoir entitled *Big Sur,* Kerouac discusses Monterey, but pretty much just as the last bus stop from San Francisco on the way to Big Sur. He had to hitchhike the last forty-five miles. He was waiting for a bus at one point in Monterey on his way back to San Francisco, and he wandered the streets of Monterey a bit, but there is no mention of him going into the city far enough to look for Steinbeck. It sounded to me like Kerouac just wandered around close to the bus station. The Steinbeck haunt is about two miles away.

I chose Kerouac's *Dharma Bums* for the first book to read. At first, his reports of the beat study of Buddhism heartened me; but, later, I was aghast at these descriptions, his depiction of the poet, Japhy Rider, in particular. Kerouac was very widely read by the beats and the hippies. The dharma bums—that is, the Buddhists who were traveling around different centers or just reading on the subject—also read a lot of Kerouac. I am sure millions of copies, at least, were sold. What bothered me was that Kerouac, in his ever-generous and gentle manner, described scenes with Japhy Rider having sex in the Tibetan ritual style on the floor, during parties and with multiple partners, and Japhy always encourages others to do the same. Kerouac never criticized Japhy; further, he reported that Japhy said that the Tibetans were like that, and that this was what Tibetan Buddhism was all about: cross-legged sex on the floor in front of other people. *A great Chinese lie,* I thought.

At first, I thought it was irresponsible for Kerouac even to report such a thing, but then I decided that, as he wasn't that much of a scholar, he might actually have believed Japhy. It would be difficult to know, as Kerouac always reported gently rather than critically; but, in the memoir, Kerouac comes off as too shy and actually too respectful of women to have tried the Japhy variation on the Tibetan practice himself. But, as Japhy had pretenses to being an expert in Zen and things Buddhist—and, as his translation of Chinese Zen Poetry into English gave him a bit of credentials in the area—I thought that he should have been more discerning and less licentious in his rapid jump to conclusions on the Tibetan lifestyle. There is certainly nothing to suggest that he had done any reading or practice that would have led him to those orgiastic conclusions—other than credulity in the face of critics of the Tibetans, those who would dismiss the entirety of the culture and the religion with that one foolish lie.

The hippies were aware of the Kama Sutra, but that was always correctly taken as a Hindu text, not a Tibetan one, and there is a significant difference between Hindu tantra and Buddhist. There may actually be more sex in Hinduism, but I sincerely doubt that they are having sex in the living room at marijuana parties with casual friends and acquaintances. Hinduism talks far more about relating to the gods as existent personages, while Buddhism takes them as archetypes. The Buddhists even criticize the Hindus, as the latter argue that the living personages of gods do indeed exist, but the heavens they inhabit are not ultimate heavens but temporary ones based on sensual pleasures rather than transcendent ones. The Tibetans I had met, both secular and religious men and women, seemed sexually conservative—perhaps even a little repressed, and certainly not wild-eyed hippies hopping from lap to lap in a drug haze at parties. I was aware that the Chinese also spread stories like this about the Tibetans, and it bothered me no end to see Kerouac and Japhy spreading these same lies about the Tibetans. I also hated that the same stupid stories were cluttering up the reputations of all the good Buddhists in America, particularly those studying Tibetan Buddhism. Even worse, the book has been read by millions of beats, hippies, literature majors, and many, many others, and this put a deep and lasting blot on the record of Tibetan Buddhism, all because of the naiveté of an oversexed culture and a couple of guys with a strong but untutored interest in Buddhism.

Every culture has their excesses I am sure, but, at the time of Kerouac's writing, the beats were experimenting, the hippies were just around the corner, and Kerouac was almost mandatory reading. Both Kerouac and Japhy seemed to have absolutely no knowledge of the years of practice that were required before engaging in the legitimate practice of Tibetan ritual sex, and they also seemed to have no idea that there would be strict, well-defined limits to it—that it was not a free-for-all at a drug-fueled party open to anybody with an amorous look.

The book also indicates that Kerouac and Japhy had very poor ideas of what constitutes a "boddhisattva." Boddhisattva is a term used to describe a kind of Buddhist saint; specifically, someone who has achieved a permanent stability in the experience of emptiness. They would sometimes half-seriously call themselves and people they met boddhisattvas out of what seemed to be a genuine and heartfelt appreciation of the concept, and a genuine effort to understand it; and yet, at other times, they seemed to believe that they and the people they encountered really *were* boddhisattvas, which is extremely unlikely, given their understanding of Buddhism and their behaviors. There was also no reason to believe that they would be good judges of the matter, and some of Kerouac's friends indicate that his character judgment was more than a little bit questionable. I had also seen that a lot in the crowds around Buddhist centers. They start by good-natured joking about boddhisattvas and enlightened people, but they end up believing it without any sound reason.

I could pretty much leave Kerouac off the hook for slandering the Tibetans and making them look like a culture of out-of-control hippies; however, I had to blame Japhy Rider and the credulous readers for spreading the lies and for so darkening the scene around the Tibetans and Tibetan Buddhist centers. Kerouac was merely reporting what he had experienced, whereas Japhy was misrepresenting an entire culture in a very careless, self-serving, and licentious manner. I now understood, though, how those crazy ideas about Tibetans and Tibetan Buddhism had gained such weight and expanded to such a miserable degree—as well as why Zennies and those in Tibetan Buddhism all thought that everyone involved in Tibetan Buddhism was some kind of Japhy Rider or a Japhy Rider wannabe. The Zennies are very educated and well read, especially in literature, and I am sure they were seeing Japhy—or looking for Japhys—in everyone who attended a Tibetan lecture.

Such stories as Japhy perpetuated only serve to invite perverts and give good ordinary practitioners a bad name. The entirety of the canon of Buddhist literature does not describe anything as tawdry as Japhy's behaviors, and the one sexual practice that does exist, is between adult men and women who have undergone years of training in meditation—the Ngondro and the *sadhanas*—none of which Japhy Rider had done. The books also do not describe the practices. They are considered highly secret practices, and they are only taught to long-term practitioners. Japhy Rider did seem to do a little Zen-style sitting in that book—not a lot compared to genuine practitioners, but some. Maybe he did more in later years. It is also unclear if he had formal training, classes, or a relationship to a qualified teacher. It more seemed that they read haphazardly on the subject, based on what was popular. D.T. Suzuki, Alan Watts, and so forth; those two, in particular, were considered hacks by serious teachers.

I saw Japhy read his poetry one time in Honolulu. His poetry was quite good, but it was more beat than Buddhist, and he seemed arrogant and dismissive to me; but, then again, that is a characterization that could apply to many, many Zen practitioners. Ann Waldman read at the same reading, and I was more impressed with her, although I found her a little aggressive and tricky. Japhy no longer seemed like the wild man described in Kerouac's books, as he was much older and perhaps more refined through actual practice; nevertheless, I still blame him for much of the problem in Tibetan centers and for much of the mistaken ideas people have regarding Tibetan Buddhism. The lamas are likely to be completely unaware of the book and its influence, because few of them have either the English skills or necessary interest to read American literature. Hence, I wonder if they have the same impression of Americans that Americans often have of them: everybody thinking there is some sort of weird sex just around the corner or in the next book they are going to read, and no one recognizing that the mainstream of both cultures simply is not that wild or careless. Both cultures must be wondering, Where the hell did all the perverts come from, and where the hell did they get these ideas about us?

The Tibetans and the followers of Tibetan Buddhism are as conservative as Catholics, but, instead, they are viewed as hippies or worse, and no one seems able to get an accurate perception on the whole of Tibetan Buddhism without the interference of the Japhy Rider–type misrepresentations. I don't completely blame Japhy, and I don't completely blame the credulous readers, but I am disappointed and embarrassed—not just for me but also for the Tibetans and the serious American practitioners of Tibetan Buddhism, as well as for the crowds' spreading of what seems to be nothing more than communist lies or hippy delusions. If people would take the time to actually read about Buddhism, they would recognize the lies and delusions for what they are; but, in the meantime, the crowds, still influenced by the Chinese, Kerouac, and Japhy, continue to misread Tibetan Buddhism in this way. As the madness in the crowds always seems to be largely about sex, I wondered if this may have been how the madness got into the culture. From the book, to the centers, and then into the wider culture through the frequent nationwide travel and gossip, giving the go-ahead to perverts, and turning off and running off those who were not.

I came to think that this one misunderstanding—this one bit of confusion, published in a book that was widely popular not only among hippies and beats but also among Buddhists and scholars and the literate, coupled with the mobility of the major Buddhist groups—had led to an outbreak in the culture of a mass hysteria. However, hysteria didn't quite cover it, and I was anxious to identify it and find a cure for it. If an individual can rid himself of a neurosis, a culture must be able to do so as well, and I thought it was of crucial importance to at least know what the neurosis was, and what the cure would be.

PHILIP A. BRALICH, PH.D.

I thought about Freud's theory of paranoia a lot. I was interested in it because it centers around a large complex of symptoms that arise from a simple underlying cause, and I suspected that the problem in the crowds had a simple underlying cause. As I thought about this and the symptoms, I began to notice a rather odd parallel in the culture that seemed to account for the problem in the crowds, as well as all the symptoms. For some reason, the entirety of the phenomena in the crowds seemed to be a direct reversal of paranoia; if this were so, there might be one simple underlying dynamic that would explain it all, and that would also suggest a cure.

In Freud's, and in most theories', estimation, paranoia is primarily characterized by a withdrawal of libido from the world. The withdrawn libido is then reattached to the ego, creating megalomania; the typical withdrawal of ego libido from objects and onto the primary narcissism then leads to the type of narcissism that characterizes all the paraphrenias. This is what Freud called "secondary narcissism," where libido that is properly attached to objects in the world is withdrawn, instead becoming attached to the normal, good self-esteem of the ego. The megalomania leads to delusions of persecution, grandeur, and reference, where the individual thinks that everyone is talking about and/or against him. There is a strong dislike of social slights, which can set off an episode and a strong feeling of being rejected. Freud states that this disease is difficult to cure, but it is easier to cure than psychosis or schizophrenia. It is easier because it is still trying to reconstruct the world, while the psychotic or schizophrenic no longer makes any effort toward repair because he is completely lost in repression. The paranoiac invents wild theories and end-of-the-world scenarios that explain the feelings of persecution, and the very fact that the paranoiac is still inventing these theories indicates he is still trying to reconnect with the world and is still interested in returning his love to the world. With schizophrenia, the situation is worse, because the mechanism of repression wins utterly; there is no attempt to reconnect or reconstruct.

For Freud, the source of paranoia is a repressed bit of infantile homosexuality that is unconsciously reinforced, causing guilt and shame and forcing the withdrawal from the world. This also explains why many paranoiacs have multiple heterosexual relationships and erotomania. Those manifestations compensate for that unconscious bit of infantile homosexuality that exists in the unconscious, and they also represent an effort to resist and disprove it.

Thus, in his view, all libido development goes through several stages: the first, called the autoerotic stage, is that of an infant; next is a homosexual stage, which is followed by a heterosexual one. The individual traverses these stages before the age of five, and then goes through them again at later on in life, each time with successively more genuine sexual overtones. The homosexual stage of infancy is the sticking point that causes paranoia. Of course, this stage does not mean that an infant is having frank homosexual thoughts; but, rather, that the original libido going through a stage as it learns to make appropriate object choices. However, if a disappointment in the world causes a fixation at that point, paranoia can result. The real sexual thoughts do not occur until secondary sexual characteristics of puberty begin, and, at that time, none of the infantile ones are in consciousness.

The entirety of the crowd neurosis seemed like a direct reversal of paranoia in this classic Freudian sense: delusions of individual grandeur are replaced with delusions of everyday membership in a grandiose elite; delusions of reference are replaced with delusions of being able to refer to complete strangers accurately; delusions of persecution and rejection are replaced with delusions of acceptance, believing that everyone accepts all the pretense, presumption, and delusion at work in the squawking. Highly developed theories are replaced with confabulation and expeditiousness; the unconscious stream of repressed homosexual impulses are replaced with a consciously expressed stream of homosexual pantomimes and acting out, and a concomitant repressed heterosexuality. The shame and fear are repressed, leading to a tolerance of the grotesque behaviors. The fear and dislike of social slights are replaced with a desire to slight others socially. I made myself a chart in order to look at this more closely. (*See* chart in Appendix 1.)

It all lined up so perfectly that I could not help but think I had discovered a major neurosis—or, better yet, a paraphrenia that Freud himself had missed—that I named "agoraphrenia," that I considered to be a cultural phenomenon similar to the mass hysteria of Nazi Germany, and that had broken out across the Judeo-Christian-Buddhist culture in the West. I coined the term from the Greek *agora,* meaning "marketplace" (as in, "agoraphobia," which is the fear of the marketplace, and, by extension, the fear of crowds and/or public humiliation) and the Greek—*phrenia,* "meaning "a disordered state of mind." Thus, "agoraphrenia" describes the problem of the disordered state of mind regarding crowds, the marketplace, the targeting, the bullying, and so forth.

Like one of the plagues released on the world by the angels in Revelations—or like "the plagues no one had seen before" predicted by Trungpa Rinpoche—I was looking at an international plague that threatens the very lifestyles of the entirety of the Western world and perhaps more. And yet, those who can do anything about it are unaware of it, and, even worse, unaware of what to do about it.

I saw it as present in communism, the madness in the crowds, in the Klan, in racism, perhaps even in the fascism of World War II, mistakenly labeled as mass hysteria rather than as mass agoraphrenia. And I saw it as caused by the deliberate refusal to feel guilt and shame in the face of defiling human dignity—or, even worse, defiling human dignity in the face of one's own commitments to man's and God's laws. I did not see it not as a wisdom or a siddhi or a God-given gift of a spiritual boon; rather, I saw it as a curse or a punishment from God, visited upon those who deliberately reversed their commitments to others and engaged in the crowd behaviors of mobbing and bullying.

As the cure for paranoia is the recognition and subsequent sublimation of the repressed stream of infantile homosexuality in the unconscious, it is reasonable to conclude that reverse paranoia could be addressed by the recognition of that conscious bit of homophobia and by a sublimation of it to a higher purpose—such as the purposes to which most of these people had already committed themselves: decency, respect, generosity, or charity—using precisely the energy of male-on-male and female-on-female sexual harassment as the fuel of decent, civilized, uplifted behaviors, instead of the constant indulgence in the grotesqueries and the constant excuses made for it. Healthy heterosexual behaviors are repressed in order to engage in the agoraphrenic behaviors, and so the cure for these behaviors must be a return to healthy dating behaviors, which will "unrepress" the heterosexuality.

It may also be reasonable to assume that the condition itself is caused by a deliberate refusal to take one's commitments to the virtues of one's vows and obligations seriously, and, instead, to take indulgence as renunciation and indiscipline as discipline; it is like a punishment from God, or bad karma in the face of deliberately defying one's own commitments. And, certainly, to abandon utterly the belief that the behaviors cannot or must not be stopped until someone else stops them, or until they wear out. They will not wear out. They can only worsen if not addressed. They can only be recognized for what they are, and until an effort is made by the sufferer to recognize and stop them, nothing will change, and the entirety of our known world will collapse into a whirlpool of primitiveness and peasant behaviors and superstitions. As they convince themselves and one another that they are some sort of a spiritual boon for the world, they are getting deeper and deeper into the underworld—and more and more into their own bad karma, squawking their way into more and more confusion, and more and more narcissism.

The cure for the condition, however, is simple. As repressed healthy heterosexuality is the cause that needs to be recognized and unrepressed, and it seems that the way to work on this is with a sexualized good self-esteem, as with vanity and a slight flirtatiousness, in order to be sure that the heterosexuality is not withdrawn or repressed. Vanity and a slight flirtatiousness should get rid of communism, the Klan, the squawkers, the evil side of the right wing, and all the problems that plague modern society, which have plagued us since the dawn of time. Collective thinking can also be mitigated with this one simple strategy. Targets may not be just those who are in shock, but also those who are fertile, fresh, and flirtatious. Freud's efforts to release the sexual frustrations of mankind are undoubtedly a great contribution to this effort. (Hugh Hefner as well, though things might be a bit overdone there.)

Freud always pointed out that object libido was an aspect of love, and, in freeing the forces of love—that is, the forces of vanity and flirtatiousness—we can defeat the enemies of mankind, and join with the Christians in creating a world based on love, not hate.

The writing of this memoir, the investigation and internalization of the cures from Freud, and, particularly, the extension of Freud's theory of PTSD, all has combined, during the past few months, to help my head begin to clear. As a result, the dark side of mind has begun to diminish, and my need to scan for potential disaster is significantly diminished. I am quite confident that this will continue. My understanding of Buddhism is improving, and it is becoming more coordinated with the Freudian system and with other Western perspectives.

In particular, I have begun to reduce all my Buddhist musings to emptiness, clarity, and noncontinuity, combined with a bit of Dante. Seeing the vastness of the sky as unending (in a Dantean sense, not a Galilean one) and as the nature of mind, and seeing all that occurs within it as nothing other than the flash of the ever-changing sights and sounds of mind, and meeting any sense of continuity of it all as an invite to agoraphrenia, I focus on noncontinuity. This further clears my head, and it makes room for the Freudian clarity to take further effect.

My head clears, the sky is blue with wisps of clouds, and the crowds seem friendly, cheerful, and welcoming. I anticipate only good things from this point on. I have begun seeking out agents and publishers for my screenplays and for this memoir, and a new friend has introduced my software to a decision maker in a nearby city. I hope to give a demonstration soon.

Colophon

. . . Peyote solidities of halls, backyard green tree cemetery dawns, wine drunkenness over the rooftops, storefront boroughs of teahead joyride neon blinking traffic light, sun and moon and tree vibrations in the roaring winter dusks of Brooklyn, ashcan rantings and kind king light of mind . . .

—Allen Ginsberg, "Howl"

Several times during both Catholic grade school and high school, I was forced to write five-hundred-word compositions after school as punishment for bad behavior. I never had any idea what to write, but I always started with the scenario of a student misbehaving as I had done, following it through the five hundred words to the end of the world because of the original misbehavior. I can now look back at this current composition to see that I may have presaged something in myself in those early catastrophic works; I have now fulfilled a life purpose by writing a composition that warns of the end of civilization as a result of seemingly harmless misbehaviors.

. . . who chained themselves to subways for the endless ride from Battery to holy Bronx on benzedrine until the noise of wheels and children brought them down shuddering mouth-wracked and battered bleak of brain all drained of brilliance in the drear light of Zoo . . .

—Allen Ginsberg, "Howl"

Appendix 1: Charts

Table 1: Comparison of Paranoia & Agoraphrenia

Paranoia	Agoraphrenia
Delusions of individual grandeur	Delusions of group elitism or mainstream membership
Delusions of reference	Delusions of being able to refer to the unknown lives of others
Delusions of persecution	Delusions of acceptance
Theory-making to explain	Confabulation and slander to confuse
Erotomania	Homophobia
Guilt and shame	A near shamelessness in all behaviors
Fear of social slights	Desire to slight others socially

Table 2: Dante & Tibetan Buddhist Cosmology

Cantos	Planets	Sights	Sign	Angel	Lights	Consciousness
XXX-XXXII	Empyrean	Elect seated on pure-white rose	River of light with flowers	Trinity	Clear Light	Clear Light
XXVII-XXIX	Primum Mobile	Moved directly by God	Nine glowing circles	Seraphim	Pink	Instantaneous
XXII-XXVI	Fixed Stars	Church Triumphant/ Christ on Cross	Angels tending to Christ's wounds	Cherubim	Blue	Alaya
XXI	Saturn	Countless lights around a ladder	Loud sudden sound	Thrones	Red	Klesha
XVIII-XX	Jupiter	Silver/gold banner and eagle	Diligite	Dominions	White	"I"
XIV-XVII	Mars	Bands of light	Red glow	Virtues	Yellow	Body
X-XIII	Sun	Two circles of saints	Yellow	Powers	Butter Lamp	Tongue
VIII-IX	Venus	Spheres	Joyful lights	Principalities	Fireflies	Nose
V-VII	Mercury	Countless lights	Countless lights	Archangels	Smoke	Ear
II-IV	Moon	Taken inside	Pale faces	Angels	Mirage	Eye
I	Flat Earth	Transhumanization	Two suns		Mélange	

APPENDIX 2

E-mails from Buddhist Email Discussion Lists and Letter from Alan Ginzberg Commenting on My Poetry.

From:	bounce-shambhala@list.shambhala.org on behalf of Philip Bralich [pbralich@earthlink.net]
Sent:	Thursday, May 26, 2011 10:40 PM
To:	'Sangha Talk'
Subject:	Poem: Seeing the Other Sky

Trungpa Rinpoche one time said that "Sky gazing is a very important practice." I have done a fair amount of this in my time in this valley of tears and have begun to think about the other sky, the sky of vast mind, rather than the sky of daily routine, foolish control, and fools gold. With my rather meager understanding of this concept, inspired by my trip to Hollywood and having a couple of beverages in Bukowski's old haunt, I thought I'd try to put it in to a poem, remembering that Allen Ginsberg told me my poetry is a head trip and that I should read more Kerouac.

Seeing the Other Sky

In the midst of truth, justice, beauty, wisdom and courage,
The sky immortalized on the Sistine Chapel,
Choirs of angels sing, and the Renaissance and Opera are born.

In the midst of the book of five rings,
The sky of the Sun Goddess Amaterasu shines
and Kami frolic, laugh and cry

In the midst of the flat earth and the spheres of heaven
The Sky of Mount Olympus opens
And the Olympian Gods mingle with the masses.

In the midst of the mind of romantic love immortalized by Dante and the legends of Arthur,
The crystal river of heaven with its bed of radiant flowers,
The Renaissance and Opera are born.

In the midst of Trungpa's efforts,
The sky of profundity and wisdom,
The fruits of spiritual materialism are transformed.

In the midst of all this, the world is refreshed and,
We begin to wonder of the glories of the wider world of Jambhudvipa and begin to dream of lost continents.

If you see the sky of wisdom, the other sky, you see the possibility of purified dependent truth
And the lessons of America, the Judeo-Christian tradition, and Shambhala,
Where there is no need to multiply theoretical entities beyond what is necessary to explain a phenomenon,
No need to dwell on UFOs but only to recognize that the Other Sky is where spiritual reality is clearly enough
To explain the spiritual traditions of the world.

1

Step Wise -- A Poem

From:	Phil Bralich <pbralich@earthlink.net>
To:	sangha-talk@shambhala.org
Subject:	Step Wise -- A Poem
Date:	Jun 22, 2009 2:24 PM

This is kind of a poem, but more of a review sheet I made to review the steps to the realization of Mahamudra. The only addition I have made from my personal experience is the view of "step wiseness" to the exercises. Mahamudra fans might find this a useful review sheet as well, so I decided to post it. Naturally as these are Kagyu notes, mahamudra transmission makes it easier.

Step Wise.

One-Pointedness: Mundane Consciousness analyzes itself

Brahman's thread without first learning tightening and loosening is not possible. Loosening the string around a sheaf of straw is not possible without the Brahman's thread.
Gazing like a child at smoke and fireflies is not possible without first loosening the string.
Preceding like an elephant pricked by thorns is not possible without gazing like a child at smoke and fireflies.

Simplicity 1: Supramundane Consciousness

The elephant pricked by thorns is itself the supramundane consciousness.
It is the union of the moving and non-moving.
Without knowing the moving and non-moving, they cannot be analyzed.
Looking at the moving and non-moving, like 2 sticks rubbed together, they consume themselves in the supramundane --
The intellect, that which looks on, is not separate from the moving, the non-moving or their union.

Simplicity 2: Supramundane Consciousness analyzes the mundane

Knowing the 3 times do not exist is not possible without the elephant pricked by thorns.
Knowing that birth, death and time do not exist is not possible without knowing the 3 times do not exist.
Knowing that mind is neither matter nor not-matter but something in between is not possible without knowing that birth and death do not exist.

Knowing that one and many, unity and plurality, do not exist is not possible
without knowing that matter and not-matter do not exist.

One Taste:

Knowing the body is sleep and phenomena dream is not possible without knowing that
matter and not-matter do not exist.
Viewing phenomena and noumena as water and ice, 2 forms of one thing, is not
possible without knowing the body is sleep and phenomena dream.
Viewing everything as an ocean and waves is not possible without knowing phenomena
and noumena as water and ice.

Non-meditation:

Nothing to do, but something to get used to.
Watch paint dry, pet a cat, play checkers, brush your teeth.

Without the step wise approach, it is possible to touch in with any of the above
(though usually just with mundane consciousness analyzing itself), but only with
the step wise approach can the yogin approach the stage where he is attached to
the path and his review sheets.

Phil Bralich

A nice quote from Evans Wentz

From:	Phil Bralich <pbralich@earthlink.net>
To:	sadhaka-talk@shambhala.org
Subject:	A nice quote from Evans Wentz
Date:	Jun 26, 2009 1:34 AM

This may not be too interesting to those who are not working with the Four Root Dharmas, but I believe it is not inappropriate to discuss on this list as it appears in many published texts and does not include any discussion of actual practices. It regards the Offspring Clear Light ("Son Clear Light" in some texts) and the Mother Clear Light. In Evans-Wentz' book, _Tibetan Yoga and Secret Doctries_, he discusses these two aspects of the clear light, saying...

"(11) By meditating thus [on the Six Rules of Tilopa]*, that which dawneth, as the Voidness and Phenomenal Appearances [the two aspects of a duality which in reality is a unity], is the Offspring Clear Light.

(12) The unobscured, primordial condition of the mind, which shineth in the interval between the cessation of one thought-formation and the birth of the next, is the Mother Clear Light."

(13) The recognition of that is the Blending of the Mother and Offspring Clear Light; and it is called 'Blending of the Nature of the Clear Light and the Path Into Oneness."

Now my question is: How does this relate to our flashing of ordinary mind? Is that flashing that we do, even for nongdro, in some sense a jump to the experience described in paragraph (13) or is it something other: a) something perhaps more preliminary? or b) Perhaps that which results in the discovery of (11)? As the flashing is the mahamudra transmission, I tend to think the flashing is (13) which, in later practices, is enhanced through discussions like the one above but am not sure. Does that ring a bell with anyone?

Also, I included the term "son clear light" because many texts have not made the translation to "offspring" and it has made me wonder if there isn't something in the relation between a boy and his mother that is different from the relation of giri to her mother that may have inspired that original form -- or perhaps just a kind of naive sexism on the part of the translator. This also has raised questions for me in the statement that "seeing the clear light at death is like a boy meeting his mother." Is "offspring" too general or is "son" just a little incautious on the part of the translators? Also if there was a note of sexism in the original, why wasn't "Mother Clear Light" changed to "Parent Clear Light."

225

Finally, the word "that" near the beginning of paragraph (13) seems a bit
ambiguous to me. I am not sure if it refers to (11) and (12) together or merely
to (12) alone, where in the former possibility you must work through both steps,
while in the latter, the recognition of the Mother Clear Light alone (rather than
just a knowledge of its existence) is sufficient to cause the blending of the 2
versions of Clear Light.

In any case, it is a very nice quote and I thought I would share it.

For those of you who are interested in more of this discussion, it can be found on
page 225 of the 1958 edition -- still available from used book stores though I
think it is no longer in print.

*This bracketing was added by me to avoid an excessively long quote, the other
bracketing is from the original. It refers to the well-known dictum of Tilopa
which appears in a variety of translations and a variety of orders and instructs
the practioner to "Imagine not, think not, analyse not, meditate not, reflect not,
keep in the natural state." That is the order provided in Evans-Wentz, I prefer
the one I saw on-line somewhere which said, "think not, imagine not, reflect not,
don't try to figure it out, don't control," which, for my money, more acurately
reflects the order one might find of the Buddha families on a mandala and may be
closer to the original statement.

Phil Bralich

Dream self and Bardo

From:	Phil Bralich <pbralich@earthlink.net>
To:	sangha-talk@shambhala.org
Subject:	Dream self and Bardo
Date:	Jun 28, 2009 2:16 PM

I was talking to a Lama a while back and asked him who travels through the Bardo, the daily conscious self or the dream self. He said it was the dream self which naturally makes us realize how difficult negotiating the Bardo might be -- we will only be as good at it as our dream self is. Thus, without rather stable success in lucid dreaming, our only judge of how dharmic we will be in the bardo is how dharmic we are in our dreams.

Still, perhaps just wishful thinking, I like to think that to some degree, I would be more conscious than my usual dream self. Has anyone else heard or read anything on this?

Phil Bralich

We the Americans Welcome We the Shambalians -- A poem

From:	Phil Bralich <pbralich@earthlink.net>
To:	"sangha-talk@shambhala.org"
Subject:	We the Americans Welcome We the Shambalians -- A poem
Date:	Jun 30, 2009 3:08 PM

We the Americans Welcome We the Shambalians

by Philip A. Bralich, Ph.D.

We of the lightbulds, telephones, and cars welcome
We of the Yumi's, brushes, and shrines

Moses, Jesus, Michaelangelo, DiVinci and Pope
Dante, Hegel, Freud and Jung our lineage holders
Welcome the Rigden Kings to the land where the iron
bird first flew.

Pianos, Suzaphones, timpani and opera (the highest achievement of mankind)
Welcome we of the ghanta, damaru and bowls

We of the Judeo-Christian-Buddhist tradition, welcome
We of the Shambhala-Buddhist tradition

We of the templars (warrior monks) welcome
We of the Shambhala warriors (warrior householders)
We of the wars that must be fought* welcome
We of the wars that must be fought.

We of truth, justice, beauty, wisdom and courange** welcome
We of profound, brilliant, just and all victorious
We of DeToquiville, Washington, Jefferson and Lincoln, welcome
We of Nagarjuna, Gesar, Trungpa and Gampopa.

We of Ginsburg, Kerouac, Hemingway and Poe welcome
We of Trungpa, Mipam and Milarepa.

We of Shakespeare, Chaucer, Spencer and more welcome
We of Marpa, Gampopa, Tilopa and more.

We of the 2500 year tradition of church and state, welcome

We of the Shambhala-Bhuddist beginnings.

We of the 2500 year tradition of church and state welcome
but also warn of wars that need not have been fought,
Picasso, Hitler and Nero.
We also warn of atomic bombs, arms races, and smog
Revolution and monarchies gone bad
Unspoken movements lurking evilly at your back door
Drunken, jealous misreadings of your views

We also warn of bad press which may at some date arise
As naysayers ignore your pianos, operas and Vaticans and look
only at your wars.

We of the 2500 year tradition welcome
We of the 10 year tradition
We of the Egypto-Greco-Roman-Dark Aged-mideaval-
classisict-renaissance-romantic-enlightement-modern
era welcome
We of the Buddhist-Kagyu-Zen-Shambhala-Buddhist tradition.

We wish us the same.

We supplicate our lineage holders. We welcome sparks of light.
We wish the best to both of us.

* "wars that must be fought" is a line from Trungpa Rinpoche somewhere where he
noted this unfortunate reality.

** "truth, justice, beauty, wisdom and courage" are for Socrates, as reported by
Plato, the 5 prime virtues which can themselves be no further broken down and from
which all other virtues arise.

YIJCSBD

Phil Bralich

229

Bullies and Mobs -- A doha of circumirential sniping

From:	Phil Bralich <pbralich@earthlink.net>
To:	"sangha-talk@shambhala.org"
Subject:	Bullies and Mobs -- A doha of circumirential sniping
Date:	Jul 3, 2009 4:44 PM

Bullies and Mobs
(or the old switcheroo*)

When birds squawk their pretenses to insight,
When vultures gather and animals lunge
When unspoken, unspeakable movements lurk evilly at your backdoor
Look at the desire for revenge as a whole,
Center yourself between angels and demons**
And relax in your everyday oridnary self

When perverts insist, they must do what they do
When they insist that it is tantric to do so
When they flash their beam of perversion at your mote
Look at your mote of perversion as a whole
Center yourself between Angels and demons
And relax in your everyday oridnary self

When slanderers and gossips insist
When kangaroo courts and vigilantes gather
Look at your sense of injustice as a whole
Center yourself between Angels and demons
And relax in your everyday ordinary self

When slanderers seek to protect you from slander with slander
When gossips seek to protect you from gossip with gossip
When inuendo mongerers seek to protect you from inuendo mogering with inuendo
mongering
When lunatics seek to protect you from lunatics with lunacy
When pretenders to kasung seek to protect you from pretenders to kasung by
pretending to be kasung
Look at your frustration as a whole
Center yourself between Angels and demons
And relax in your everyday ordinary self

When your good practice is met with hostile glares
When your ettiquette is greeted with backward bows
When your healthy social skills are met with unspoken, unspeakable movements

230

When your clear comments are dismissed with muddled thinking
When your straight speech is met with spin and double talk
When your single meaning is met with a double
Look at your desire for revenge as a whole
Center yourself between Angels and demons
And relax in your ordinary everday self

When tantra is treated as perversion
When right speech is passive aggressive
When right living is secretly perverse
When discipline is said to be indiscipline
And indiscipline the highest discipline
Look at your mote of indiscipline
Center yourself between Angels and demons
And relax in your ordinary everday self

Philip A. Bralich, Ph.D.

* "the old switcheroo," a muddled reference to something Trungpa Rinpoche once
said.

**"Angels and demons," meant to be taken as giving up clinging to good and evil.
Inspired by the quote from the
Sadhana of Mahamudra where it says something like, "As long as you cling to the
concepts of good and evil,
the world will continue to manifest as harmful demons and helpful goddesses."

Japanese Zen/American Zen: A Koan

From:	Phil Bralich <pbralich@earthlink.net>
To:	sadhaka-talk@shambhala.org
Subject:	Japanese Zen/American Zen: A Koan
Date:	Aug 14, 2009 12:06 AM

An American in Japan took up the study of Zen. He went to a teacher and was
introduced to the first Koan. "Does a dog have Buddha-nature?''
He knew full-well that Buddhism teaches that all sentient beings have Buddha
nature, but he knew the koan had a deeper purpose in mind.
He asked the accomplished teacher, "Does a dog have Buddha-nature." The teacher
replied "mu," a negation that does not translate well
into English. It is like "non-" or "un-" or "not" or "no" or some undefined
combination of all four. It is not the simple "no" as it is sometimes
translated. The American had no real response and no real illumination, so the
teacher sent him back to meditate. He would call him back on a semi-regular
basis to answer, "What is 'mu'"?

A Japanese in America wanted to learn English. He went to the ESL teacher and
asked "What is 'it'"? The teacher replied, "A third
person, singular, neuter, objective or subjective, indefinite, (im)personal
pronoun." The Japanese replied politely, "Thank you" and went out to
practice his English.

As the Japanese wandered the streets and coffee shops and bars and restaurants in
search of friends with whom to practice his
English, he would hear people sort of calling out to him, "that's it", "you've got
it," "tag, you're it," "you're it," they cried. He also heard others
call in repsone, "No, we've got it," "He hasn't got it," "I've got it," "He's got
it." "He's it," "That's it." He was somewhat confused by the exuberance
with which these statements were uttered. The speakers were so convinced they
knew what "it" was and who had it, and he honestly had no
idea what "it" was. He was no less clear on what "it" was from this practical
experience then he was from the explanation from the grammar
teacher. A cruel looking bartender moved toward him and said, "Now you're going
to get it." "We're getting it," wailed some strangers. He
heard a sister call to her brother, "Boy are you going to get it." His classmate
said, "I love Professor X. I always get it when he teaches." This experience
didn't help so much either, but it provided him with more to think about.

"What's mu?" mused and contemplated the American on his cushion in Japan.

"What's it?" mused and contemplated the Japanese on the streets and in the

establishments of America. "What's it?" he asked us. "What's
mu?" the American asked of the Japanese.

"It" and "mu." The American wanted to understand Japanese culture. The Japanese
wanted to understand American English. Some
Japanese believed that only Japanese could understand "mu." Some American's
believed that no Japanese could understand "it."

"What's mu?" wondered the American -- other's called out, "you've got it."

"What's it?" wondered the Japanese -- other's called out "that's not it."

The Japanese went to dokusan to explain his response to "mu" to his teacher, "It"
was all he said.

The American went back to his teacher and said nothing.

On a quiet mountain top, somewhere in the Himalayas a Tibetan yogi was
meditating. "Twain" cried the Tibetan on the mountain top for no apparent
reason. A Zen master in Hawaii quietly whispered "mu" on his out breath in spite
of his 50+ years of practice.

A Koan.

Philip A. Bralich, Ph.D.

Addendum to Japanese Zen/American Zen: 2 old poems

From: Phil Bralich <pbralich@earthlink.net>
To: "sadhaka-talk@shambhala.org"
Subject: Addendum to Japanese Zen/American Zen: 2 old poems
Date: Aug 15, 2009 2:12 AM

Poem written for Aitken Roshi's retirement ceremony about 10+ years ago and, while no one was looking, pinned
to the Diamond Sangha Palolo Zen center''s kitchen bulletin board, which he established ...

(No title)

No mirror, no dust
No robe, no bowl
What precious teachings flow
From the body speech and mind of this great teacher.

This second poem was written in about 1998 or around there after attending my first VY
fire puja. Be careful, the title is important.

For the Eyes of the Solitary Warrior Only

The War was never begun.
The Battle never ends.
Winning and Losing are costly Illusions.

The Solitary Warrior knows when to Engage.
Male a good dinner;
Be sure and place flowers.

Philip A. Bralich, Ph.D.

My Demented Fat Aunt; My Slender Poised Aunt

From:	Phil Bralich <pbralich@earthlink.net>
To:	"sangha-talk@shambhala.org"
Subject:	My Demented Fat Aunt; My Slender Poised Aunt
Date:	Jun 11, 2011 6:12 AM

I was raised Catholic in a family with six siblings. My father was from a family of 10 siblings, my mother of 4. They all got married and had lots of Catholic kids. We would frequently get together in our many big back yards where the men would drink beer, the women would chat and the many, many cousins would romp and play.

My demented fat aunt would always be watching the boys: she was terribly concerned that they were masturbating and wanted them to confess to her in great detail what they were doing. My slender poised aunt was always on the lookout for her and would warn the boys not to tell her the slightest thing even if such an unfortunate thing were to occur.

My demented fat aunt forgot that Catholics had priests and confessions or that somehow she knew better than the priests. My demented fat aunt constantly was saying that she knew what the boys did and wanted them to confess in detail and only she cold show them what to do. She would try to teach gross behaviors as a cure. My slender poised aunt would encourage the boys to sit up straight, play nice and be fair. My demented fat aunt wanted to tell the boys that she should arrange their dates and she would undoubtedly fix them up with lazy girls who didn't want to try and jobs that were well below their ability. She said they were following the scent of money and that the weight gain and lack of make up were the result of that. As soon as the money came they would clean up good. (I thought they were smelling the scent of butt and would only end up in latrines, but I never spoke like that in front of my slender poised aunt. My girlfriends and students hardly know I am capable of speaking like that.) My slender poised aunt would tell the boys that you win girls' hearts with gentlemanly behavior and interesting accomplishments.

When it came time to look for a girlfriend and go to the prom, my fondness for my slender poised aunt caused me to look for slender poised girls.

My parents seemed totally unaware of this and seemed to like both aunts equally or at least seemed to have little choice in the matter. I thought I caught my mother tearing up when she saw the slender poised aunt one time, but I was quickly redirected to a game of go fish. One time I saw my demented fat aunt wipe her brow toward my mother as if to say, "Phew that was close." I was quickly redirected to a group of kids who were picking raspberries in my grandfather's victory garden.

Do Buddhists/Shambhalians have anything like this?

Phil Bralich
A Judeo-Catholic Buddhist

From:	bounce-shambhala@list.shambhala.org on behalf of Phil Bralich [pbralich@earthlink.net]
Sent:	Wednesday, October 27, 2010 10:11 PM
To:	Sangha Talk
Subject:	Looking for a poetic response

Follow Up Flag:	Follow up
Flag Status:	Flagged

I wrote the poem "This" in response to John Tisher's poem "That." I was wondering if there was someone out there who could respond to my poem and address the problem expressed therein. The two poems are below my signature. A poetic response may actually be helpful to me a long term sangha member and practioner.

Phil Bralich

In response to John Tisher's poem, "That."

        This

This is clinging.
That is letting go.

No referernce point is that.
The poet is this.

Center and fringe are this.
No center and fringe is that.

That is compassion.
This is wronged.

I spend all day thating my this.
and yet I still this.

Dang.

Here is Jonn's original poem, which inspired the above.

That

is not this…
but, is it other than this?
is this part of that,
or is it separate from that?
this is merely a knot in that
that thinks therefore it am…
nothing personal…
nothing lasting….
nothing real other than
the illusion of That!

Philip Bralich

From: bounce-shambhala@list.shambhala.org on behalf of Philip Bralich [pbralich@earthlink.net]
Sent: Thursday, May 26, 2011 10:40 PM
To: 'Sangha Talk'
Subject: Poem: Seeing the Other Sky

Trungpa Rinpoche one time said that "Sky gazing is a very important practice." I have done a fair amount of this in my time in this valley of tears and have begun to think about the other sky, the sky of vast mind, rather than the sky of daily routine, foolish control, and fools gold. With my rather meager understanding of this concept, inspired by my trip to Hollywood and having a couple of beverages in Bukowski's old haunt, I thought I'd try to put it in to a poem, remembering that Allen Ginsberg told me my poetry is a head trip and that I should read more Kerouac.

Seeing the Other Sky

In the midst of truth, justice, beauty, wisdom and courage,
The sky immortalized on the Sistine Chapel,
Choirs of angels sing, and the Renaissance and Opera are born.

In the midst of the book of five rings,
The sky of the Sun Goddess Amaterasu shines
and Kami frolic, laugh and cry

In the midst of the flat earth and the spheres of heaven
The Sky of Mount Olympus opens
And the Olympian Gods mingle with the masses.

In the midst of the mind of romantic love immortalized by Dante and the legends of Arthur,
The crystal river of heaven with its bed of radiant flowers,
The Renaissance and Opera are born.

In the midst of Trungpa's efforts,
The sky of profundity and wisdom,
The fruits of spiritual materialism are transformed.

In the midst of all this, the world is refreshed and,
We begin to wonder of the glories of the wider world of Jambhudvipa and begin to dream of lost continents.

If you see the sky of wisdom, the other sky, you see the possibility of purified dependent truth
And the lessons of America, the Judeo-Christian tradition, and Shambhala,
Where there is no need to multiply theoretical entities beyond what is necessary to explain a phenomenon,
No need to dwell on UFOs but only to recognize that the Other Sky is where spiritual reality is clearly enough
To explain the spiritual traditions of the world.

1

```
------
Sangha-talk policy: one post per day.
More at http://www.shambhala.org/members/lists.html
```

... They Lied to the Buddhas

From: Phil Bralich <pbralich@earthlink.net>
To: "sangha-talk@shambala.org"
Subject: ... They Lied to the Buddhas
Date: Jun 15, 2011 4:36 AM

THEY LIED TO THE BUDDHAS
(Chanted like chanting the sides of cereal boxes on dathun day off.)

1.
2.
3. They lied to the Buddhas.
4. They lied to the Boddhisattvas.
5. They lied to Plato's forms.
6. They lied to the Protectors.
7. They lied to the Gods, the Kami, and God.
8. They lied to the asuras, the pretas, the demons, and animals.
9. They lied to the Kasung.
10. They lied to the humans.
11. They lied to themselves.
12. They lied to their friends.
13. They lied to their enemies.
14. They lied obsessively.
15. They lied pathologically.
16. They lied through their teeth.
17. They chortled with glee.
18. They's not Buddha; They's Rudra.
19. Offer warm-hearted Tong-len.
20. Don't forget the dissolve in the middle, as warm-hearted as you can.

Phil Bralich
"The only thing you own is attachment", sticky fingers.

(That was particularly difficult to punctuate and annotate. I have never seen an
appositive attached to a quote before, which is why I put the comma outside the
close quote. It was said by that Shambhala guy: you know that Tibetan son of that
guru guy in Boulder and now guru-ing himself Mr. Mipam Sakyong or something like
that.)

Specify your antecedents.

Philip A. Bralich, Ph.D.
26 Gartley Place
Honolulu, HI 96817
(808)595-8980

email: bralich@hawaii.edu

Allen Ginsberg
P.O. box 582
Stuyvesant Station
New York, NY 10009

November 20, 1996

Dear Allen,

I have been a student of the Vidyadhara since 1982 I have done Ngondro, Vajrayogini (up to
first fire puja) and I have been doing Zen koan practice with Aitken Roshi in Honolulu for about
six years. You and I met briefly (Summer of 82?) and we have nodded hellos occasionally since
then. I noted one of your poems on the bulletin board that year. Poetry has always escaped me
somehow, but recently (notably since fire puja), I find myself writing poetry, and it seems to be
somewhat in the Kagyu tradition. I would like to continue in this vein, but I know no one who
can comment or direct me in this interest.

I know you are a very busy man and you probably get tons of unsolicited poetry, but I wondered
if I couldn't impose on your good nature and our mutural membership in the sangha to ask you to
help me find someone who could help me develop in poetry writing. I have included the first
poem on this page and the others in the booklet that is inlcuded with this letter.

Thank you for your consideration.

Sincerely,

Phil Bralich

Phil Bralich

Dear Mr B — Not possible
to "help you find someone" — got a poet whose
work you like & study with him to the situation's
possible.

I don't like abstraction in poetry &
Can't stand dharmaspeak abstractions even
Vajrayanaspeak.

Even vidyadhara's poetry got more grounded
as he moved over mudra & First Thought, Best Thought
books (with Shambhala the latter out of print)
One Catalyst for his change of style was
a reading aloud of J. Kerouac's (over)

241

Mexico City Blues, which he said was "a perfect manifestation of mind", having laughed all the way from Teeth of the Tigers Vt. TO N.Y.C. as I read them aloud — there's now a 2 casette 3 hr. version published by Shambhala (audio) (or whatever they call it. That might be a good beginning.

Then I'd say forget about abstract Dharmic verbal Paradoxes as usually a head trip anyway, and read the Objectivist poets William Carlos Williams, 2 Vols. Paper <u>Collated Poems</u> New Directions, NY

Charles Reznikoff — <u>Collated Poems</u>, Black Sparrow Press, Santa Barbara

Carl Rakosi — <u>Collated Poems</u> American Poetry Foundation U. of Maine Orono Maine

That's a beginning, You asked my advice & that's it. Or take a summer off for the mid June to Mid July Poetics summer every year at Naropa Institute 2130 Arapahoe Ave Boulder Colorado

AGinsberg
12/2/90 9PM

242

A FABLE, SOME POEMS, AND OTHER PROJECTS BY THE AUTHOR.

Fable:

Where There's Smoke, There's Fire: or Drive All Blames Into One

A near-sighted young eagle dove from a precipice toward the rocky waters below for a fish he thought he saw. He caught his right wing as he dove and broke it. He tumbled clumsily into the water but was able to painfully pull himself onto the shore. He was unable to fly, in great pain, and alternately stumbled and rested about the shore at the bottom of the precipice.

A young yogin looking for a place to meditate heard of a cave called Kelly-Taco-Tom-Tap in the mountains surrounded by villages. He heard the villagers were Buddhist and would be helpful and sympathetic with his interests. He moved into the cave and began to practice.

The villagers heard of this and became curious. They went to Black Bear, the village shaman, and asked what he thought. The villagers reported that the yogin seemed to be talented and genuinely interested in the scene. Black Bear, who never practiced very much, was jealous and said, "This could not be true; I have seen this yogin's type before and know that type to be nothing but trouble," even though he had never met or seen him. The villagers didn't pay too much attention, and Black Bear felt threatened and even more jealous, so that evening, Black Bear went outside the village and started a fire of wet leaves and twigs to create a lot of smoke. The smoke rose to the height where the young yogin was meditating. The next morning the villagers awoke and saw the smoke and became afraid. Black Bear walked among them, leaving the fire to burn. "I told you," he said. "It's that yogin. That type is nothing but trouble." "Where there's smoke, there's fire," he cried. They looked aghast at the smoke and said, "Something must be done." They gathered below the cave and cawed. They raised their hoes and shovels menacingly. They shouted at the yogin. The yogin continued to practice thinking it must be some sort of mistake. They raised their shovels and hoes. They shouted; they cawed. Black Bear walked among them. "Where there's smoke, there's fire," he said again and again, raising the villagers voices to a feverish pitch. The smoke got in the yogin's cave. He coughed. His eyes teared up. "They're Buddhists, he thought. This will pass. They'll recognize everything is fine." As the smoke grew thicker and the day grew longer, the villagers fashioned nooses, built a pillory, hooted and cried. A kangaroo court was established, vigilante and vagilante parties were formed. The talk got more brazen. Those secretly belonging to gangs, said the yogin secretly belonged to gangs. Those who secretly molested, said the yogin secretly molested. Those who secretly killed, said the yogin secretly killed. The crowd became more determined.

Black Bear called out, "Where there's smoke; there's fire; where there's smoke there's fire" and snuck back down the mountain top to stoke the fire. While there, he burned the bars, the brothel and the tobacco shop. "These are evil," he said. "From now on they will have to come to me for lessons in secret drinking, secret prostitution, and secret tobacco. They will have to kow-tow to me for those things, for now I am in charge. The government regulations made everyone soft and simple. I'll teach them to fear their indulgences, whatever it takes." He never noticed his behaviors were indulgent, instead he thought of his indulgences as a kind of special discipline. He stoked the fire and went back up the hill.

The villagers pointed and hooted at the yogin. They showed their rumps in defiance. They raised their hoes. They threatened with their nooses and pillories. "That's what he needs," cried some. "That's what he wants," called others. "We got him." "He's ours." "That' it." "You've got it." They congratulated and encouraged each other shamelessly. They made threatening gestures. The yogin said, "Except for the ego problems, I'll bet they're quite nice" and continued to practice (and cough). He had heard somewhere that Buddhists would recognize that someone who can sit is highly unlikely to be criminal and figured the villagers must all know this, and if he just continues to practice quietly he'd make some friends and all would quiet down.

Black Bear didn't notice, but the fire he started to burn down the bars, the brothel, and the tobacco shop, burned down all the crops and the rest of the houses in the village. The smoke continued up the mountain as did the chant, "Where there's smoke, there's fire. Where there's smoke, there's fire." Someone looked below and called out, "The village and the crops are gone! We're lost! We'll starve! We'll freeze!" The crowd ran to the village and saw Black Bear standing in the center of the devastation. They turned to him for a comment. "It's that yogin," he said. "I told you he was trouble." "It's that yogin," they all cried in response. Their eyes teared up. They could not bear to look at their past, their present, or their future. They were too disheartened to go after the yogin. Their heads hung. Their bodies went limp. They stared at their village reduced to a smoldering ash. "That yogin, that yogin, that yogin," they muttered.

At that moment, a cloud covered the moon and left the village in utter darkness. Laments, wails and cries were heard. Simultaneously, the near-sighted bald eagle with the broken right wing took his last breath.

A fable.

Moral #! The smoke goes to the heavens; it comes from below: follow the smoke the other way.

Moral #2: Laws do not only tell you what you approve of and disapprove of but also what you feel needs to be regulated to prevent the likes of Black Bear from arising. A particularly challenging example of this is abortion: it is easy to be against abortion, but it is difficult to be against both legal and illegal abortion. The yogin is against both legal and illegal abortion but certainly does not want the mountains of criminality that would surround illegal abortion: He'd rather the politicians, judges, lawyers, doctors, priests, rabbis, lamas, and ministers take care of regulating it. He is not pro-life; he is not pro-choice; he is pro-education, maturation, inspiration, motivation, teaching and parenting; and of course, regulation of an unfortunate human reality: let the doctors, lawyers, judges, and religious do the regulation; not the abusers, criminals, mobs, and bullies; he just wants out of the whole issue, cowardly as that may seem.

If the laws are too strict, people will be cunning, if the laws are light, people will be simple and will likely turn toward maturation, inspiration, motivation, and intelligent regulation.

Moral #3: If you can't make it on tobacco, alcohol, caffeine and healthy dating behaviors (the Judeo-Christian version of Yab Yum), you just haven't got it.

Poem #2:

Leaning on a Lamp Post, Flipping a Coin

To the beats and their beat: Vesuvio's, City Lights, the Beat Museum, North Beach, China Town

Every coin has two sides: it is best to know who is on your flip side.

Neurotic	←→	pervert
Vic	←→	perp
Sinner	←→	devil
Nut case	←→	whack job

I'll stay with the heads myself: those on the left.

Poem #3:

(Be careful the title is very important.)

For the Eyes of the Solitary Warrior Only

> **The War was Never Begun.**
> **The Battle Never Ends.**
> **Winning and Losing are Costly Illusions.**
> **The Solitary Warrior Knows When to Engage.**
>
> **Make a Good Dinner.**
> **Be Sure and Place Flowers.**

Poem #4:

In a mood to have some Zen fun, and on the occasion of Aitken Roshi's retirement, I decided to respond to the famous poem dual of the 6th Patriarch (repeated below). My response follows.

身是菩提樹	The body is a Bodhi tree,
心如明鏡臺。	The mind a standing mirror bright.
時時勤拂拭，	At all times polish it diligently,
勿使惹塵埃。	And let no dust alight.

菩提本無樹	Bodhi is fundamentally without any tree;
明鏡亦非臺	The bright mirror is also not a stand.
本來無一物	Fundamentally there is not a single thing —
何處惹塵埃	Where could any dust be attracted?

Untitled:

No Mirror No Dust
No Robe No Bowl
What precious teachings flow through the body, speech and mind of
this great teacher.

Other Projects by the Author:

**TaxTheRichDotName a website and political economic
movement.**

http://www.taxtherich.name

Petition to get the tax the rich plank on a 2012 platform:
http://www.thepetitionsite.com/1/a-tax-the-rich-plank-in-the-2012-
presidential-platforms/
Support the TaxTheRichDotName effort to make or break the 2012:
http://www.kickstarter.com/projects/1118562472/tax-the-rich-
performance-art-documentary-rally-and